Analyzing the Cultural Unconscious

Also Available from Bloomsbury

Ordinary Literature Philosophy: Lacanian Literary Performatives between Austin and Rancière, Jernej Habjan
Beckett, Lacan and the Mathematical Writing of the Real, Arka Chattopadhyay
Lacan Contra Foucault: Subjectivity, Sex, and Politics, edited by Nadia Bou Ali and Rohit Goel
Lacanian Realism: Political and Clinical Psychoanalysis, Duane Rousselle
Pixar with Lacan: The Hysteric's Guide to Animation, Lilian Munk Rösing

Analyzing the Cultural Unconscious

Science of the Signifier

Edited by
Henrik Jøker Bjerre, Brian Benjamin Hansen,
Kirsten Hyldgaard, Jakob Rosendal,
Lilian Munk Rösing

BLOOMSBURY ACADEMIC
LONDON · NEW YORK · OXFORD · NEW DELHI · SYDNEY

BLOOMSBURY ACADEMIC
Bloomsbury Publishing Plc
50 Bedford Square, London, WC1B 3DP, UK
1385 Broadway, New York, NY 10018, USA
29 Earlsfort Terrace, Dublin 2, Ireland

BLOOMSBURY, BLOOMSBURY ACADEMIC and the Diana logo are trademarks of Bloomsbury Publishing Plc

First published in Great Britain 2020
This paperback edition published in 2021

Copyright © Henrik Jøker Bjerre, Brian Benjamin Hansen, Kirsten Hyldgaard, Jakob Rosendal, Lilian Munk Rösing, and Contributors, 2020

Henrik Jøker Bjerre, Brian Benjamin Hansen, Kirsten Hyldgaard, Jakob Rosendal, and Lilian Munk Rösing have asserted their right under the Copyright, Designs and Patents Act, 1988, to be identified as Editors of this work.

Cover design by Jade Barnett

All rights reserved. No part of this publication may be reproduced or transmitted in any form or by any means, electronic or mechanical, including photocopying, recording, or any information storage or retrieval system, without prior permission in writing from the publishers.

Bloomsbury Publishing Plc does not have any control over, or responsibility for, any third-party websites referred to or in this book. All internet addresses given in this book were correct at the time of going to press. The author and publisher regret any inconvenience caused if addresses have changed or sites have ceased to exist, but can accept no responsibility for any such changes.

A catalogue record for this book is available from the British Library.

A catalog record for this book is available from the Library of Congress.

ISBN: HB: 978-1-3500-8836-8
       PB: 978-1-3502-6228-7
       ePDF: 978-1-3500-8837-5
       eBook: 978-1-3500-8838-2

Typeset by Integra Software Services Pvt Ltd.

To find out more about our authors and books visit www.bloomsbury.com and sign up for our newsletters.

Contents

Figures   vii
About the authors   viii

Introduction   1

Part I   Science and the Signifier

1   The Cunning of the Signifier   *Henrik Jøker Bjerre*   17
2   The Echo of the Signifier in the Body: How Drive Works (or Not) Today   *Juliet Flower MacCannell*   27
3   The Secret in the Body: The Fantasy Structure of Genes and Brains   *Renata Salecl*   47

Part II   From Couch to Culture

1   Of Drives and Culture   *Mladen Dolar*   65
2   Lars von Trier's *Nymphomaniac*. Boredom and Knowledge as Defense. The Discourse of the University and the Discourse of the Hysteric   *Kirsten Hyldgaard*   85
3   Courtly Capitalism   *Center for Wild Analysis*   95
4   Is There a Way out of the Capitalist Discourse?   *René Rasmussen*   109

Part III   Application

1   The Materialist Use of Examples: Relocation, Repetition, and Reconceptualization   *Brian Benjamin Hansen*   121
2   On Ethics and the Unconscious in J.M. Coetzee's *Disgrace*   *Kari Jegerstedt*   131
3   When I Am beside Myself; or, Why Beckett Is Good for Nothing   *Linus Nicolaj Carlsen*   149
4   Analysis Sounds Boring   *Anders Ruby*   159

Part IV Materiality and the Signifier

1 Lol V. Stein to the Letter *Ida Nissen Bjerre* 173
2 Lacan and the Archeology of the Subject *Carin Franzén* 187
3 The Signifiers of *Cherry Ripe*: On the Repetition of an Art Historical Motif *Jakob Rosendal* 197
4 Color between Materiality and Signification *Lilian Munk Rösing* 215

Index 225

Figures

15.1	LI190.1 Joshua Reynolds, *Portrait of Penelope Boothby*, 1788. 75 × 62 cm. Oil on canvas. Lent from a private collection. Image © Ashmolean Museum, University of Oxford	207
15.2	John Everett Millais, *Cherry Ripe*, 1879. 134.6 × 88.9 cm. Oil on canvas Private collection. © Bridgeman Images	208
15.3	John Everett Millais, *Cherry Ripe*, 1880. A supplement from the 1880 Christmas Number of the journal *The Graphic*. 70 × 45 cm. © The British Library	209
15.4	*Cherry Ripe*, 1897. Poster from the Christmas publication *Pears' Annual*. 84 × 54 cm. © Jakob Rosendal	210
15.5	L. T. Peele, *Cherry Ripe*, 1866. From *The Illustrated London News*, March 24, 1866. © Jakob Rosendal	211
15.6	Rowlands' advertisement, 1880. Printed in the 1880 Christmas Number of the journal *The Graphic*. © The British Library	211

About the authors

Henrik Jøker Bjerre is Associate Professor of Applied Philosophy at Aalborg University, Denmark, and a member of the philosophical collective Center for Wild Analysis. His research focuses on subjectivity and culture, specifically on the work of Kant, Kierkegaard, and Lacan. His publications include books on Kantian moral philosophy, the concept and practice of cultural analysis, and the philosophy of action. His most recent book is *Handl! ("Act!")*, coauthored with Brian Benjamin Hansen (2017).

Linus Nicolaj Carlsen is External Lecturer at the Department of Arts and Cultural Studies of the University of Copenhagen. His research interests include Samuel Beckett, Maurice Blanchot, robotic fiction, and early Soviet culture. He has previously written on voice and dissonance in the works of Scott Walker, narrative strategies in Agota Kristof, and issues of eroticism and subjectivity in *Westworld*.

Center for Wild Analysis is a philosophical collective that has existed since 2006. It has produced two books, a year-long national radio show, weekly newspaper columns, and a number of interventions at conferences and other events. Its members are Brian Benjamin Hansen, Henrik Jøker Bjerre, Kasper Porsgaard, Rasmus Ugilt, and Steen Thykjær. The center exists when two or more of these write or speak in its name.

Mladen Dolar is Professor and Senior Researcher at the Department of Philosophy, University of Ljubljana, and Professor at the European Graduate School in Switzerland. His principal areas of research are psychoanalysis, modern French philosophy, German idealism, and philosophy of art. Apart from over 150 papers in scholarly journals and collective volumes and a dozen books in Slovene, his book publications include most notably *A Voice and Nothing More* (MIT 2006, translated into nine languages).

Carin Franzén is Professor and Director of the Graduate School in Language and Culture, Linköping University. She has a PhD in comparative literature. Her research explores the relations between formations of subjectivity and cultural hegemonies. She has published various articles and books on literature and psychoanalysis as well as on medieval and early-modern literature, most recently "Subjects of Sovereign Control and the Art of Critique in the Early Modern Period," in *Control Culture: Foucault and Deleuze after Discipline*, ed. Beckman (Edinburgh University Press, 2018).

Brian Benjamin Hansen is Associate Professor at VIA University College and a member of Center for Wild Analysis. His research interests focus on subjectivity (enjoyment, disgust, freedom, the act, madness), collectivity, the psychopathology of culture, and philosophy of science (the use of examples, the concept of analysis). His latest book is *Handl! ("Act!")*, coauthored with Henrik Jøker Bjerre (2017).

Kirsten Hyldgaard is Associate Professor at the Danish School of Education, Aarhus University (Campus Emdrup), Denmark. Her research interests are psychoanalysis, philosophy, epistemology, and gender studies. She has published on the philosophical implications of Lacanian psychoanalysis, Heidegger, educational philosophy, epistemology, and on feature films and documentaries. Her most recent book (2014) is *Eksistensens galskab. Freudo-lacanianske tilgange til videnskab, kunst, culture* [Madness of Existence. Freudo-Lacanian Approaches to Science, Art, and Culture].

Kari Jegerstedt is Associate Professor at the University of Bergen at the Centre for Women's and Gender Research. Her research interests focus on postcolonial literature, feminist and intersectional gender theory, psychoanalysis, and posthumanist. She has published on Angela Carter, Norwegian and South African literature, as well as on gender theory. Her most recent book is *Exploring the Black Venus Figure in Aesthetic Practices* (co-ed 2019).

Juliet Flower MacCannell is Professor Emerita of English and Comparative Literature at the University of California, Irvine. Her books include *Figuring Lacan* (1986/2014), *The Regime of the Brother* (1991), and *The Hysteric's Guide to the Future Female Subject* (2000); her edited collections are on philosophy and psychoanalytic theory. Her recent essays focus on violence, sex, law, perversion, war, capitalism, space, fashion, architecture, cities, suburbs, and "The Regime of the Brother Today." She has been awarded Outstanding Professor Emerita, UCI (2015); Honorary Fellow, Institute for Advanced Study, University of London (2009); Artist in Residence, Headlands Center for the Arts, Sausalito, California (1993); and Resident Artist, Moonhole, Bequia, ICA, Boston/Engelhard Foundation (1994).

Ida Nissen Bjerre is PhD fellow at Copenhagen University. Her research focuses on Lacanian readings of literature, in particular Marguerite Duras and William Shakespeare. She is the cofounder and chairman of the Danish Society for Theoretical Psychoanalysis, and the editor-in-chief of its journal, *Lamella*, and has edited the first three issues (2016–2018). Her most recent publication is a Lacanian analysis of August Strindberg's *The Defence of a Fool*.

René Rasmussen is PhD and Associate Professor in Danish literature at the Department of Nordic Studies and Linguistics, University of Copenhagen, and psychoanalyst, Copenhagen. He does his research and writing in the cross fields of literature, psychoanalysis, capitalism, and consumerism. His most recent book is *Kærligheden til det uden navn* [Love to That without Name].

Jakob Rosendal holds a PhD in Art History from Aarhus University and is conducting postdoctoral research at The Women's Museum in Denmark as part of the group project "Gender Blender –Everyday Life, Activism, and Diversity" in collaboration with Aarhus University. His research focuses on everyday visual culture and the repetition of images, and his postdoc project deals with images of children and children's drawings in relation to the issues of children's (a)sexuality, sexual difference, and transgender childhood. His latest publication "Det pædofile blik? Om seksualitet i billeder af børn" ("The Paedophile Gaze? Sexuality in Images of Children") questions the relatedness of paedophile fantasies and contemporary mainstream images of children.

Lilian Munk Rösing is Associate Professor at the Department of Arts and Cultural Studies, Copenhagen University, and a literary critic. She does her research and writing in the cross field of aesthetics, psychoanalysis, and cultural criticism. Her most recent book is on the painter Anna Ancher (*Anna Anchers rum*, Gyldendal 2018). She has a book published in English: *Pixar with Lacan. The Hysteric's Guide to Animation* (Bloomsbury 2017).

Anders Ruby is a music producer and has an MA in History of Ideas from Aarhus University. He is currently working on a PhD thesis on subjectivity and machine music in a Lacanian context. His most recent publication (2018) is on disgust and musical fantasies ("Musik er en ækel fantasi" in *Det ækle*, ed. Hansen, Brian Benjamin, and David Mayntz).

Renata Salecl is a philosopher and sociologist. She is Senior Researcher at the Institute of Criminology at the Faculty of Law in Ljubljana, Slovenia, and Professor of Psychology and Psychoanalysis of Law at the School of Law, Birkbeck College, the University of London. She is also Recurring Visiting Professor at Cardozo School of Law in New York. Her last book *Tyranny of Choice* (Profile Books 2011) has been translated into fifteen languages and was featured at TED Global. Her forthcoming book is *Passion for Ignorance* (Princeton University Press).

Introduction

Henrik Jøker Bjerre, Brian Benjamin Hansen, Kirsten Hyldgaard, Jakob Rosendal, Lilian Munk Rösing

This book addresses the methods and problems of "applied psychoanalysis" as it moves from couch to culture, focusing on "the signifier" as the royal road to the unconscious. While Lacanian-inspired analyses of cultural and social phenomena have for the latest decades enjoyed a certain success within Academia, not least thanks to the "Slovenian" school, the methods and problems of "applied psychoanalysis" still need to be addressed and discussed. What are we actually doing when taking psychoanalysis from the couch to the analysis of society, culture, and arts? Is there such a thing as a "cultural unconscious"? How is it possible to move from the singular experience on the couch to universal structures to be detected in culture and society, or to the aesthetic experience of an artwork? In this book, we will propose applied psychoanalysis as a "science of the signifier," insisting that the analysis of the signifier is the royal road to the understanding of the unconscious, whether individual or cultural.

With this approach, we take it that the concept of the signifier is what connects the domains of the private and the public. In Lacanian theory, the subject is the product of the cut of the battery of signifiers—or what is called (symbolic) castration. The subject is constituted through signifiers; it is never "itself" plain and simple. As Lacan once emphatically said, "Man does not think with his soul, as the Philosopher imagined, he thinks as a consequence of the fact that a structure, that of language, carves up his body" (Lacan 1987: 10). With the notion of a structure, we already leave the simple division of the private and the public. Following the lead of the signifier in all its dimensions—its work of castration, its chains and structures, its complicity in the creation of desire, its material side, its ideological function, etc.—causes us to think the domain of private pathologies and the domain of public discourse in a new way. Even for Freud, it was never just an individual lying before him on the couch but also the very question of the subject as constituted by an "inherited" language. Just as culture, on the other hand, was not just a question of "dead" structures, but of structures carried by desire, infested with libido.

Psychoanalysis is often disclaimed as nonscientific, because its main object, the unconscious, has no positive existence. But if we define the object of psychoanalysis as the signifier, we might speak of psychoanalysis as a science, even if perhaps closer to linguistics and semiotics than to biology or psychology. The unconscious may be found in that which escapes the signifiers—the gaps between them, the principle of their production, the surplus that they produce, their materiality—but the way to track it goes through the signifier. The signifier may be what subjects us to cultural norms, but it is also able to set us free if we stick to its materiality and follow the associations that it produces.

In our time, science is commonly understood as natural science. The relation between psychoanalysis and natural science is complicated, as Freud saw himself as a natural scientist, arguing for the existence of the unconscious and the functioning of the drives in ways and models inspired by biology. Today we rely on brain studies to explain human behavior, and contemporary brain studies do regard the determining forces of our behavior as unconscious, but they locate these unconscious forces in genes and neurons. Here we must remember Lacan's definition of the unconscious as the echo of the signifier in the body ("Drive is the echo in the body of the fact that there is speech" (Lacan 2016: 9)).[1] The psychoanalytical unconscious is not the biological processes at work in our bodies without our knowledge; it is produced in the body by the signifier, when sign and materiality, *sema* and *soma* meet.

The unconscious is structured like a language

Lacan insists that the unconscious is structured like a language. This claim results from his combination of Freudian psychoanalysis with structural linguistics and anthropology. From the founding father of structural linguistics, Ferdinand de Saussure, he takes the identification of the two different internal aspects of the sign: its signifying side (the "signifier") and that which it signifies (the "signified"), as well as the understanding that signification is produced by the difference between signifiers rather than by each signifier's "naming" of some object. From the founding father of structural anthropology, Claude Lévi-Strauss, he takes the idea that human communities are based on the exchange of objects (gifts, women, money) and adds that even language is such an object of exchange. In both cases, rather than merely applying insights from structuralism to psychoanalytical questions, Lacan reinterprets the structuralist heritage itself.

Saying that the unconscious is structured like a language thus does not mean that it is structured like a well-formed language with univocal relations between signifiers and signifieds. On the contrary, language itself is much less "ordered" and predictable than Saussure described it, and the key to this unruliness is precisely the priority of the signifier over the signified. Saussure was right in identifying two different "internal" aspects of the sign and liberating language from its traditional role of being (merely) a nomenclature of objects in the world, and he was right in describing language as a system of differences, in which each sign gets its meaning from its nonidentity with other signs (and not from some essence or correspondence with objects). But he underestimated the unruly character of the signifier: There is never such a thing as a closed system of signifiers in steady, synchronic stability. A science of the signifier in this sense, of which Saussure was sometimes dreaming, would be utopian. Instead, signifiers have to be followed in the chains they form in speech, sometimes leading us completely astray, fatally supplementing the original meaning, and they have to be taken seriously with regard to the problems they present for us. "A signifier represents the subject for another signifier," as Lacan puts it (Lacan 1998: 207). A signifier does not represent meaning, and it does not represent meaning for us, so that we can understand something. A signifier represents the subject—the "something" that we try to convey, maybe even our soul—for another signifier. The signifier has something to do with meaning, but there is a continual slippage of the signified underneath the signifier. The signifier creates its own signification through its mingling with other signifiers, it means nothing or everything, and it is shaped and misappropriated by social interaction. This is precisely why it needs to be interpreted.

As Lacan vehemently insists, the unconscious is structured like a language, not because the unconscious *is* a language (and thus we should simply learn how to speak this language, like learning to speak Esperanto), but because it is subject to or even an effect of "structural" inconsistencies just like a language. The unconscious and language overlap in their common failure, to be realized or to convey meaning without loss (or surplus). In a powerful passage in *What Is Sex?*, Alenka Zupančič describes this as the interplay of subject/unconscious/gap and discourse.

The subject (of the unconscious) is… the name of the *gap* pertaining to discourse, as well as the name of the *effect* that takes place *because* there is this gap in discourse. In this precise sense we can say that for Lacan the subject is both "identifiable within the uniform networks of experience" (that is, fairly common, presumed by the functioning of the signifier), *and rare*—that is, emerging only from time to time. Psychoanalytic examples of the latter—that is, of sudden and *surprising*, unexpected emergences of the subject—range from slips of the tongue, dreams, jokes, to shattering love encounters. (Zupančič 2017: 132)

The materiality of the signifier

Also when it comes to the heritage from structural anthropology, Lacan does not simply follow Lévi-Strauss, but reinterprets his points. Lacan notices that the gifts founding social relations are typically objects that have lost their use ("vases made to remain empty, shields too heavy to be carried, sheaves that will dry out, lances that are thrust into the ground" (Lacan 2006: 225)). Likewise, the value of words is less their use value than their value as objects of social exchange. The exchange of words is less a communication of useful information than a way to create social bonds. To Lévi-Strauss, the patterns and rules of the exchange of gifts are a kind of social grammar, testifying to a fundamental, but not explicitly articulated social structure. To Lacan, the principles ruling our combination and exchange of words have a similar status, testifying to the unconscious structure of our social bonding. This is why Lacan claims that Lévi-Strauss is "conquering the very terrain in which Freud situates the unconscious" (Lacan 2006: 236). What distinguishes Lacan from structural anthropology, nonetheless, could be said to be the difference between looking for anthropological constants working behind the backs of the (individual) subjects of a culture and looking for effects of the signifier working behind the backs of subjects, without any possible reference to a common "human nature." In any case, it is this "terrain," this "other scene," that Lacan is exploring with the assistance of his structuralist predecessors.

The obviously useless part of the sign is its material quality, such as the letters and sounds of the verbal sign, detached from their meaning. But this material dimension of the sign was Freud's royal road to the unconscious in his *Interpretation of Dreams*. When analyzing his own famous dream of "the botanical monograph," for instance, he followed the trace of the letters "KO" and "KÖ" to find out how this was very much a dream about his relation to paternal figures. His associations slide from his own monograph on the anesthetic effect of COcaine to his elder colleague, Dr. KOller, who introduced cocaine as an anesthetic without referring to Freud, and who was the anesthetist when Freud's father was operated for glauCOma by Dr. KÖnigstein, whom Freud had met the night before the dream (Freud 1953: 170–2). The story of Freud's rivalry with and wish for recognition from paternal figures has taken its refuge in the seemingly insignificant syllable KO, which is part of the signifiers' material and has nothing to do with their reference.

Unconscious connections and structures cling to the seemingly meaningless "material" of language, language as letters and sounds. This is why Lacan (at a press conference in Rome in 1974) could claim the pun to be the key to psychoanalysis: "I do attribute an enormous importance to puns, you know. This seems to me to be the key to psychoanalysis." The pun plays a central role in Lacan's own writings: "Hommelette" (meaning both omelette and "little man") for the infant before the differentiation from its surroundings, "lituraterre" for literature, containing the word "terre," earth or dirt, to indicate how literature takes care of the dirt, the materiality, of language; "sinthome" mixing "symptom" and "Saint Thomas" to suggest the "holy" and epiphanic quality of the symptom. The pun makes it clear how language carries a surplus of meaning, usually unintended, unconscious.

The work of the signifier

The project of this book, of a "science of the signifier," could be summarized in the catchphrase of the "work of the signifier." A central discovery of psychoanalysis is that the signifier performs some kind of work; a work that we have to analyze and theorize, without totalizing the concept of the signifier, binding it to one definition. That the signifier performs some kind of work was evident already for Freud—even without the technical term of the "signifier"—in his famous "talking cure." The medium of psychoanalysis is "language" in the broadest sense of the term; what psychoanalysis proposes is that there is something about setting language in motion, which already in itself relates to the cure (even if the cure requires touching on delicate, anxiety-ridden matters). There is "full speech," as Lacan said, stating that: "Analysis is not a matter of discovering in a particular case the differential feature of the theory, and in doing so believe that one is explaining why your daughter is silent—for the point at issue is to *get her to speak*" (Lacan 1998: 11).

The signifier works in mysterious ways, one could be tempted to say, but these mysteries are there to be analyzed. There are first and foremost some very basic conditions of interpretation that hinges on the signifier. You have to analyze chains and networks of signifiers; you have to beware of the retroactive effect of the signifier—one signifier can completely alter the preceding ones: "See you," the man jubilantly says as he exits the door, but when in his car, driving away, he mumbles, "never again." You have to beware of gaps, breaks, inconsistencies in discourse: "Impediment, failure, split. In a spoken or written sentence something stumbles. Freud is attracted by these phenomena, and it is there that he seeks the unconscious" (Lacan 1998: 25). Analysis really only begins when something of this character pops up; something that does not fit, that cannot be spoken of directly, but nevertheless demands to be said. You also have to follow odd connections of signifiers, only carried by sounds and homophonies, you have to be willing to follow the "superficial associations," "by assonance, verbal ambiguity, and temporal coincidence, without inner relationship of meaning," where no connection is "too loose and no witticism too objectionable to serve as a bridge from one thought to another" (Freud 1953: 530).

Analyzing chains and networks of signifiers is one thing. But the signifier can in itself be a powerful tool for analysis. Lacan's notations of the four discourses and his formulae of sexuation are signifiers to be used as tools by analyzing how subjects instantiate these signifiers in their social bonding or sexual positions. In order to track the cultural unconscious, this book will be doing both: analyzing chains of signifiers and analyzing positions and bonds as instantiations of signifiers.

To discuss the method of analyzing the cultural unconscious and define it as a science of the signifier, we have divided the book into four sections. Part I, "Science of the signifier," discusses, from a philosophical and theoretical angle, what kind of science arises from taking the signifier as its object, and not for instance genes and neurons. Part II, "From couch to culture," examines the step from analyzing the individual to analyzing the cultural unconscious partly by deconstructing the opposition between drives and cultures, arguing that culture has the structure of the drive, partly by presenting Lacanian analyses of social and cultural positions and structures. Part III, "Application," argues that psychoanalysis is fundamentally an applied science, living from the split between its concepts and examples, and then presents examples of psychoanalysis "applied" to literature and music. Part IV, "Materiality and the signifier," discusses the relation between psychoanalysis and materialism, arguing that psychoanalysis has a (dialectical) materialist strain by presenting analyses of art and literature focusing on the materiality of the signifier.

Part I: Science and the signifier

In the opening chapter of Part I, Henrik Jøker Bjerre defines a motto for the science of the signifier by replacing just one word in Hegel's *Lectures on the History of Philosophy*: "It is what we may call the cunning of the signifier that it sets the passions to work in its service." The chapter argues that the history of philosophy is not unfamiliar with the thought that the actions of human beings contain a surplus of meaning unknown to the human beings themselves. This thought plays a role in metaphorical and speculative concepts like Adam Smith's "invisible hand" or Hegel's "cunning of reason," but Freud's investigations of the unconscious gave a concrete sense of the ways in which we produce meaning that escapes our conscious intention. The ambition of the chapter is to show how the Lacanian linguistic turn of psychoanalysis made it possible to formulate a precise, materialist version of the trope: It is the signifier itself that works behind the back of the speaking subjects. The great advantage of the science of the signifier, compared to Hegel, is that it relies less on a concept of divine intent.

With the second chapter of Part I, we move from "the cunning of the signifier" to "the echo of the signifier." The title of this chapter, written by Juliet Flower MacCannell, is Lacan's definition of drive: "The echo of speech in the body." MacCannell shows the lineage between, on the one hand, Saussure's revolutionary discovery of the "signifier" and, on the other hand, Jacques Lacan and Jacques Derrida. The theory of the signifier resonated for each with their understanding of Freud. Derrida used Parisian psychoanalytic work on the signifier to argue against any idea of a transcendental signified, and Lacan linked language to the drive. The chapter questions whether Lacan's definition of unconscious drive as the echo of the signifier is losing something vital in our current age. The enjoyment that capitalist society promises us is the enjoyment of an individual who needs no partner, no social link, no other who responds, and no other for whom one is responsible.

The biological sciences that dominate the scientific discourse of our time do not listen for the unconscious in the echo of the signifier in the body, but rather looks for the secret in the physicality of the body, in genes and brains. Still, the terms of genetics and neuroscience are signifiers that produce echoes—fantasies, anxieties—in our bodies. This is Renata Salecl's concern in the third and last chapter of Part I: "Secret in the Body—The Fantasy Structure of Genes and Brains." Salecl argues that the advances of biological sciences have opened new ways to reflect on the nature of subjectivity. On top of bringing new knowledge about our bodies, genetics and neuroscience incite anxieties and paranoia, while also giving rise to new forms of social control. The chapter uses Lacanian theory to analyze the fantasies people create concerning genes and brains. Second, it analyzes the fascination with DNA in the judicial system and the way movies and TV series contribute to the perception of the all powerfulness of forensic science, exemplified by new forms of neurosis and perversion observable in the legal domain. Finally, it looks at the way the desire to see the secret in the body goes hand in hand with the spread of the belief that genes are responsible for crime. Salecl argues that, paradoxically, psychoanalysis perceives the subject as more responsible than law often does. Freud's concept of "Neurosenwahl," choice of neurosis, perceives the subject as "author" of his or her suffering.

Part II: From couch to culture

In Part II, Mladen Dolar sets out to dismantle the common assumption that drives and culture stand at opposite ends. On the contrary, by extracting six defining traits of culture from Freud's epochal essay on the "discontent in culture," Dolar shows how they are all closely connected to the basic traits of drives to the point of coinciding with them. In each case, the trait that seems to oppose the drives turns out to be a drive itself, or the effect of drive, whether it be the case of mastering of nature by means of tools as prosthesis of human body; embellishments that don't serve the survival function; cleanliness and disciplining of bodily functions; order in its connections with the compulsion to repeat; spiritual elevation and sublimation; or social restrictions that demand renunciation and inhibition of the drives. The last part of the chapter deals with the paradoxical placement of psychoanalysis in this divide: it is neither a natural science nor does it belong to social sciences and humanities; its object is rather the impossible overlap of the two.

In the second chapter, Kirsten Hyldgaard takes on a concrete cultural product, Lars von Trier's *Nymphomaniac*, and shows how psychoanalytical concepts are already at work in culture itself. The clinical categories in psychoanalysis do not represent a differentiation between pathology and normality but rather describe formal ways of forming social bonds; that is, they serve to analyze how speech is structured—inside as well as outside the clinic. The focus of the analysis is how the principal characters of *Nymphomaniac* speak, how they address the Other, and how this relates to the status of knowledge. The contention of the chapter is that when knowledge is in the position of agent (as it is the case in the discourse of the university), speech protects against the desire of the Other and produces hysteria, that is, lack of knowledge. This description exactly fits the principal character, Seligman.

The science of the signifier could thus, among other possible things, be a systematic investigation of cultural phenomena that say more than what they immediately seem to say. In the third chapter of Part II, this is the explicit agenda of the Center for Wild Analysis, when they engage with the 1990 romantic comedy *Pretty Woman*. It is argued that the film is not just a romantic comedy about the perfect relationship between a cynical businessman and a beautiful prostitute but nothing less than a foundational myth of post–Cold War capitalism. The film thematizes the relation between romantic love and economy, and while it raises more serious questions than one would expect, it also succeeds in explaining how one handles a really offensive, obscene amount of money.

While the Center for Wild Analysis investigates the foundational myth of contemporary (financial) capitalism, René Rasmussen, in the last chapter of Part II, asks the question whether there is a way out. To this purpose, he takes his point of departure from Lacan's less-known "fifth" discourse, the discourse of the capitalist, which he describes as the (master) discourse of our time. In the structuring of this discourse, we are subjected to the illusion that our desires can only be satisfied if the other does not prevent us from enjoying what is contained in this satisfaction. The capitalist discourse thereby much more effectively than the other discourses runs in a closed circuit, because it contains its own counter-move as a part of the logic of the discourse itself. The chapter stresses how this discourse gives rise to the idea of "us" (who can enjoy what "we" are entitled to) as opposed to "them" (who steal our *jouissance*) and how it gives us the idea of an unlimited enjoyment. The question about a possible escape from this discourse is answered rather pessimistically, although the chapter ends with an investigation of art and psychoanalytic practice as more "local" emancipatory practices or breathing spaces.

Part III: Application

An established term for the move from couch to culture, or from the analysis of the individual subject to the analysis of art works and cultural phenomena, is "applied psychoanalysis." In the opening chapter of Part III, "The Materialist Use of Examples: Relocation, Repetition and Reconceptualization," Brian Benjamin Hansen argues that psychoanalysis is from its beginning an "applied science," implying a necessary misfit between the concept applied and the example to which it is applied. Hansen sees a necessary connection between Freud's use of examples in his three books on the unconscious and his theoretical edifice, founded on the concept of the unconscious. The unconscious resists exemplification, as it is always in another place, and yet Freud constantly turns this failure into its opposite, so that the only way to investigate the unconscious goes through nonfitting examples and the surplus meaning they produce. Hansen argues that the non-fit of the example to the concept is the only way to fully employ the concept.

In the second chapter of Part III, the central psychoanalytical concept is Lacan's conceptualization of the masculine and feminine positions. The "example" is J. M. Coetzee's novel *Disgrace*. Kari Jegerstedt performs a Lacanian reading of the novel, in which the decisive acts of the protagonist, Lurie, and his daughter, Lucie, are shown to be ethical acts of subtraction in respectively a masculine and a feminine mode. Jegerstedt insists on psychoanalysis as an ethics and on the fundamental link between the question of ethics and the question of sexual difference in Lacan. Furthermore, the chapter rephrases the question of moving from singular to cultural as a question of moving from the singular literary work to general social and cultural structures, in this case the structures of post-Apartheid South Africa.

The third chapter, "When I Am beside Myself, or: Why Beckett Is Good for Nothing," aims at proving the Lacanian point that language is not spoken by the subject; rather language produces subjectivity, to the point that poetic language may produce a voice of subjectivity without a subject. The example is Samuel Beckett, more specifically Beckett's middle and later works, in which Linus Nikolaj Carlsen analyzes the recurring "murmuring" as a terrifyingly present failure of language—a speaking absence produced by language itself. Carlsen argues that the psychoanalytic contribution to cultural criticism revolves around a kind of present absence or positive "nothing," and regards the Lacanian conception of the unconscious as a way to understand a literature that drills holes in language. By way of Beckett, the chapter explores the importance of absences for the subject as a cultural being.

The final chapter in Part III, "Analysis Sounds Boring," turns to an art form that has not received much attention from psychoanalysis: modern electronic music. Whereas musical genres are conventionally analyzed on the level of audio (musicology) or cultural positions (sociology, psychology), Anders Ruby insists on analyzing electronic music on the level of the signifier, comparing the "setting" of the electronic concert to the setting of (clinical) psychoanalysis, finding both to stage the "fall of the Other." Ruby's "example" of the fall of the Other (and the rise of the signifier) is what is called in electronic music "the drop."

Part IV: Materiality and the signifier

The science of the signifier could seem to be opposed to materialism, insisting on language rather than matter as that which matters. In Part IV we want to deconstruct this opposition by insisting on the (dialectical) materialist strain of psychoanalysis as a science of the signifier, not least trough focusing on the material dimension of the signifier itself.

The first chapter of Part IV, Ida Nissen Bjerre's analysis of Marguerite Duras' novel *Le ravissement de Lol V. Stein*, follows Lacan's encouragement from his exploration of the same novel in his "Homage to Marguerite Duras" and reads the novel "to the letter"—literally, by reading in the contours of her writing. As an attempt to take this somewhat mysterious request serious, the article zooms and tunes in on the graphic patterns and sound-images in Lacan's unfolding of "Lol V. Stein," thus shifting the emphasis from the semantic meaning of the signifier to its materiality. This allows the analysis to show how the equivocal "ravissement" evoked in the title—the feminine *jouissance* of Lol V. Stein, as well as the masculine *jouissance* she gives rise to—is not just a theme in (Lacan's essay on) Duras' novel but also something that makes itself manifest in the very texture of (his and) her writing.

The second chapter—Carin Franzén's "Lacan and the Archeology of the Subject"—argues that the subject in Lacanian psychoanalysis has a specific materiality that differs from both naturalistic materialism and post-human new materialism. Franzén approaches Lacan to Michel Foucault and his "archeological" take on the subject by showing how Lacan's work engages with certain historical occurrences of the subject of the unconscious, in particular in the medieval tradition of courtly love poetry. Franzén argues that Lacan, like Foucault, uses history "to cut diagonally through contemporary reality." The chapter shows how Lacan's "linguistic turn" is not a turning away from materialism and points to Lacan's own definition of a specific "Freudian materialism," which is to be distinguished from "naturalist materialism" because of its "symbolic form."

The two last chapters of Part IV turn to the art of painting to investigate the signifier lingering between signification and materiality. Jakob Rosendal analyzes John Everett Millais' painting *Cherry Ripe* (1879), arguing that this painting breaks up metaphoric signifying relations and turns conventional signs into signifiers by representing the child in its liminality, resistance, and tension vis-à-vis the symbols and sexuality of the adult world. In the dark void of the painting, Rosendal sees a transformation of representational signs into pure signifiers (the materiality of the paint). The chapter goes against the standard reading of the painting as an image of English girlhood innocence and addresses the reproductions and reception of the painting as various defensive formations that screen out the traumatizing aspect of the child and the signifier.

In the final chapter—"Color between Materiality and Signification"—Lilian Munk Rösing links psychoanalysis to aesthetics through their common attention to the material dimension of the signifier. The chapter focuses on color as a clear example of the signifier's lingering between representation and materiality. Color may represent something, either through mimesis or as a conventional symbol, but color also draws attention to the material presence of the artwork. The chapter critiques Merleau-Ponty's concept of *color as flesh* as an imaginary healing of the cut of the signifier and counters with Eric Santner's and Georges Didi-Huberman's concepts of *flesh, incarnation,* and *pan* as explorations of the real of color in its excess and materiality. In doing so, the chapter also rehabilitates the notion of color as feminine by seeing color as belonging to the feminine in the Lacanian sense of an opening in the meaning-making fabric of the symbolic.

Through all chapters, the book claims the analysis of the cultural unconscious to be a science of the signifier. Following Lacan, it understands the unconscious as the echo of the signifier in the body, and it deconstructs the oppositions of drive and culture, materiality and language. It not only asks what happens when we move from couch to culture but also performs this move in analyses of social and cultural structures and positions, and of art works. It shows how psychoanalysis was always an "applied" science and applies Lacan's formulae and notations to literary, visual, and musical art works, insisting not least on the materiality of these works, the materiality of the signifier.

The concept of the signifier provides ample opportunity to think once again some of the basic challenges of Lacanian psychoanalysis. What is the status and function of the master-signifier—the signifier that in its meaninglessness grounds the other signifiers? What kind of materiality can be ascribed to the signifier; how can it be virtual-differential and actual-material at the same time?

What are the relations between the signifier and the lack of desire, on the one side, and enjoyment, on the other? Can one enjoy signifiers?

If there is a science of the signifier, its role is not simply to answer these and related questions; it is to keep on posing them in relation to ever-new constellations of signifiers. We could even say with Lacan that it is not our intention to discover differential features of a theory (of the signifier); it is rather to get the signifier to speak.

Note

1 Our modification of translation. Price translates: "of a fact of saying" (French: "du fait qu'il y a un dire").

References

Freud, S. (1953 [1900]), *The Interpretation of Dreams*, in Standard Edition of the Complete Psychological Works of Sigmund Freud, vols. IV–V, trans. and ed. J. Strachey, London: The Hogarth Press.
Lacan, J. (1987), "Television," trans. Denis Hollier, Rosalind Kraus, Annette Michelson, in *October*, vol. 40, Cambridge, MA: MIT Press.
Lacan, J. (1998), *Seminar XI: The Four Fundamental Concepts of Psychoanalysis*, trans. A. Sheridan, London/New York: W. W. Norton.
Lacan, J. (2006), *Écrits: The First Complete Edition in English*, trans. Bruce Fink, New York: W. W. Norton.
Lacan, J. (2016), *Seminar XXIII: The Sinthome*, trans. A. R. Price, Cambridge/Malden: Polity Press.
Zupančič, A. (2017), *What Is Sex?* Cambridge, MA: MIT Press.

Part One

Science and the Signifier

1

The Cunning of the Signifier

Henrik Jøker Bjerre

It is no unfamiliar thought to the history of philosophy that the actions of human beings contain something more, a kind of surplus of meaning, than what is clear to the humans themselves, something that escapes the consciousness of the subject(s) producing it. Mostly, though, such a conception has been relying on a notion of foresight, providence, or a spiritual power that "wants something" with history, such that its course gradually unfolds on the back of its subjects, making use of their actions and intentions as the material content of history, but developing beyond what they intended or could even imagine. What I want to do in this chapter is to suggest that there is an interesting line of thought to be found particularly in Leibniz, Smith, and Hegel that might inspire the scientists of the signifier in this regard, and, furthermore, that the great advantage of the science of the signifier is that it relies less on a conception of divine intent than they do.

Invisible forces

In Leibniz, we find the thought of a surplus of meaning to human actions (not in so many words, but by implication) in the idea of the best possible world. Leibniz's theodicy includes a magnificent vision of all the infinitely many possible worlds that God scrolled through before creating the world—and of the least flawed one that he would allow to come into existence. The argument for the world being the "best possible" is strictly logical: Out of love God wanted to create a world, but he could only create it on condition of it not being perfect, for if it was, it would be identical to himself (for only God is perfect), and so nothing would have been created at all. Having seen all the ways in which such a world could turn out, God then chose the best possible path, the one *closest* to perfection.

Thus, the actual course of the world we live in, with all its events and actions, is the best possible that could have been, given its necessary imperfection, and if we think that something shouldn't have happened, it is only because we cannot see the bigger picture.

> One must judge the works of God as wisely as Socrates judged those of Heraclitus in these words: What I have understood thereof pleases me; I think that the rest would please me no less if I understood it. (Leibniz 1990: 215)

If, for example, I experience loss, it is only because any alternative world without my loss would have included even greater suffering for me or someone else. If I hadn't spilled coffee, maybe I would have walked into a door and hit my nose. If there were no storms and earthquakes, maybe there would be no fertile land either, and people would starve.[1] God has seen the other possible world, and he has seen that it is worse than this one. On a strict reading of Leibniz, I think we can extend this even to actions that appear to be unmoral: If I make mistakes or damage something, this action contains a kind of moral value nonetheless, although unknown to me, because it is literally the lesser evil. My action contributes to a general development that is overall better than it would have been, if I hadn't acted so. A mistake or an evil is to Leibniz therefore always what we might call a wrong step in the right direction. We secretly contribute to a better world, even when we do something wrong. (This, of course, has very intricate implications for the concept of freedom, but I will have to leave those aside here.)

In Adam Smith, there is less metaphysical grandeur, but still a well-known case of silent workings behind our backs. The infamous concept of an "invisible hand" guiding our economical behavior toward the best interest of all relies precisely on some surplus meaning that works best, when we remain completely unconscious of it. Smith does not have a vision of the infinite totality of all possible worlds that God saw before creation, but he does offer a theological justification of the current state of affairs, or more precisely of the distribution of wealth. Following his own interest in industry, the producer is "led by an invisible hand to promote an end which is no part of his intention," as it is called in the *Wealth of Nations* from 1776 (Smith 2012: 445). Already in *The Theory of Moral Sentiments* (1759), we are told that the rich naturally share their wealth with the poor, because they employ them to further other, more abstract aims than their own immediate needs. The rich are thus "led by an invisible hand to make nearly the same distribution of the necessaries of life, which would have been made, had the earth been divided into equal portions among all its inhabitants, and thus without intending it, without knowing it, advance the interest of society"

(Smith 2009: 215). Although the invisible hand can to some extent be explained in "scientific terms" by the secondary effects of individual consumption (even the rich can only eat so much), Smith does in fact invoke nothing less than "Providence" to explain why this is so, or maybe rather to reassure us that it is so: "When Providence divided the earth among a few lordly masters, it neither forgot nor abandoned those who seemed to have been left out in the partition. These last too enjoy their share of all that it produces" (Smith 2009: 215).

It is a curious fact that Smith here actually himself seems to be saying more than he intends. In his *History of Astronomy*, which was published posthumously in 1795, but was written some time before 1759, that is, before the *Theory of Moral Sentiments*, he uses the concept of an invisible hand *ironically* to mock those superstitious explanations of nature that assume some inscrutable force behind phenomena that we do not immediately understand. No one ever apprehended "the invisible hand of Jupiter" as an explanation of natural phenomena, as he puts it (Smith 1795: 25). But only a few years later, it is as if this ironic concept slips into his pen, when he seeks to explain how the generation of wealth *somehow* must come to benefit all—a deus ex machina much like the one he himself ridiculed in the realm of astronomy.

The problem with the invisible hand, however, is not that it relies on explanations that go beyond that which can immediately be observed. Rather, it is that it is a *bad* theory about that which goes beyond what can immediately be observed. In spite of its speculative justification of inequality, I think there is something right about Adam Smith's slip: Obviously, the significance of an economic transaction cannot be reduced to the conscious intention an actor has for doing it. Such reductionism would invalidate the Marxist analysis of surplus value as well, or Bourdieu's conception of classes, etc. There *is* in a way an invisible hand guiding our economic behavior, or there are a number of hands, probably pulling in various directions. The problem is the unification of these hands into one hand belonging to a benevolent free market deity. (As Mladen Dolar has elegantly put it, the invisible hand turned out to be a fist performing an uppercut.)

But it is in Hegel that we find the most systematic and integrated conception of a surplus of meaning in human behavior that contains effects beyond what the subject itself had imagined or intended. In his lectures on the *Philosophy of History*, Hegel is very explicit about this, and even at times, he seems quite cynical about the endeavors of human subjects. They tend to think of themselves as masters of their own conduct much more than they really are. True, "*nothing great in the World* has been accomplished without *passion*" (Hegel 2004: 23), and it is clearly the passion and engagement of individuals that have pushed history forward, but the direction of history, its true significance and thereby also the significance of those passionate individual actions, is nonetheless progressing unbeknownst to the actors themselves. The famous concept of the "cunning of reason" says precisely this:

> The special interest of passion is thus inseparable from the active development of a general principle: for it is from the special and determinate and from its negation, that the Universal results.... It is not the general idea that is implicated in opposition and combat, and that is exposed to danger. It remains in the background, untouched and uninjured. This may be called the cunning of reason—that it sets the passions to work for itself, while that which develops its existence through such impulsion pays the penalty and suffers the loss. (Hegel 2004: 32–3)

It is this view that led to the remarkable statement that the great merit of the Peloponnesian War was that it gave occasion to the wonderful historical account given by Thucydides ("his immortal work is the absolute gain which humanity has derived from that contest" (Hegel 2004: 266)).

Hegel's conception of history, like that of Leibniz and Smith, relies on a divine necessity or self-realization ("God governs the world; the actual working of his government—the carrying out of his plan—is the History of the World" (Hegel 2004: 36)), but unlike his predecessors, he insists on the scientific investigation of the structure and movement of this plan and refrains from installing "inscrutable" forces that mysteriously fill out the gaps of our understanding.

The plan, which is carried out, is the realization of freedom, and Hegel shows how the consciousness of freedom has developed throughout human history to its culmination in German thought (and in the German state); in the early Eastern cultures, One was free; in Greece and Rome, some were free; but only in Germany, all are free. This is the idea, which establishes the fundamental structure of history, while human intentions and passions make the content. In a striking metaphor, Hegel describes the idea as "the warp" and the human passions as the "woof" in "the vast arras-web of Universal History" (Hegel 2004: 23). Human passions are thus woven into an already pre-established structure. There is no history without them, but they are not occurring in an empty space; they are always already placed in a web that gradually unfolds and gets its shape from the repeated "*Einschlag*" and from the idea that is there to be woven in.

I think one can overemphasize the Platonic tendency in these remarks. Marx is of course right (in his critique of Hegel's *Philosophy of Right*) that it sometimes seems that the idea is the subject of history, while (what Marx calls) the "actual subject" is reduced to a predicate to this idea (Marx 1970: 209). But, on the other hand, one might ask, What is a subject without its predicates? "[A] meaningless sound, a mere name," as Hegel himself puts it in the *Phenomenology* (Hegel 1977: 12); that is, no concept or idea or substance would be anything without that through which it is something specific. Even God himself is nothing without his self-othering, that is, without the realizing activity made up of human history.[2] Hegel is clearly presupposing a fundamental rationality that unfolds in history, but he just as much sees the actual unfolding of history as that which makes the rational real or through which alone it "is translated into the domain of objectivity," as he says (Hegel 2004: 27). Freedom is *produced*, in other words, and rather than saying that there is freedom, which realizes itself through history, on the back of human suffering, one should say that it is humans themselves who produce freedom, even when they are not aware that this is what they are doing. Or put in another way: What escapes us in the mastery of our own conduct is, paradoxically, not that we are less free than we think or that we cannot realize ourselves as free beings as much as we think, but on the contrary, that we actualize freedom in the course of our actions even more than we are aware of. The "warp" that human action is woven into is thus not a preconceived *course* of history, like in Leibniz, but much more something like the dialectical ground rules that push development forward through negation of the "special and determinate."

> The connection of events above indicated, involves also the fact, that in history an additional result is commonly produced by human actions beyond that which they aim at and obtain—that which they immediately recognize and desire. They gratify their own interest; but something further is thereby accomplished, latent in the actions in question, though not present to their consciousness, and not indulged in their design. (Hegel 2004: 27)

So, there is something fundamentally right about the intuition in Leibniz, Smith, and Hegel that the conscious intentions of an agent are not enough to explain what it is that he or she is out to achieve, and maybe even that they are not enough to explain what it is that he or she really wants. What they also share, however, is a spiritualized personification of the secret master behind the curtain pulling the strings behind the backs of the (human) agent. There is moral value, utility, or progress beyond the scope of the agent's intentions, because a divine foresight, providence, or plan is being realized through the medium of historical actions. This is where I think psychoanalysis offers a stricter and more materialist form of explanation. Indeed, what psychoanalysis offers is precisely what Adam Smith himself requested in his *History of Astronomy*: more "philosophical" and less speculative explanations that connect the gaps in our understanding, which metaphysics or religion fill in with divine intervention or inscrutable forces.

The science of the signifier

Psychoanalysis is closely tied with the acknowledgment of a certain hierarchy and asymmetry between the signifier and the signified. If a sound image were always unequivocally related to a specific and distinct idea, there would be a lot less ambiguity, insecurity, and openness of meaning, and probably also less neurotic problems. One would imagine, for example, that children were initiated into the broad field of language by gradually taking in more and more signs, calmly relating each signifier to an appropriate signified. Any question could be answered with a precise definition: "X is called… " or "Y means…." Maybe in some cases confusion could arise, when certain signifiers obtained several possible meanings, but such confusion could then be sorted out and clarified. Some people would of course still mess up things and confuse categories or meanings, because they were stressed or had experienced something traumatic, or because they were just stupid, but it would be clear to a competent language user that this was what they were doing.

Of course a lot of language does function more or less unproblematically, and one could certainly argue that for the normal and reasonably smooth functioning of culture, it is necessary that most of us most of the time behave as if there really was no problem between the signifiers and the signifieds. But there is, and the question is not really whether or not we pretend that there isn't, but rather *how* we pretend that there isn't, and how well this strategy works to keep the problem at bay. (According to psychoanalysis, there are three basic strategies: repression, disavowal, and foreclosure.)

If we take the ontogenetic route of explanation once again, isn't it quite literally so that in the beginning there is simply a massive network of signifiers that do not have any clear meaning at all? To the child, there is inevitably a "too muchness": an overwhelming reality of signifiers that someone seems to intend something with, but which makes no clear sense to the child. They are sounds that are directed at the child, but do not correspond to anything. "What is it that the Other wants?" is a question that comes up as a natural reaction to this presence of a load of signifiers that don't mean anything or the meaning of which we have to grasp for and cling on to when we seem to have found something that apparently works to satisfy the Other. Therefore, it is the Other who really knows what *we mean* when we start to speak. I do not have authority over the meaning of the sounds that I utter, and so to every utterance, there is attached a fundamental ambiguity, a question, even, of its legitimacy: Is this what it is called? Is this the right expression? Do these words make any sense at all? The signifier is simply there, and we feel that we have to do something with it. So, we start producing meaning, guessing, mimicking, inventing, while it stays in the background, unmoved, pushing us forward toward a meaning that it never grants us completely. To rephrase Hegel: "This may be called the cunning of [the signifier]—that it sets the passions to work for itself, while that which develops its existence through such impulsion pays the penalty and suffers the loss."

In a quite literal sense, I therefore always say more than I am aware of. I am producing meaning without knowing exactly why I am doing it and not knowing exactly what it is that I am saying. In analysis, a single sentence that one says can be the cause of hours and hours of work. In *Seminar V*, Lacan himself maintained that the fact that there are unconscious signifying chains that act on the organism and "influence what appears externally as a symptom" is "the heart of the analytic experience" (Lacan 2017: 388). But while it is true that analysis is in a way "just" about finding out what that, which I say, really means, this meaning cannot be reduced to a semantic implication that can be unraveled by a therapist with thorough knowledge of the language spoken, because it includes the important question of what this means *when I say it* with my particular history and in this precise context. The paradox is that it is the Other that knows what my speech really means, but the Other is not there, since it is rather an expectation or an imaginary tie between the speakers of a language than an actual agent, and so it is the subject itself that must produce the answers. The analyst has to play the role of a stand-in for the Other, but there is no right answer to be found in the analyst. Analysis is more about un-tying perceived necessities in the relation between the signifier and the signified than about finding the "right" relation between them. It is a re-search of the effect of the signifier on the subject.

What a science of the signifier should do is therefore two things. Firstly, it should be a science of the signifier itself—an investigation of the status of the material dimension of the sign, its contingency, and its genesis and function, even its ultimate meaninglessness. "A mere sound," as it were. Secondly, it should investigate the effects of the signifier: The labor and suffering it subdues us to, the surplus semantic meaning that we produce. Maybe one could say that the confrontation with the signifier is the confrontation with the ultimate meaning*less*ness of the foundation of any discourse, whereas the investigation of the effects of the signifier on the subject and culture is a way of dealing with the "meaning-*excess*ness" that is generated by the lack of unambiguity that characterizes the signifier.

First attempts at a semiodicé

Returning to our initial investigation of the secret working of history behind our back, the question that remains to be addressed is then maybe, whether it is possible to consider something like a thought of progress or direction in an account that maintains the insight into the surplus of meaning of human conduct, but refuses to acknowledge a divine intent behind it. Can there be a *telos* of a science of the signifier? In a way, we have already answered this question in the emphasis on the analytical work with the signifier. Partly, analysis, and I think this goes for cultural analysis as well, can unfold, elaborate, bring forward, elucidate realms of meaning that were not clear to the analysand or speaker or writer or artist or politician himself or herself. The *telos* would, in this respect, be a kind of full speech or an uncovering of the truth of the speech that has been uttered. Partly, this work implies a confrontation with the signifier as such.

On a more solemn note, and taking the comparison with Leibniz, Smith, and Hegel in a somewhat different direction, the question would be, if there could be a sense of purpose or direction in the work with the signifier that would somehow resemble the justification of God in Leibniz as well as in Hegel's philosophy of history (which he himself explicitly calls a theodicé)? Can there be something like a "semiodicé," that is, a justification of the sign? If we answer this question in an evolutionary sense, there is no doubt that the sign represents a massive progress, if not even a turning point in history; indeed, it marks the precondition of history as such (since history is defined by being recorded in writing). Gottlob Frege compared the use of signs to the invention of tacking in sailing, that is, the ability to use the wind to sail up against the wind (Frege 1964: 156). Instead of merely passively receiving sensual input from our surroundings, signs made it possible to erect posts that gradually formed patterns and insights that allowed us not only to systematize this input but also to prescribe laws to nature itself, to put it in Kantian terms. Hegel has a rather beautiful metaphor for the way we construct edifices that work against our own immediate interests. When building a house, we make use of the elements in order to shape the material, iron, wood, stones that we build the house from. We exploit gravity in the stones that naturally press downward—to carry up high walls. "Thus," he writes, "the elements are made use of in accordance with their nature, and yet to co-operate for a product, by which their operation is limited" (Hegel 2004: 27). Wind is ultimately used to protect us from the wind, etc. Something similar goes for the construction of society in general, Hegel says: "Thus the passions of men are gratified; they develop themselves and their aims in accordance with their natural tendencies, and build up the edifice of human society; thus fortifying a position for Right and Order *against themselves*" (ibid.). (One is reminded here of the passage from abstract law to morality in the *Philosophy of Right*, where the subject of the legal state realizes that he *would want to be punished*, if he should violate the law (Hegel 1999, 5: § 100).) The signifier is the primordial erection, the inscription of an absence into the flux of sensual impressions. Lacan precisely described the signifier as something very different from an imprint of sensual impressions (such as it may be defined in the empiricist tradition). The signifier is not the trace left behind by a footprint, for example, but *the effacing or erasure* of the footprint. In this sense, the signifier is an "Aufhebung," as he says, playing on the double meaning of this expression in German: simultaneously a cancellation and a sublimation or "raising to a higher power" (Lacan 2017: 323).

So, the signifier carries with it not only immense practical advantages but also an elevation of the very existence of human beings. We are not merely referred to the "code," as Lacan calls it, which is the communication system that allows nonsignifying animals to exchange information and data, but to a signifying chain that both cancels and elevates that which it marks itself upon. Is there progress in this history? Undoubtedly. Can we make sense of a concept of the absolute that occurs in the realm of the signifier? Why not? The concerto to end all concertos, full speech, truth events. But is there a *telos*, a direction, or an end to this history? Maybe the good news of the science of the signifier is that the end is essentially defined by being a beginning. In analysis, the end is marked not by the complete transparency of the symbolic order, nor of the answer to the question of what the Other really wants, but much more by a kind of realization that one might move more freely in this order, relate to the Other differently. The destination of analysis is in this sense precisely the signifier itself. "You have arrived at the signifier. You may now make use of it."

Notes

1 Kant actually suggested something like this to explain a possible positive dimension of the earthquake in Lisbon in 1755. He later abandoned such moral explanations of natural events—a change which, in Susan Neiman's description, "marks the beginning of the modern" (Neiman 2002: 246).
2 This use of the concept self-othering relies on Mladen Dolar's interpretation of the *Phenomenology of Spirit*, as unfolded in an interview with the Center for Wild Analysis (Radio 24/7, week 31, 2012). Hegel uses the term *Anderswerden* (Hegel 1999, 2: 19)—or *becoming-other* in the English translation (Hegel 1977: 11).

References

Frege, G. (1964 [1882]), "On the Scientific Justification of a Concept-Script," *Mind*, 73 (290): 155–60.

Hegel, G. W .F. (1977 [1807]), *Hegel's Phenomenology of Spirit*, Oxford, New York, Toronto, Melbourne: Oxford University Press.

Hegel, G. W. F. (1999, 2 [1807]), *Phänomenologie des Geistes*, Hauptwerke in sechs Bänden, Frankfurt: Felix Meiner Verlag.

Hegel, G. W. F. (1999, 5 [1820]), *Grundlinien der Philosophie des Rechts*, Hauptwerke in sechs Bänden, Frankfurt: Felix Meiner Verlag.

Hegel, G. W. F. (2004 [1837]), *The Philosophy of History*, New York: Dover Philosophical Classics.

Lacan, J. (2017 [1998]), *Formations of the Unconscious, The Seminar of Jacques Lacan, Book V*, Cambridge: Polity Press.

Leibniz, G. W. (1990 [1710]), *Theodicy: Essays on the Goodness of God, the Freedom of Man and the Origin of Evil*, Chicago: Open Court.

Marx, K. (1970 [1843]), *Kritik des Hegelschen Staatsrecht*, Berlin: Dietz Verlag.

Neiman, S. (2002), *Evil in Modern Thought*, Princeton University Press.

Smith, Adam (1795), *Essays on Philosophical Subjects*, London: Cadell/Davies.

Smith, Adam (2009 [1759]), *The Theory of Moral Sentiments*, London: Penguin Books.

Smith, Adam (2012 [1776]), *Wealth of Nations*, London: Wordsworth Classics of World Literature.

2

The Echo of the Signifier in the Body: How Drive Works (or Not) Today

Juliet Flower MacCannell

Is the signifier losing—if it has not already lost—the power to create and sustain the domain of the human? Is the labor of the signifier—to shape us and our societies—still beyond doubt today? And if it is indeed waning, what is taking its place? Here I explore the implications that the current fate of the signifier has for our bodies, our social orders, and our creativity.

The relation of the signifier to meaning

There is no meaning that is supported except by the relay to an other signification: touching at the extreme the remark that there is no extant language for whom the question of its insufficiency in covering the whole field of meaning is asked—being a fact of its existence as language that it responds to all needs (Lacan 1966: 498; 1977: 150).

Ferdinand de Saussure's revolutionary discovery of how language creates meanings from meaningless sounds by the mechanism he termed *the signifier* was for me the confirmation of the line of thought about language that I had studied closely in my second year of doctoral work at Cornell University (1965–6): theories of language in the eighteenth century, especially Jean-Jacques Rousseau's *Essay on the Origin of Language* (1990).[1] Rousseau demonstrated what Giambattista Vico had earlier argued: That just as humans have created our own history, we originated language independently of Adamic language (God's granting Adam the power to name the animals).

Rousseau likewise did not take words as God-given names for things. Words, he argued, were created to *respond* to whomever and whatever we encountered, to cope with the distance (physical or social) between us and them—or it. Rousseau took an openly expressive stance on the originating impulse of language. Words were devised to reach across a divide between oneself and others. Though words could not actually bridge the abyss separating us, they could mediate (while also symbolically marking) the space between us. In rhetorical or literary terms, the original word is thus "poetic": a metaphor, a "carrying across."[2]

Metaphor relates disparate things by conveying a sense of a fundamental affinity between them. As Aristotle put it, "a good metaphor implies an intuitive perception of the similarity in the dissimilar" (*De Poetica*). It is a linkage, however, that implicitly depends on differentiating its object from other (unstated) things: To say, "My love is like a red, red rose" is tacitly to say it is not like a weed or an onion. The origin of language was not a simple act of generating names for things; it was the original symbolization of likeness and difference.

Saussure's semiology—the "science of signs in the heart of society—carried on this Enlightenment project, whose basic premise was that language is the product of a human society whose precondition is the existence of language—a language that is ironically completely unknown outside of human society. Language generates signs that respond, in the strongest sense—including emotionally—to our experiences, especially of other human beings. Signs are formed by linking a sound to a concept, a signifier to a signified. A signifier is articulated to another signifier by traversing a void between them to make articulate speech. Articulation is based on the absence of sound, that is, on the consonantal stops that cut off the streaming of undifferentiated noise when tongue touches teeth or lip touches lip. Closing a physical gap produces a signifying gap.

In Saussure's account, the succession of signifiers alone generates meaning (the combination of the signifier and the signified), since in language there are only differences, without any positive terms. Indeed, if there is to be any sign, it is only by virtue of being addressed to an other who responds, and it is only their concurrence about its meaning (or the signified) that makes a sound into a sign. In fact, it is this agreement (or social contract) alone that makes the sign into a symbol, symbolic of the social tie that establishes it. (Which is also why it is language that socializes the infant: when addressed, the infant is called on to respond.)

The ongoing addition of signifiers retroactively produces the impression of "meaning" and prospectively anticipates ones that may later modify the sense just fashioned. There is no transcendent meaning outside the process of a second signifier's (S_2) endowing a prior one (S_1) with a significance it cannot nor would not have on its own. And because meaning is structured solely by adding yet one more signifier to the total of already created signifiers, Saussure underscored the incompleteness of language and the need for creative additions to keep it alive (Saussure 1959: 75).

This is the essence of the citation above from Lacan: Language is what responds to all contingencies; any focus on meaning that excludes consideration of the work of the signifier, Lacan goes on, "leads to the absurd impasse logical positivism finds itself in, searching for the 'meaning of meaning'" (Lacan 1966: 497 my translation and emphasis).[3]

The year after my study of Rousseau, Jacques Derrida published his book, *De la Grammatologie* (1967), which treated Rousseau's *Essai* along with Saussure's semiology. Derrida notes early in his book (1967: 35) that Parisian psychoanalysis was at that time doing the most original work on linguistics anywhere in the world. He did not mention Lacan by name (1967: 33–5).[4] But of course it was Lacan who had brought Saussure's "exact study of the liaisons proper to the signifier and of the scope of their function in the *genesis* of the signified" to French psychoanalysis (Lacan 1966: 497; 1977: 149).

Derrida adopted (as Lacan had earlier) the thesis that the signifier generates meaning strictly through deferrals and differential relays (Derrida 1967: 35; 1974: 20–1). But Derrida demanded a stringent theory of the signified, criticizing Saussure for thinking there is even the slightest material difference between the signifier and the signified: The "difference between the signifier and the signified is *nothing*," he says (1967: 36; 1974: 22–3).[5] And if there is no ontological distinction between the signifier and the signified—if all we have are signifiers—then we must question whether the concept that makes a signifier into a sign even exists.[6] A decade before Derrida, Lacan took a different attitude toward the signifier while also recognizing its capital importance. In 1957, he said the signifier carries the whole weight of meaning, but its materiality should not be overlooked: "the signifier enters into the signified, namely, in a form which, not being immaterial, raises the question of its place in reality" (Lacan 1966: 500: 1977: 152). Lacan remarks:

> [W]e will fail to pursue the question [of the nature of language] further as long as we cling to the illusion that the signifier answers to the function of representing the signified, or better, that the signifier has to answer for its existence in the name of any signification whatever. (1966: 498; 1977: 150)[7]

But Lacan also said something more important than Derrida did when it came to the signified, the concept. Lacan never lost sight of a power and an energy in the signifier that Derrida misses, a subjective, unconscious authority that produces beyond conscious meanings other meanings incapable of articulation, meanings that insist, although they can never be spoken.

> [O]nly someone without eyes could not see from what radiating center the signifier sends forth its light into the shadow of incomplete significations... For the signifier by its very nature, always anticipates meaning by unfolding its dimension before it... From which we can say that it is in the chain of the signifier that meaning "insists" but that none of its elements "consists" in the signification of which it is at the moment capable. (1966: 500–1; 1977: 152–3)

The "meaning" that "insists" in the chaining of signifiers is what Lacan comes to call "truth" (disparaged by Derrida among others in today's political sphere), the never more than half-spoken and never fully articulated truth of the speaking being that nonetheless exercises real impact on its life. Instead, Lacan said that there remains a *bar* not only between the signifier and signified and another *signified*, beyond the signifier's ostensible concept, another signified that the signifier represses, an unconscious response that it alone evokes.

Lacan calls attention to a dimension of language that Derrida later dismisses in emphasizing the nothingness of the signified. Lacan could never subscribe to Derrida's argument that the signifier is aconceptual, that is, that there is no distinction between the signified and its signifier except for the difference between them. That is because Lacan recognized, in the effect of the signifier, something more explosive and more generative, more reflective of human experience, than a mere concept: its continued relation to the *thing* the signifier has displaced, substituted for.

> If we try to grasp in language the constitution of the object, we cannot fail to notice that this constitution is to be found only at the level of concept, a very different thing from a simple nominative, and that the *thing*, when reduced to the nothing, breaks up into the double, divergent beam of the "cause" (*causa*) in which it has taken shelter in the word *chose*, and the nothing (*rien*) to which it has abandoned its Latin dress (*rem*). (1966: 498; 1977: 150)

Unconscious drive as the by-product of the signifier

Lacan tied the "radiant energy" of the signifier to what it produces *beyond* its main task, that of generating symbolic, conscious meanings: It constitutes a dimensionless arena beyond time and space, where insistent (non-)meanings, "Things," haunt the very "no-thingness" of the chain of signifiers that dislodged them from their dwelling in the Real.

No multiplication or proliferation of symbolic "meanings" can ever completely bury the signifier's true impact—its generation, alongside overt meanings, of unspoken ones with immense affective impact.[8] The meaning-effect of the signifier, its "signified," is thus not only symbolic; it is *unconscious*.[9]

The signifier is the repression that produces the unconscious because of the body's response to speech. Every positive speech act implies carving an aperture that simulates the original physical exit and entry points of pleasure: the orifices of the natural body are simulated by the after-effect of the signifier, as fake openings to be "filled in" with fantasies of enjoying the Real Thing (that unspeakable real thing the signifier had tried to reduce to "no-thing," to a mere symbol). When the signifier banishes the thing, it unwittingly births another, ghostly Thing, a phantom animated by the excess of the energy expended by the signifier. The cuts made by the signifier supercharge the libidinal passion for the "thing" lost to the signifier and which returns to the body in fantasy form. This is why Lacan says clearly, "Drive is the echo in the body of the fact that there is speech" (2016: 9).[10]

Internal bars or breaks/brakes placed on the mental energy that overstimulates the organism never constitute a total repression: A "hyper-energy" (Freud 1956a) of undischarged stimulations from within becomes an insistent demand to discharge the libido dammed up by repression. Libidinal passion vibrates in us, unconsciously, as hyper-energy accumulates, pooling in our mental apparatus to become *drive*, which Freud defines as "a concept on the frontier between the mental and the somatic… the psychical representative of the stimuli originating from within the organism" (Freud repeats this exact definition twice, 1953: 168, 1957: 122).[11]

Drive, the astonishing by-product of the signifier, thus turns out to be of capital importance for us as human, speaking beings. Why? Because drive, too, has its own rebound, its own reverberation, its own echo to which we must respond. Freud puts it thus: Drive pushes us to exert our minds, to do the mental labor necessary to redirect drive's insistent urging toward livable rather than lethal ends. When drive reaches the mind, Freud says, it is "as a measure of the demand made upon the mind for work in consequence of its connection to the body" (Freud 1953: 168). The work demanded is, of course, the satisfaction of needs that are more than bodily, that are fantasmatic.[12]

As speaking beings, we must constantly and ingeniously devise ways to sublimate (and partially satisfy) drive's incessant demands.[13] If we do not, we risk yielding to a fantasized *jouissance* while our real needs go unmet: to give way on our desire (lack of full enjoyment) is literally to give in to death drive. So we must continually invent new ways of duping death drive. But how? We have by and large reconciled ourselves to the ongoing productive/destructive work of adding new signifiers to reenergize our drives and animate creative responses to them. New signifiers can then strike us the way a gong or a bell is struck, with a resonance more than acoustic. They must reverberate within us, for only if they unleash fresh unconscious drives can they also renew our mental resistance to those drives.

Lacan warns that any aspiration to halt the process is ultimately a variant of death drive—the end of meaning-making. Fulfilling the dream of totalizing knowledge and finalizing language by quantifying "meaning" is ultimately a nightmare of stagnation.

> This other signifier is not alone. The stomach of the Other, the big Other, is full of them. This stomach is like some monstrous Trojan horse that provides the foundations for the fantasy of a totality-knowledge [*savoir-totalité*]. It is, however, clear that its function entails that something comes and strikes it from without, otherwise nothing will ever emerge from it. (Lacan 1975: 33)

A next signifier must "strike it from without" with a resonance that echoes—not only through our physical body but throughout the linguistic body.

> There must be something in the signifier which resonates. It is surprising that this has been in no way apparent to English philosophers. I call them philosophers because they have a rock-solid belief that language has no effect. They imagine that there are drives and so on… for they don't know what a drive is: the echo in the body of the fact that there is speech. For speech to resonate,… the body must be sensitive to it. (Lacan 1975: 4)

Language or code? The fate of the signifier today

In what follows, I argue that signifiers seem to have to work harder and harder these days to provoke any response of the kind Lacan describes. Does the signifier, indeed, continue to constitute the most singular, evocative force in the formation of our bodies, our psyches, and our social ties? Can it continue to maintain the symbolic order as a living entity, open to change? Has that crucial *next* signifier now lost this tone? Or have we simply become tone deaf to it?

It is true that, under the rubric of postmodernism, the value of the *new* has recently come strongly into question. Lacan nonetheless remains faithful to the thesis that only the advent of a *new* signifier (that permits the *next* to emerge from the "Order") grants knowledge (S_2) *and* the linguistic formations that support its true Symbolic standing. If this Order becomes (as it so often does) sclerotic, it is no longer enough simply to add on a signifier that has lost touch with its link to meaning: that would offer neither promise nor hope.

Human language has never been a simple stockpile of ready-made meanings. Yet today this fundamental assumption has come into question. Has the Babel of globalized late capitalism radically altered the form(ul)ation of us as speaking beings, split by the signifier and subject to the pressures of unsatisfiable unconscious drives that force us to create alternative ways of enjoying?

After all, today we have accumulated a great many ready-made meanings that as they are piled up become fodder for meaninglessness. We witness capitalist economies devising the quasi-automatic generation of as many intentionally meaningless names for things as one could imagine: for example, those names of automobile models with a vague aura of a signification they do not possess (e.g., "Sentra" and "Elantra" are Japanese-made car models sold in America; a pseudo-Italian word, "Miata" names a sports car by Mazda in the USA while in its country of origin, Japan, it is named "Roadstar," etc.). Not to mention the seemingly endless proliferation of terms for new gender identities (cissexual, transsexual, bisexual, and more)—all now *consciously chosen*. (A recent *Bizarro* cartoon by Dan Piraro shows parents telling their children that right now they have the choice of being LGBT, "but surely there will be many more by the time you grow up." Indeed, there is already an expansion: LGBTIQ.)

When language loses to imaginary satiety, the pen is no longer mightier than the sword and its erstwhile productions (poems, metaphors, songs, lovers' discourses—and even psychoanalysis) can no longer resonate with us or move us. Indeed, late capitalist culture already seems to require that we *not* be driven from within, and that drive should emanate exclusively from the external economic order. Capitalism promotes the belief that it handles our drives for us, thereby releasing us from the requirement to do the work necessary to fend off the lethalness of fantasmatic *jouissance*.

The takeover of the crucial functioning of drive in our lives has now become a literal triumph of death drive: consider the recent demise of 40-year-old John Brown, a former Navy SEAL, who put his Tesla Model S on autopilot so he could watch a Harry Potter film on his car's video screen. The vehicle's radar sensor showed no problems ahead—but the autopilot was misreading the white side of a large truck turning in front of the car, categorizing it as "sky," while the camera, aimed at the pavement beneath the truck, showed the road ahead as "clear." The automobile drove into the van, or rather under it, shearing off its top along with the driver's head, as it continued driving autonomously for some miles before it came to a halt.[14] Witness as well the two men in Northern San Diego County in California who fell off a bluff recently while playing the cell phone game Pokémon Go (*The San Francisco Chronicle* 2019, 7/15/16: D8).

What better figure for giving over your mental labor to the semantic/categorical machine imperatives—yielding to imperatives that can never birth even a single new metaphor, let alone a new signifier? (Zukovic (2006: 25) says a computer chokes on metaphor). If unconscious drive insists we devise ever-new ways to satisfy it, there is not much evidence of an anxious desire for novel ways of "pursuing happiness." Indeed, capitalist discourse seems to rely on recycling old, used-up meanings to advertise its provision of E-Z *jouissance*.

Lacan already noted (*Seminar XVII*) that in late capitalism we bathe in an aura of satisfaction, as if our drives need no longer be frustrated by the limits placed on us by language and the symbolic social contract. This is, of course, a false aura based on flooding our world with what Lacan called the "fake satisfactions" or *jouissances en toc* embodied in proliferating gadgets (he said this before the plethora of i-gadgets like iPhones, iPods, iPads, etc. were invented) (Lacan 2007: 162; MacCannell 2006: 205).

To sum up: the implicit claim made by the endless proliferation of part-words, sound-bites, made-up names, and the like, names detached from signification, is that we have achieved a final victory over the disruptive, disturbing impact of unconscious drive. Even many educational institutions are busily consigning language, narrative, literature, and the work of the signifier to blissful oblivion: after their second year of high school in the United States, "English" courses no longer teach works of fiction; instead, students learn how to read business reports and other data-filled material. This clearly limits the signifier by cutting off its "poetic" or metaphoric side.

The question remains as to why this implicit claim of "satisfying all drives" became a hallmark of our era? Let me take perhaps a more subtle example, one completely word-based, of an assault on the signifier that shows up in a recent advertising campaign for a new perfume.[15] The scent industry might be seen as in the business of re-establishing the olfactory as indispensable to sexual attractions: Once human beings attained erect posture, the close association of smell with sexuality was broken. Smell was displaced in favor of sight as the means of attracting a mate. Bodily odors (and not only those from our sexual parts) came to seem base and unpleasant, while visible beauty became the dominant factor in sexual appeal.

The vast amount of retail space devoted to perfume counters might lead one to assume the return of the repressed olfactory. But if we study closely the commodification of scent, we find the perfume industry is not really in the business of making smell indispensable to sexual attraction. We also find the capitalist system of commodification in which this industry participates actually dismisses sexual difference as something to be overcome.

Consider Chanel's recent marketing for a new perfume, *Allure*. It illustrates my first caution that the nose is not what is really being promoted, not even displaced by the eye (as Freud thought), but by the ear. *Allure*, the perfume's name, is obviously intended to imply that the woman who uses it will attract men (and, since Polge—Chanel's "nose"—later created *Allure pour homme*, we imagine that he had women in mind).

Yet it can only suggest this if we hear the name with an English-speaker's ear. *Allure*—for the Anglophone—hints at temptation and lure, at an attractiveness that may be deceptive, and it is most usually applied to a woman. To the French-speaker's ear, however, *allure* is gender neutral, and simply means someone's natural or customary way of doing something: neither marked as feminine nor related to the seductive deceptiveness the word denotes in English.

Second, the perfume is described as being an almost overwhelming profusion of aromas that would bring about outright olfactory confusion and void the particularity of this invented scent.

> Like all Chanel perfumes [*Allure*] has a rich and complex composition. Fresh and citrusy at the beginning, it opens in lavishing floral heart to wooden and vanilla nuances and leaves lingering and fickle scent. It is best to describe it by the various accords it possesses.

One has to wonder at this fantasized blending of differences, at the odorous and at the conceptual level (opposites harmoniously coexist, e.g., "fickle" yet "lingering"). Its marketing has the scent accomplishing a miraculous, impossible reconciliation of irreconcilable differences: flower and tree, fruit and flower, trunk and root. *Allure*'s "accords" are a sustained erasure of contrasts, oppositions, and differences.

Out of this plethora, the verbal description of the fragrance, as much as or perhaps more than the physical ingredients, blends a single aroma (or fantasy of an aroma; we are not told whether these are natural fragrances or chemically concocted ones) in order to introduce it into the global market as the purest commodity, conjured chiefly by words. These words, please note, are exclusively names for things: they evoke sense images (visual and olfactory) without resonance beyond. As such they are cleverly designed to mask, yet hint at, their ultimate source: globalized trade and its twin, colonialism.

Each aroma contributing to *Allure* is an exotic scent that originates in plant life outside of Europe, brought there by international trade and colonial adventures. The specific fragrances making up the advertised "accords" are "lemon and bergamot; mandarin and peach" (all originating in Asia); "rose of May/jasmine" (Asia for rose of May; only one species of jasmine is native to Europe, while the water lily is the national flower of Bangladesh and Sri Lanka); "peony/magnolia" (these come from Asia, Southern Europe, western North America; and the West Indies); "sandalwood/vetiver" (South India and Asia); "orange/vanilla" (orange is native to China and was brought to Europe by Arabophone peoples, while vanilla comes from Mexico and Central America).

With its global credentials established, this perfume is ready for a worldwide economy, whose miraculously universal appeal transcends all minor differences of nation or even of sex. The perfume's concoction and its marketing scheme operate at a level well beyond the division of the sexes, so *Allure* thus decidedly does *not* signal a return of the nose to sexual attraction. For women the perfume bears no real linkage to the sexual difference Lacan described—to the logical divide under which masculine and feminine line up, regardless of their biological bodies.

The muting of all natural/symbolic differences merged into a single smell in *Allure* is analogous to the merging of cultural and sexual differences into the artificially bound "global order," ruled by only one side of sexual logic, a masculine universal that recognizes *no difference*—and where, we might add, "society doesn't exist."

Slavoj Žižek claims ours is the era of the obscene or sadistic superego, where an "anything goes" mentality combines with intensifying self-imposed regulations against (guilty) pleasures (like "giving up" sugar or more recently gluten). Žižek repeatedly argues that symbolic law simply hides its true origin in the obscene superego, and he exhibits very little interest in symbolic social ties and their formations because he sees them as ultimately rooted in obscenity. Any limits placed on enjoyment today are individual (not moral) choices (we can just deny ourselves certain pleasures and thus restrain the dominant imperative to just "Enjoy!"). No need, that is, for socio-symbolic laws to modulate our behavior. Ironically, of course, if these self-denials (which somehow are always a collective trend or fad) are our "own" doing, then we can logically dispense with the need for expending mental effort on finding sublimated or creative alternatives to the problem of satisfying unconscious drives.

Žižek is insightful at the level of individual psychology, especially since today's capitalist order has established the ego and its superego in domains well beyond their origination in the unconscious. He does not address corresponding alterations in the constitution of *society* itself—material changes in what Lacan called "discourse" or varying forms of the social tie—the tie between subjects, represented by the signifier to other signifiers, symbolic ties, because he sees those ties as simply between egos based on images, not subjects.[16] Žižek's oversight is not inadvertent, however, as it is entirely consonant with the direction I have been detailing in the discourse of capitalism: its claim that there is no unconscious, no drive that *it* cannot satisfy—and above all that "society doesn't exist."

In contrast, in his seminars from the 1950s to the 1970s, Jacques Lacan began to hold "discourse"--the "form of the social tie"--to be an alternative axis to the simple oppositions of language to speech and writing to authentic voice, twisting these oppositions until they reveal their unconscious substrate: discourse both supports and alienates its subjects in its pretended embodiment of the finite whole of language (in contrast, perhaps, to the infiniteness of code/numbers). But every discourse has an impediment, a truth it cannot articulate. The discourse Lacan targeted in his seventeenth seminar, *The Other Side of Psychoanalysis*, was "university" discourse, which imperceptibly shades into and becomes indistinguishable in his view from the discourse of capitalism.

Capitalism, Lacan said, begins by doing away with sex (1974: 51).[17] As he expanded on the singular feature of the modern "artificial" group, that "everyone must have the same and be the same" (Freud 1956b: 120–1), Lacan took very seriously Freud's insight that in such groups even sexual differences are banned: to the point where the "sexual couple" is actually a protest *against* group life.

What this means, and it is time to say it clearly: the *enjoyment* that capitalist discourse promises you is what is indeed only satisfiable as an *individual* who needs no partner, no social link, no other who responds to you or that you are responsible to and for (such as children). No sex, in short, just the *jouissance de l'idiot*[18]—idiosyncratic, purely individual, sans society, and completely meaningless.

In "Instincts and Their Vicissitudes" Freud proposed that "two groups of… primal drives should be distinguished: the *ego* or *self-preservative* drives and the *sexual* drives." He hypothesizes that the "conflict between the claims of sexuality and those of the ego" is at the root of psychoneurotic disorders (Freud 1957: 124). What distinguishes Freud's "sex drives" from "ego drives" is that the former must link to someone or something *other* to seek out its satisfaction—in all its vicissitudes (Freud details the others involved in sado-masochism, scopophilia, exhibitionism, and even in taking oneself as another: "turning round upon the subject's own self"). The sex drive is not only what makes one a link in a longer reproductive chain, tying you to your forebears and progeny. It also means that in terms of attaining organ pleasure beyond self-pleasuring, you need another, a partner, to whom you are linked as well.

So, it seems, to be consonant with the demand that society not exist, we simply set aside the sex drive in favor of the ego drives.

This is the actual basis for the now faddish claims that we are indeed in a post-human society.[19] Consider the many apocalyptic alarms raised these days by the discourse of techno-capitalism, its takeover of creativity (and I claim, the drives), and the resignation most thinkers feel before it. Let me here turn once again to Derrida's *La Carte Postale* (1980) to illustrate: Derrida says in this text that everything we have considered the very heart of what the signifier has created in our human history (literature, philosophy, love letters, and psychoanalysis) is about to vanish under the weight of technology's displacement of the work of the signifier. With their loss, the "human" in our history vanishes as well.

Can we not ask Derrida, however, if his early refusal to divide the signifier from the signified has influenced his later pronouncements in *La Carte Postale* about the end of the human and of literature, philosophy, psychoanalysis, and love letters? How are we to deal with such an apocalypse? Must we resign ourselves to the fate of being defined exclusively by how we are encoded in a cybernetic field and unable to use the signifier to represent us as subjects for another signifier?

My colleague J. Hillis Miller had an exemplary response to Derrida's observations about the looming technological eclipse of literature and love. He cites Proust's image of seeing his grandmother eerily split in two by the invention of the telephone:

> The introduction of a new technology, while it still overlaps with the old, provides inadvertently, by allowing Marcel to juxtapose the two grandmothers [one telephonically near, the other real and far away], a striking confirmation of Marcel's assertion that we superimpose upon or project into the dark and forever impenetrable shadow that is another person this or that set of assumptions about what is "really there"
>
> ...
>
> It also provides a way to understand what Derrida means when he says that the new regime of telecommunications will put an end to literature, philosophy, psychoanalysis, and love letters. (Miller 2001: 147 and 193)

Miller's response to Derrida's "new regime of telecommunications"?

> The comment Derrida makes through his protagonist in *The Post Card* [on the end of literature, et al.]... is truly frightening, at least to a lover of literature like me... the comment arouses in me (by an efficacious performative effect) the passions of anxiety, fear, disgust, disbelief, and perhaps a little secret desire to see what it would be like to live beyond the end of literature, love letters, philosophy and psychoanalysis. It would be like living beyond the end of the world. (Miller 2001: 155–6)

The "response" evoked in Hillis by Derrida's thesis is not mere conventional anxiety. Anxiety is avowedly part of it, but this fear is supplemented with a surprising jubilation, an unexpected anticipation of incalculably *new things to come*. It is also supplemented with a remarkable desire to know what cannot, according to the current logical arrangement of things, actually be known ("perhaps a little secret desire to see what it would be like to live beyond the end of literature, love letters, philosophy and psychoanalysis. It would be like living beyond the end of the world").

Hillis Miller anticipates, that is, a *next* signifier that might emerge from the ruins of literature, love, and philosophy. The anticipation he articulates here is no shallow, casual, or even rational reaction. What Derrida prompts Hillis to desire is no less than the desire to witness strange new events, and to do so from the point where the literary writer always stands: at a point "beyond the end of literature."

If my attention to tonality as a "poetic" alternative to seeing language as a treasury of ready-made meanings consternates you,[20] I can refer you to the 1938 essay by American critic Kenneth Burke, who described semantic meaning (as opposed to poetic meaning) as an "aim to evolve a vocabulary that gives the name and address of every event in the universe" (Burke 1994: 122). (Could anything more aptly describe the deep intention behind the Internet, the basic assumptions of "coding"?)

Poetic meaning ignores the boxes around semantic meanings by attending instead to what lies beyond pigeonholed individual meanings: poetic meanings. Burke says poetic is the "kind of meaning [which] *impinges* upon semantic meaning ... [and] cannot be encompassed with perfect fidelity to the *semantic ideal*":

> When you have isolated your individual by the proper utilizing of the postal process, you have not at all adequately encompassed his "meaning"... because he means one thing to his family, another to his boss, another to his underlings, another to his creditors, etc. All such meanings are *real* enough, since at every point people act towards him on the basis of these meanings. (Burke 1994: 124–5)

Dare we say that such relational, situated "meanings" that Burke terms "poetic" are the "*next*" signifiers awaited by Lacan and by us—and by Hillis Miller?—the signifiers that emerge when established ones are displaced from their semantic categories, and put together in ways that stir new responses?

What I find exemplary in Hillis Miller—and a challenge to us all as students of language, literature, psychoanalysis, and the signifier—is the way he positions his response as an ideal "demand from the other," a demand to answer back. Miller productively saves literature from the dustbin of history—to which postmodern theorists and cybernetic prophecies often readily consign it. The poised prose of Hillis Miller's response removes "all the sting of unanswerability that automatically resides in powerful theoretical assertions about how code displaces language as we have known it" (MacCannell 2005).

Hillis' own critical performance suggests that after each and every apocalypse, the signifier will still be standing--if only in the form of a responsible questioning—and it may continue to evoke that drive to deny its power, the drive that may still be the strongest resource for evoking the *next* signifier.[21]

Notes

1   I studied Rousseau's multifaceted *Essay On the Origin of Language*. It is filled with striking ideas—that language could only have been invented on an island, that the first words uttered in mild southern climes were « *Aimez-moi,* » ("Love me!"), while in harsher northern regions they were « *Aidez-moi* » ("Help me!"). The charming picture Rousseau painted was that language was really invented to express love for or a reaching out for another: In one scenario he describes a metaphorical crossing of the distance between two would-be lovers from opposing groups who meet at a well that both groups must use for water, and they fall in love. (Why did they not settle for gestures or facial expressions to convey their passion? Why trouble themselves to invent words as a means of bringing them closer while still marking the distance between them? These are Rousseau's real questions.)

2   Metonymy is the variant that emphasizes a connection between things rather than their difference from each other. Rousseau says that figurative language precedes conceptual or literal language; the first "meaning" evoked as a response--fear or love or pity—precedes the literal meaning, which comes later, after reflection on the experience, as in his example of a man running through a forest who spies an unfamiliar figure, and out of fear, pronounces him a "giant." Later he realizes their equality of stature and invents a word/concept to cover both of them: "man."

3   The published English version reads, "That leads logical positivism in search of the 'meaning of meaning,' as its objective is called in the language of its devotees" (1977: 150). Lacan refers to I. A. Richards's *Mencius on the Mind.*
4   The English translation renders the passage this way: "Outside of linguistics, it is in psychoanalytic research that this breakthrough seems at present to have the greatest likelihood of being expanded" (Derrida 1974: 21).
5   In the original French: « *la différence entre le signifiant et le signifié n'est rien* ».
6   I was particularly struck by a passage on Babel from Lacan's "Rome Discourse": "Let he who cannot reach at its horizon the subjectivity of his epoch therefore rather renounce it [analysis]. For how could he who knows nothing of the dialectic that engages him in a symbolic movement with so many lives possibly make his being the axis of those lives? Let him be well acquainted with the whorl into which his era draws him in the ongoing enterprise of Babel, and let him learn his function as interpreter in the discordance of languages." (Jacques Lacan, "Function and Field of Speech and Language" (Lacan 1977: 106-7)). Babel shows up again later in Derrida's The *Ear of the Other*—and this then led me to formulate (for this essay) just what has been so glaringly missing in psychoanalytic method. That is the way for psychoanalysis, theoretically and practically, to account for how the subject is linked to discursive regimes that alter, rapidly or slowly, in the course of history. How is it linked to his social and symbolic others: that is, how the subject is, quite literally, *written*?
7   After Derrida ironized Lacan's seminar on *Poe's Purloined Letter* in "*Le Facteur de la vérité*", few ever looked at them together on the matter of "the letter" or writing, again. The critique cemented Lacan's critical reception as having missed the boat on writing and having missed the point that *écriture* (the graphic) does not directly convey truth: there is no *aletheia* in or of writing. Lacan, of course, distinguished between "meaning" and "truth," and made the inability to convey a truth the cornerstone of his discourses: truth is precisely what a discourse is designed *not* to say; every discourse is formed around an unspeakable impossibility, a sticking point the discourse can neither express nor avoid. His examination of the *parlêtre*, the horizon of the speaking being's immersion in discourse, is hardly very far from Derrida's graphematic universal.
8   Thus distilling Freud's insights on the construction, of the child's erotic body in the *Project for a Scientific Psychology* (MacCannell 2013: 73-89).
9   Lacan, *Seminar XVII* (2007, 81: 1991: 93). See MacCannell 2006: 205.
10 Author's modification of translation. Price translates: "of a fact of saying" (French: "du fait qu'il y a un dire"). Lacan will ascribe to language the very shaping of the infant's erotic body as well: "L'homme… pense de qu'une structure, celle du langage—le mot le comporte—de qu'une structure découpe son corps, et qui n'a rien à faire avec l'anatomie" (1974: 16). "Language--the word implies it (*language/*

tongue/blade)--carves up [the] body"--but what precisely has it carved away? The animal body "lost" to language returns to it in fantasies of unlimited enjoyment--fantasies that shape our sexuality by zoning our bodies erogenously. *Blade* is the root sense of *la langue*. This is, by the way, entirely consistent with Freud's view of the origin of mental life and of the drives: i.e., the infant responds to what is closest to it—the Mother, the *Nebenmensch, Das Ding*, maternal speech. Freud (1956a: 317 ff.) writes about it in the section "on satisfaction," where the "helpful person" and the "hostile object" are two ways of characterizing the "*Nebenmensch*."

11 Drive is "a measure of the demand made on the mind for work," Freud, "Three Essays on Sexuality" (1953: 168). Also from Freud's "Instincts and Their Vicissitudes": "drive appears to us as a concept on the frontier between the mental and the somatic, as the psychical representative of the stimuli originating from with the organism, and reaches the mind, as a measure of the demand made upon the mind for work in consequence of its connection to the body" (1957: 121–2).

12 Lacan's approach to the infant seems a far cry from Freud's. Yet if we look back to the early *Project,* we find Freud too tracing the growth of the infant's mind as its body is altered by conceptual (metaphoric) thought (Freud 1956a: 283–399). Technically, this is the same as Freud's thesis in the *Project* that the organism makes a primitive judgment on what to keep and what to expel of incoming energy from its surroundings. Selection requires that raw physical energy's *quantity* be transformed (conceptualized or metaphorized) into mental *quality*. Physical energy is converted into both qualitative nervous mental energy (conceptual thought) and hyper-energized unconscious thought (drive) via one set of neurons, that permit energy to flow in, be stored up or discharged, and another set that blocks portions of the conceptualized energy from exiting the organism at all. The *Aufbau* or elaboration of mind occurs chiefly by way of a quantity of physical energy that, in primordial sentience, gets absorbed, deflected, and/or transformed by incipiently "neuronic" structures. What permits sentience at all is quite simply the act or fact of shielding the organism from a portion of the energy that passes through it.

13 Drive (translated "Instinct" by Strachey) is "a measure of the demand made on the mind for work," Freud says in "Three Essays on Sexuality"; it is "the psychical representative of an endosomatic, continuously flowing source of stimulation, as contrasted with a 'stimulus,' which is set up by single excitations coming from without" (Freud 1953: 168).

14 http://ktla.com/2016/07/03/tesla-autopilot-death-driver-may-have-been-watching-harry-potter-at-time-of-crash-witness-tells-ap/(accessed May 18, 2018).

15 I was offered this example by artist Sharon Kivland (2015), who asked me to comment on it for her exhibit inspired by Karl Marx's description of women as "folles de leur corps." Her installation consisted (among other things) of tiny

perfume bottles converted into miniature Molotov cocktails. I thought back to Freud's notion of how the olfactory sense affects sexual attraction among animals, whose females habitually exude odors, signaling readiness for sexual congress with a male, and how this is lost once humans walk upright.

16 The theory of discourse as a form of the social tie is developed systematically in Lacan's *Seminar XVII* (1969–70) and in subsequent seminars. *Seminar XX* presents its final form. For Lacan, language and the symbolic are embodied in *discourses*. The *discourse* is a set of concrete commands that organize or frame each of its subjects. Now, each *discourse* has a certain slippage that eventually, and over time, rotates its axes—a "revolution" that (non-violently) goes mostly unremarked as a rupture or break, but that nonetheless inexorably moves its components into a new situation. The unconscious evoked and carried by these little letters goes against the grain of the discursive dominant (current symbolic and linguistic powers), but what must be understood is that the two—discourse and unconscious—together create a text: a *tissu* of lines interwoven in opposing directions—a *writing* Derrida would call it.

17 "Autant donc pour le sexe, puisqu'en effet le capitalisme, c'est de là qu'il est parti, de le mettre au rancart" (1974: 51).

18 Lacan says this is the ultimate outcome of the masculine universal in the logic of sexuation: masturbation as the truest and only complete satisfaction. While Todd McGowan tries very hard to define capitalism as deploying a simple mechanism (promising you satisfaction and then sadistically withholding it), the question seems to me to be much more complex than what *Capitalism and Desire* depicts it. After all, desire is defined as and structured as unsatisfiable; it always misses its objective, according to Lacan. McGowan does not grasp that capitalism purveys a tremendous number of satisfactions in an effort to "free us" from desire. Recall Lacan's remarks on Alexander and Hitler: "What is Alexander's proclamation when he arrived in Persepolis or Hitler's when he arrived in Paris? The preamble isn't important: 'I have come to liberate you from this or that.' The essential point is 'Carry on working, work must go on.' Which of course means: 'let it be clear to everyone that this is on no account the moment to express the least surge of desire.' The morality of power of the service of goods is as follows: 'as far as desires are concerned, come back later, make them wait'" (Lacan 1992: 315).

19 I have proposed that we have transitioned to an Imaginary from a Symbolic version of society, an Imaginary that has yet to develop the necessary *metaphoric* distinctions that language can. See MacCannell (2015).

20 Tzvetan Todorov once wrote that only literature has the power to resist language. If the "body" of language requires the addition of a new signifier to remain a living,

open, and generative system, the same is also true for our bodies and the creative *work* we must do to remain human.

21 I have addressed this moment in an earlier essay, "*J is for Jouissance*" (MacCannell 2005).

References

Burke, K. (1994), "Semantic and Poetic Meaning," in *The Philosophy of Literary Form: Studies in Symbolic Action*, 138–67, Berkeley: The University of California Press.

Derrida, J. (1967), *De la Grammatologie*, Paris: Éditions du Minuit.

Derrida, J. (1974), *Of Grammatology*, trans. Gayatry Chakravorty Spivak, Baltimore and London: Johns Hopkins University Press.

Derrida, J. (1980), *La Carte Postale: De Socrate à Freud et au-delà*, Paris: Flammarion.

Freud, S. (1953), "Three Essays on Sexuality," in *The Standard Edition of the Complete Psychological Works of Sigmund Freud VII*, 135–245, ed. James Strachey, London: Hogarth Press.

Freud, S. (1956a), "Project for a Scientific Psychology," in *The Standard Edition of the Complete Psychological Works of Sigmund Freud I*, 283–399, ed. James Strachey, London: Hogarth Press.

Freud, S. (1956b), "Group Psychology and the Analysis of the Ego," in *The Standard Edition of the Complete Psychological Works of Sigmund Freud XVIII*, 67–143, ed. James Strachey, London: Hogarth Press.

Freud, S. (1957), "Instincts and Their Vicissitudes," in *The Standard Edition of the Complete Psychological Works of Sigmund Freud XIV*, 117–58, ed. James Strachey, London: Hogarth Press.

Kivland, S. (2015), "*Folles de leur corps*/Crazy about Their Bodies," London: Café Gallery Projects & Ma Bibliothèque, Aldgate Press.

Lacan, J. (1966), *Les Écrits*, Paris: Éditions du Seuil.

Lacan, J. (1974), *Télévision*, Paris: Éditions du Seuil.

Lacan, J. (1975), *Le Séminaire XX: Encore*, Paris: Éditions du Seuil.

Lacan, J. (1977), *The Écrits: A Selection*, trans. Alan Sheridan, New York and London: W. W. Norton.

Lacan, J. (1991), *Le Séminaire XVII: L'Envers de la Psychanalyse*, Paris: Éditions du Seuil.

Lacan, J. (1992), *The Seminar of Jacques Lacan: Book VII: The Ethics of Psychoanalysis (1959–60)*, trans. Dennis Porter, New York: W. W. Norton.

Lacan, J. (2007), *Seminar XVII: The Other Side of Psychoanalysis*, trans. Russell Grigg, New York and London: W. W. Norton.

Lacan, J. (2016), *Seminar XXIII: The Sinthome*, trans. A. R. Price, Cambridge/Malden: Polity Press.

MacCannell, J. F. (2005), "*J Is for Jouissance*," in Barbara Cohen and Dragan Kuzundjic (eds), *Provocations to Reading: Essays on J. Hillis Miller*, 3–13, New York: Fordham University Press.

MacCannell, J. F. (2006), "More Thoughts for the Time on War and Death: The Discourse of Capitalism," in Justin Clemens and Russell Grigg (eds), *Jacques Lacan and the Other Side of Psychoanalysis: Reflections on Seminar XVII*, 194–215, Durham and London: Duke University Press.

MacCannell, J. F. (2013), "The Abyss of Mind and Matter: Sexuality on Edge," in Insa Härtel (ed), *Erogene Gefahrenen Zonen: Aktuelle Produktionen des (infantile) Sexuellen*, 73–89, Berlin: Kulturverlag Kadmos.

MacCannell, J. F. (2015), "Lacan's Imaginary: A Reader's Guide", in S. Tomsic and A. Zevnik (eds.) Jacques Lacan: Between Psychoanalysis and Politics, 72-85, London: Routledge

Miller, J. H. (2001), *Speech Acts in Literature*, Palo Alto: Stanford University Press.

Rousseau, J.-J. (1990), *Essai sur l'origine des langues: où il est parlé de la Mélodies, et de l'Imitation musicale*, éd. Jean Starobinski, Paris: Gallimard.

The San Francisco Chronicle, "Two Pokemon Players Catch Bad Luck; Fall off Cliff," p. D8, July 14, 2016. Available online: https://www.sfgate.com/news/article/2-Pokemon-Go-players-catch-bad-luck-fall-8379101.php (accessed February 8, 2019).

Saussure, F. de (1959), *Course in General Linguistics*, Bally, C., Sechehaye, A. and, Reidlinger. A. (eds), trans. Wade Baskin, New York: McGraw Hill.

Zukovic, B. (2006), "Four Ways into a Vortex: Metaphor and Machine Logic," *(a): The Journal of Culture and the Unconscious*, VI (1): 15–30.

3

The Secret in the Body: The Fantasy Structure of Genes and Brains

Renata Salecl

In Agatha Christie's novel *The Mysterious Affair at Styles* (1983), Hector Poirot says, "It is the brain, the little grey cells on which one must rely. One must seek the truth within—not without." Poirot means it metaphorically: He is pointing out that it is with the help of our reasoning that criminal cases can be explained. Nowadays, however, we are more and more thinking this literally—namely, that it is in the brain or the genes that the truth of subjectivity can be found.

The attempts to find the answer to one's actions and even political beliefs in the body are nothing new. During the late eighteenth and early nineteenth centuries, Franz Joseph Gall established phrenology, also referred to as crainology, which held the belief that an individual's character and mental faculties correlate with the shape of his or her head. As one of the early biological theories of criminology, phrenology laid the foundation for other schools of thought that were searching for biological roots of criminal behavior. Moreover, in the late nineteenth century, Cesare Lombroso, the founder of the Italian school of positivist criminology, became famous for his description of "born criminals." Although these theories about biological causes of criminal behavior have been heavily criticized, the attempts to find biological explanations for people's behavior have persisted.

In the 1970s, when Germany experienced attacks orchestrated by the radical left movement Red Army Fraction (RAF), the question about the biological cause of political beliefs emerged when one of the leaders of this organization, Ulrike Meinhof, in 1977 allegedly committed suicide in prison. The pathologist Jürgen Pfeiffer (Third 2010), who performed the dissection of Meinhof's body, secretly removed her brain and stored it in a container with formaldehyde in hopes that the future development of science might provide an answer to the question of why someone becomes a terrorist. At the end of the 1990s, Pfeiffer imagined that such an analysis could be done by his colleague, psychiatrist Bernhard Bogerts, who researched the biological roots of schizophrenia, which is why he passed the container with Ulrike's brain to this colleague. Dr. Bogerts placed the container in the basement of the University of Tübingen, where it was by chance discovered in 2002. Meinhof's daughter was appalled that her mother had been buried without her brain. She thus filed a lawsuit, and after the court decision, the brain was finally buried in Meinhof's grave.

Why was there such an interest in Meinhof's brain? Meinhof was considered to be the "brain" of RAF. The question, however, was raised why Meinhof, a well-known journalist in her twenties, suddenly became radicalized. One theory tried to find a biological cause for that. When Meinhof was six months pregnant, she started experiencing strong headaches. The doctors diagnosed a brain tumor and suggested immediate surgery, but Meinhof decided to wait till after having delivered her twins. At the time of the surgery, however, it turned out that Meinhof had a benign cyst. Because of some complication, doctors had to install a metal clip into Meinhof's head. The procedure was considered a success, but Meinhof's personality presumably changed. Increasingly, she started getting close to the ideology of RAF. In 1970, she even helped its leader, Andreas Baader, escape from prison. When the police caught Meinhof and Baader, they, due to the lack of her fingerprints, confirmed Meinhof's identity with a brain scan that showed the metal clip in her head.

The question usually posed regarding terrorism is, how do people get radicalized? Often, the perception is that they have somehow been "brainwashed" when they started identifying with a particular ideology. Previous convictions of a person have been washed away, and then his or her head has been "charged" with new ideology. Both the perception of brainwashing and the search for brain deformities as the cause of a person's embracement of political beliefs dehumanize the terrorist. Jacques Lacan (1996), in his early work, took dehumanization as one of the main problems of criminology and insisted that the criminal needs to be perceived as a subject and not as someone determined by some innate biological instincts or social influences.

The new turn to neuroscience and genetics for the explanation of people's actions presents an opportunity for psychoanalysis to question how people imagine their brain and their genes, what kind of fantasies they create around them, and which new imaginary and symbolic register they engage with. And the new biological turn in criminology calls for the return to psychoanalytic interpretation of criminal acts.

Secrets of the body

The whole discourse of neuroscience, the institutions and the rituals that go together with this new establishment, is creating a new symbolic order. We have a new language and new disciplines: neuro-law, neuro-marketing, neuro-architecture, etc. At the same time, we have the emergence of a very strong imaginary. What exactly are PET scans and fMRI images? They are images that are trying to discern what is in us more than ourselves, the core part of our corporality—our brain. We often forget that these images are computer generated. In the legal domain, we use the term "Christmas tree effect." When fMRI images are, for example, presented to the members of the jury, they are blinding them with their colors and shapes. These images promise to create a map of our brain that will enable us to discern that x in us which is linked to puzzling questions—who are we, why did we do what we did, are we consciously in control or not, or did we lie or not? However, they very much depend on the power of the interpretation and the authority of the scientist.

Genetics also relies heavily on a new set of symbols, a symbolism underpinned by the terms DNA has brought to the lexicon. Genes themselves have become an aspect of the body we regularly try to visualize in the same way; we might picture for ourselves the condition of internal organs or muscular tissue. Because science has taught us that they are so important, it is vital for us that we "see" our genes. This means, however, that the picture we develop of our genes belongs more to the realm of imagination rather than biological science and reflects the state of our psyches more than the latest results from the laboratory.

Concern about what the dark insides of our bodies might look like, and what they might be doing, is a long-standing preoccupation of the modern age. Each of us carries an image of the body as the entity with which we identify, but which still seems separate to "us," and which seems to hold power over us. Despite all that experimental science has taught us, we follow an ancient form of thinking in our speculations about the body. Lacan (1953) observes that psychoanalysts have to recognize a mode of thought in their patients that modern science rejected long ago. For people still tend to understand their bodies according to what Aristotle (1991) called a "substantial form" (morphe)—a concept in some ways similar to the Platonic Idea. In thinking about the state of their bodies, people believe that their physical condition is dictated and controlled by an underlying form, a defined state to which they correspond. The form, as Aristotle saw it, is thus an "explanatory cause" of the physical state in which people find themselves.

Our genes are now implicated in the idea each one of us carries of our body's "substantial form": in our minds, that is, they are a big part of the "explanatory cause" by which we understand who we are. Thinking about genes as a cause of this kind also affects the way we see our parents and families, from whom we got those genes in the first place. At a time of illness, this genetic link can be reimagined, and as a result, a person may search for new explanations of what was passed on to him or her from one's parents.

Dr. Allan Hobson (2011) wrote a memoir after suffering a stroke. In it, he says that his genes presented him with a particular kind of "Hobson's Choice" when he thought about the bad alternative fates he had been allotted genetically—Alzheimer's on his mother's side of the family or cardiovascular disease on his father's. Sadly, he had the impression that both fates had reached out to claim him.

After his stroke, Hobson had the feeling that his brain owned him as much as he owned his brain and that a little bit of him had died as a result of an aneurysm. So far as all external physical indicators could be discerned, he seemed to be recovering well; but on the inside, he felt worse and worse. When he described his sensations to his doctors, who expected him to make a complete recovery, no one believed his symptoms were real. Hobson felt that his subjective experience of the aftermath of the stroke was utterly ignored and that his doctors only looked at the data that indicated he was in good health. The trauma he suffered at this time led Hobson to apologize to his patients. In the past he had often disregarded the suffering they reported when their charts suggested they were okay or responding well to treatment.

When Hobson suffered his second stroke, he began to wonder whether his father's genes were now speaking to him as they once, he guessed, spoke to his father. Through the perception that the inherited genes were causing his illness, he felt connected to his father in a new way. The progress of Hobson's clinical recovery after this second stroke very much resembled a psychological—or psychotherapeutic—process of working out his relationship with his father. The genes Hobson was concerned about during this process became what psychoanalysts would call a "transitional object," a means for Hobson of rethinking his family ties.

Anxiety over death might in some cases take the form of a question concerning the genes that were passed from the parent to the child; while in other cases, it involves fixating on the particular age at which a parent died. A Russian man started experiencing strange attacks of breathlessness and at one point even fainted on the street. When doctors could not find any physical cause for his illness, he was sent to a psychiatric hospital. A consulting psychologist there asked about the man's family background and learned that his father had committed suicide at the age of 39. When the psychologist looked up the patient's age, she noticed that he was 38. In discussions with the patient, it became clear that the anxiety over dying at the same time as the father played an important role in this patient's anxiety attacks.

Calvin Colarusso (2010) describes a similar case, that of Mr. B, who sought help through psychoanalysis because of acute anxiety over death. This anxiety became especially pronounced when Mr. B turned 49 since his father had died ten days before his fiftieth birthday. With this loss, the family was suddenly pushed into poverty. As an adult, Mr. B strove to build a successful and prosperous career to "bullet-proof his family," so that, in case he died, they would not suffer in poverty as he himself did after his father's sudden death.

When Mr. B turned 49, his physician noticed a significant lowering of his testosterone, which was taken as the possible cause of his depression. Mr. B was prescribed antidepressants, but they did not seem to help. On the fearful day when Mr. B turned 50, his mother suddenly fell into a coma and died two days later. After this tragic event, Mr. B started remembering how as a child he wished his father would die and how horrified he was when his wishes came true with his father's premature death. But at one point in the analysis, he said, "I am beginning to see him as a man, not just my Dad." From then on, Mr. B slowly gave up on antidepressants and started feeling better. To his doctor's surprise, his testosterone levels also went back to normal.

The year before his fiftieth birthday, Mr. B started to "close everything down," and the falling levels of his testosterone were a physical consequence of his "preparation" for death. The psychoanalyst took the change in testosterone as a form of an unusual self-imposed "hormonal castration" related to the infantile wishes to kill his father and take his place. One, however, has to question what role his mother's death played in the lifting of Mr. B's anxiety. Did she in some way die instead of Mr. B? Did her death alter something about the incestuous wishes he had fostered as a child?

If Dr. Hobson heard his father's genes as a voice that announced his mortality, with Mr. B it was the number 50 that was the anchoring point for his anxiety about death. In both cases, the fear of death covers up the way each man had identified with his father: in one case that fear fixated on the idea of genes taking control of his life and in the other with the prospect of reaching a certain age. The point to be made here is that Dr. Hobson's anxieties about his genetic inheritance are no more or less "scientific" than Mr. B.'s profound concerns about his fiftieth birthday. Both men looked to the object of their anxiety as an "explanatory cause" of the state in which they found themselves.

Anxiety and genes

People usually consult the geneticist not because they are ill, but because of the possible risk that they might get sick in the future. They take the geneticist's answers as objective information. Psychoanalyst Andree Lehman (Mieli, Houis, and Stafford 2000) observed that women who consult geneticists out of their fear of breast cancer often already had questions about their future or the origin and transmissibility of genes. They were often full of doubt and uncertainty, hence already in the grips of anxiety. When women were informed that they were not in danger of developing genetically linked breast cancer, some seemed satisfied, evinced feelings of relief, proffered their thanks, and resolved to follow preventative recommendations; others looked just as anxious as before, if not more so. The latter would then demand more tests or focus on other organs, which they fear might become cancerous soon.

Many people find it hard to deal with genetic information: Even if people grasp it, they might not understand it. Where the knowledge brings intellectual comprehension, it may still fail to override preexisting anxieties or beliefs. Lehman observed three important aspects at work in the way a person deals with genetic information: first, the way a person deals with doubt; second, her fear of illness; and third, the state of her family equilibrium.

Psychoanalysts dealing with people with cancer anxieties observe that cancer often evokes fantasies of both physical and mental decline, of abandonment, loss, and mourning. These fantasies are linked to how cancer is perceived within the larger family constellation. For some, family relationships are thoroughly revisited and thrown into turmoil when they go through genetic testing. They might suddenly remember past family events or particular sets of family beliefs, and some might engage with previously abandoned family traditions. While some experience anger over genes they have inherited, others feel guilt for having passed on something terrible to their offspring.

The way information about genetic predisposition is absorbed and worked through differs from person to person. Often people need to undergo a crucial subjective change to assimilate new ideas and be able to live their lives after receiving traumatic information. While some people might find ways to ignore relevant information that comes from the domain of genetics, others struggle to make a cognitive adjustment and absorb this knowledge as something that is not fixed or determining. The problem develops when knowledge about genes is perceived as certainty and when people strongly identify with the language of statistical likelihood in which genetic information is often presented to them. When unconscious beliefs, fantasies, and desire also come into play, people's symptoms and anxieties are reformulated.

In the relationship between a doctor and a patient, transference plays an important role. The way doctors present information influences a patient's anxieties, and how the patient hears this information, and whether he or she listens at all, also makes a difference as far as the patient's reaction is concerned. The question, however, remains whether patients have the right to ignorance, that is, whether they can in advance inform doctors that they do not want to know if the news about their health may be traumatic. Discussions on the right not to know are also part of scientific studies in the domain of genetics. They also involve the issue of so-called incidental finding (Lanzerath et al. 2013). When, for example, people agree to be part of scientific research, they cannot easily opt out of learning about some surprising findings that came up in the research process. The ethical question is whether a person can in advance inform the researcher that he does not want to know about incidental findings. Is the doctor obliged to keep this promise also in the case when there is a possible treatment of the disease that was discovered by accident?

Geneticists deal with issues related to transmission of knowledge when they by chance find that family members are not genetically related. A family, for example, agreed to be part of genetic research, and the geneticist discovered that they were not genetically related to the child. In the hospital where the child was born, there was a mix-up that the family was not aware of. The geneticist might decide not to tell the family about his discovery in case there was no genetically transmitted illness discovered among these volunteers. However, if he were to find one, he would have been under pressure to inform the family about his finding and also about the fact that they are not genetically related.

Genes—The new real?

Molecular biology borrowed the term "program" from computer science to describe the genetic information an organism may contain. The term "information" in itself tells us that we are dealing with semantic data that can be communicated. One can easily get the impression that this information can be taken as an imperative or as a cause: If we possess information, we are obliged to interpret or suppress it, act on it or ignore it. Additionally, advances in science give us hopes that we will soon be able to control and amend our genes. One of the founders of Human Genome project claimed that with the decoding of the genome, a living creature can understand its origin and can undertake to design its future. Evelyn Fox Keller (2002) warned that when life is relocated in the genes and redefined according to their informational content, the project of refashioning life or redirecting the future course of evolution could be cast as a manageable, doable project.

We live in times of the so-called "neurogenetic real." While we hope to find truth in the body, we forget that human subjectivity with its imagination, fantasies, self-damaging behavior, and *jouissance* related to transgression cannot be reduced to a neuronal machine driven by the complex firing patterns of the cells in our brains or to a genetic code. New knowledge related to the body is, however, affecting the way people relate both to their bodies and to their ancestors.

Genes as a cause of crime?

While for some people the question of genes is anxiety provoking and linked to doubt and uncertainty, for others it presents a point of certainty—an answer, for example, to why they have behaved in a particular way or why they have committed a particular act. In the legal domain, genetics has played an important role in the last decade in discussions about determinism, free will, as well as responsibility and punishment.

A number of judicial cases nowadays feature experts in genetics who are willing to testify that someone might have had a genetic predisposition for crime. One such example is the trial of Abdelmalek Bayout, an Algerian national, in Trieste (Italy) in 2009 (Feresin 2009). Bayout was accused of killing a person who mocked his make-up. Bayout had been diagnosed with a mental disorder, and this was taken into account when he was sentenced to nine years in prison. Bayout appealed, and at his retrial, an expert in genetics testified that the defendant might have been genetically predetermined to commit the crime. The expert pointed to changes in the MAOA gene, which regulates neurotransmitters, among them serotonin and dopamine. From the studies (Caspi et al. 2002) that suggested the link between the malfunction of this gene and violence, the expert concluded that genes might have played a role in Bayout's behavior. The court accepted this claim and reduced the defendant's sentence.

In the last decades, studies concerning genetic predisposition for crime have been highly contested. Old debates about the relationship between nature and nurture have resurfaced in the studies about epigenetics. The question thus shifted from the analysis of genes to the analysis of the way the environment affects the expression of the genes.

In the United States, the idea of genetic determination for violence gained strength after the publication of Adrian Raine's book *The Anatomy of Violence* (2013). As an example of genetic predisposition for violence, Raine takes the case of Jeffrey Landrigan, a man who was put on death row for double murder and whose biological father faced the same sentence.

Landrigan's story is an incredible saga of violence and criminality in a single family. Jeffrey's great-grandfather was a bootlegger who illegally sold alcohol. His son, Jeffrey's grandfather, died in a shootout with the police while he was robbing a bank. His son, Darrel Hill, observed this shootout. Later, Darrel also became a criminal. He committed two murders and was sentenced to death. Darrel had a son called Billy, whom he only saw when he was a baby. When Billy was two, his mother abandoned him in a daycare center (Malone and Swindle 1999). Billy was later adopted into a stable family, where he was well taken care of and loved. This family renamed him Jeffrey. From his youth on, Jeffrey had problems with drugs and alcohol and then ended up being placed in various institutions for delinquent youngsters. As an adult, Jeffrey killed two people, as his father had, and was also sentenced to death.

Darrel Hill, on death row, said about his biological son:

> I don't think there can be any doubt in anyone's mind that he (Jeffrey Landrigan) was fulfilling his destiny… I believe that when he was conceived, what I was, he became… The last time I saw him he was a baby in a bed, and underneath his mattress I had two .38 pistols and Demerol; that's what he was sleeping on. (Raine 2013: 79)

Adrian Raine concludes: "Placing that gun and drugs under his baby boy's pillow foreshadowed what was to come. Like father, like son—whether it is violence, drugs, or alcohol. Landrigan was seemingly doing little more in life than acting out the sins of his biological father" (Raine 2013: 60). For Raine, the very fact that Jeffrey was adopted and loved later in his life could not change the biological determinism of his genetic makeup.

Jeffrey's story can, however, be interpreted in other ways. First, there is the possibility of brain damage resulting from substance abuse performed by Jeffrey's mother, who admitted that she took drugs and consumed alcohol throughout her pregnancy. Thus the judge, who later condemned Jeffrey to death row, said that she would have sentenced him to life imprisonment had she known that harmful neurological change had been inflicted as a result of his mother's drinking and drug taking during pregnancy.

Psychoanalysis offers another interpretation of Jeffrey's behavior. From various accounts, we know that Jeffrey spent years trying to track down his biological father, Darrel. Not long after he committed his first murder, he found his father due to surprising circumstances. This happened when Jeffrey was 20 years old and had just been released from prison. He got married and soon learned that he was going to become a father. One day, Jeffrey went drinking with an old childhood friend, Greg Brown, whom he had earlier asked to stand as godfather to his child. A verbal fight ensued between the two when Greg called Jeffrey "a punk," and the latter stabbed his friend to death.

Jeffrey was sentenced to twenty years in prison. When he was serving his sentence, a fellow prisoner told him that in his previous prison, he had met Jeffrey's biological father, Darrel Hill. Paradoxically, Jeffrey had found his father by committing a crime, and the two men started exchanging letters when serving sentences in different prisons.

Symbolically, Jeffrey was already following in his father's footsteps, since in his adopted family and his school, it was well known that he was a son of a criminal. One should also not neglect the fact that Jeffrey as a baby was already caught in the web of anxiety related to breaking the law. The very fact that his father was hiding a gun and drugs under the baby's mattress could have important consequences for the development of this baby. We know very well that little children are influenced by their caregivers in a myriad different ways and that unconsciously they also take in the anxieties present in their caregivers. What can be more anxiety provoking than sleeping on a gun? We should pay equal attention, moreover, to the fundamental lack of care the weapon in this story represents. Psychopathic character traits have been traced both to brain injuries suffered in childhood and to chronic neglect on the part of caregivers to interact and demonstrate empathy for the infant at the symbiotic stage of development.

The term "father" plays an essential role in Jeffrey's story. The facts that he committed his first killing when he was about to become a father and that he killed a man who was to become his child's godfather have important ramifications for the psychoanalytic understanding of this crime. Jeffrey was searching for his biological father throughout his childhood, and the moment he was about to take on the symbolic role of a father might have triggered something in him that contributed to his violent outburst toward the man who was supposed to take on another symbolic paternal role—that of a godfather.

Darrel had also long been haunted, quite literally, by his own father. Jeffrey's grandfather, whom Darrel had seen shot dead by police, would often appear to him in hallucinations. Already in his youth, he was hearing the voice of his father telling him that he cannot escape being killed, which is why he should kill first. Another preoccupation for both father and son were homosexual impulses, which they resolved by committing acts of horrific violence. Darrel, like Jeffrey, became enraged when someone called him a "punk" in prison. After the insult, Darrel stabbed this man to death while later claiming that he acted in self-defense against a sexual approach.

When Jeffrey was serving his sentence, despite his murder charge, he was put in a minimal-security work crew, which allowed him to escape from the prison facility. Once outside, his first desire was to find his biological mother, who lived in Yuma in Arizona. On his way to Yuma, Jeffrey stopped off in Phoenix, where he met a man by the name of Chester Dyer, who worked in a health club and was known for picking up men and having sex with them at his home. A few days later, Dyer was found strangled by an electrical cord and stabbed to death in his apartment. A deck of pornographic cards was strewn over the bed, and the ace of hearts was dramatically propped up on Dyer's back. Police rearrested Jeffrey when he was caught robbing a petrol station. His shoe prints matched those found at the scene of Dyer's murder. Jeffrey denied killing Dyer; he claimed that Dyer had made sexual advances toward him, but that another man had murdered him.

In their account of the Landrigan story, Dan Malone and Howard Swindle ask, "Do chromosomal cards dealt at birth determine whether a person becomes a sociopath or a productive member of society? Or does the world in which the child is reared cast the mold that forms the adult?" (Malone and Swindle 1999). Some theorists understand Jeffrey as a genetically predetermined criminal; others see his acts as being similarly predetermined by social background. Neither explanation accounts for the very particular form of enjoyment Jeffrey experienced while committing his murders. His murder of Dyer was highly distinctive, artful even, rather than the raw response to present conditions in biology or culture. His neat and highly demonstrative arrangement of the playing cards at Dyer's home suggests that Jeffrey was not merely a tool in the hands of some higher power—his genes, for example—but that he was very much a subject who wanted to leave a symbolic mark at the scene of his crime.

Psychoanalytically, the ace of hearts that he placed on his victim's back looks very much like an attempt to resolve the anguish he experienced about both his sexuality and his paternity. In psychoanalytical literature, some forms of homosexuality in boys are understood as a profound response to a sense of rejection or abandonment by their fathers. Jeffrey's tortured family background—and homophobic social context—prohibited him from resolving this formative problem by seeking a loving and stable relationship with another man. His murder of Dyer, however, should not be seen as a simple perpetuation of a genetic pattern, or indeed an inevitable response to social circumstances. As an act, sexual and criminal, it differs profoundly from his father's instinctive and reactive killing of the man who triggered his dormant or suppressed sexual wishes by calling him a punk. Jeffrey murdered Dyer, it seems, after agreeing to go to his home and have sex. The card he left on his victim's body was a sign that this murder was very much about a matter of the heart, one that he had solved in the only manner the frame of his life permitted. Jeffrey sought homosexual union with a father-substitute, on his way to visit his mother, and then brutally murdered him: Understood psychoanalytically, this murder was Jeffrey's way of rejecting his father's legacy. Rather than following the dictations of a line of genetic code, Jeffrey committed an act, which tried to confront such determinants. He was working within the family tradition of psychotic violence but modified the unthinking brutality of his father and grandfather with a viciously sophisticated strain of criminal behavior that was quite his own.

A geneticist's—or even a sociologist's—view of the Landrigan family's criminality fails to recognize such distinctions between the actions of one generation and those of another. Criminal acts, from the genetic point of view, are merely "criminal," to a lesser or greater extent. A police psychologist, or even a detective with a broader view of things, knows otherwise. Different criminal acts—different murders—often play out very different psychological dramas and preoccupations. Unlike his criminal forebears, Jeffrey at some level understood that his life was largely about a search for something or someone with which or with whom he could identify. He was executed in 2010, and his final words were "Boomer Sooner." This is the rallying cry for the supporters of the University of Oklahoma football team, the Sooners. His farewell to the world indicated one field of activity in which Jeffrey might have thrived, had he been spared the psychological inheritance of the Landrigan family. Sociologically speaking, his foster home may have given him every advantage but could not compensate for deprivations he suffered in the earliest phases of infancy. His guardians also could not know that he might seek to compensate for those deprivations in his own way and seek out the "tribe" in which they made a dysfunctional sort of sense.

When genetic science stresses the importance of epigenetics and points out that the expression of the majority of genes depends on the social and environmental factors, it also emphasizes the power of the family and other intersubjective relationships in the person's life. Even studies, which are trying to find the genetic basis of impulsive behavior that might contribute to a person's transgression of the law, point out that an unstable emotional environment at home, and especially domestic abuse, influences the expression of the genes linked to impulsivity. Such studies, however, need to take into account that the proliferation of media writings, which often digests genetic research related to behavior into claims that we have found the "gene for crime," create a symbolic setting that has effects on the subject, his body, unconscious fantasies, and identifications. With the spread of the belief that genes are responsible for the crime, we are paradoxically creating an epigenetic setting—language and culture—which is something that any study of genes and behavior needs to take into account.

Conclusion

One of the main challenges for psychoanalysis regarding crime is to deal with the issue of responsibility. Paradoxically, psychoanalysis perceives the subject as much more responsible than law often does, since it tries to carve out a space for human responsibility that goes beyond the nature-culture divide.

When Freud invented the term "Neurosenwahl" (choice of neurosis), his idea was not to perceive the subject as someone who rationally chooses his or her neurosis, but rather to point out how the subject is in a paradoxical way "author" of his or her suffering. He or she is thus not fully determined by nature (biology) or culture (family)—in the midst of these important factors, the subject finds his or her own answers; that is, he or she remains a subject and is not simply an object, that is, a tool in the hands of other mechanisms that determine him or her.

The subject is thus perceived as someone who always in a particular way creates his or her symptom. This authorship of the symptom is not understood in a rational way. Unconscious mechanisms are very much present in the way neurotic symptoms are formed. However, when we use the term "choice of neurosis," we also open up a space for change. The symptom can change, and the subject can make changes in his or her life.

Criminology usually explains a criminal act either by locating the instigating causes in external factors (such as poverty, family dysfunctions, peer pressure, etc.) or with the help of psychological factors (such as addiction, aggression, manic-depression, or other psychiatric personality disorders). Significantly, such an explanation tends to dehumanize the criminal: The criminal is perceived as an irresponsible entity caught in the interplay of either social or unconscious psychic mechanisms, or both. In this scientific approach to crime, as well as in the legal treatment of the criminal, the offender is not perceived as a subject, but as an object in the hands of some external or internal operations over which he has no control. Consequently, the only task of the experts dealing with crime is to locate those mechanisms and thereby to determine the responsibility of the criminal.

In contrast to this approach, psychoanalytic theory tries to explain a criminal act in terms that do not dehumanize the criminal. Psychoanalysis agrees that crime could be explained by a variety of causes. For example, murder could be linked to psychosis, and shoplifting could be a reaction to the lack of love or other traumas of childhood. However, psychoanalysis perceives these kinds of acts as a specific mode of subjectivization, a means by which the subject tries to resolve his or her inner tensions, inhibitions, and traumas. Specifically, in the case of theft, such an act could be perceived as resulting from a lack of love or as repaying a certain symbolic debt. But according to such an explanation, the criminal is not dehumanized; he or she is not reduced to being a cog in the interplay of some mechanisms. On the contrary, the criminal's theft emerges as the way in which the subject, through committing the crime, subjectivizes oneself in a new way. Psychoanalysis regards crime as a *passage à l'acte*, as an act by which the inner tensions of the subject are resolved. The essential psychoanalytic consideration is thus what role theft plays in the libidinal economy of the thief.

Psychoanalytic answers to the attempts to ground subjectivity in the brain or in the genes should also be able to look at how the search for the truth in the body presents a particular form of subjectivization. As a result, the subject remains fully responsible for the fantasy and anxiety that he or she experiences concerning the question: What is in me more than myself?

References

Aristotle (1991), *The Metaphysics*, trans. J. H. McHahon, Buffalo, NY.: Prometheus Books.

Caspi, A., J. McClay, T. E. Moffitt, J. Mill, J. Martin, I. W. Craig, A. Taylor, and R. Poulton (2002), "Role of Genotype in the Cycle of Violence in Maltreated Children," *Science*, 297 (5582): 851–4.

Christie, A. (1983), *The Mysterious Affair at Styles*, New York: Bantam.

Colarusso, C. A. (2010), "Living to Die and Dying to Live: Normal and Pathological Considerations of Death Anxiety," in S. Akhtar (ed), *In The Wound of Mortality : Fear, Denial, and Acceptance of Death*, 107–23, Lanham: Jason Aronson.

Feresin, E. (2009), "Lighter Sentence for Murderer with 'Bad Genes,'" *Nature*, published online October 30. Available online: https://www.nature.com/news/2009/091030/full/news.2009.1050.html (accessed February 8, 2019).

Fox Keller, E. (2002), *The Century of the Gene*, Cambridge, MA, and London: Harvard University Press.

Hobson, J. A. (2011), *Dream Life: An Experimental Memoir*, Cambridge, MA: MIT Press.

Lacan, J. (1953), "Some Reflections on the Ego," *The International Journal of Psycho-Analysis*, 34 (1): 11–17.

Lacan, J. (1996), "A Theoretical Introduction to the Functions of Psychoanalysis in Criminology," trans. M. Bracher, R. Grigg, R. Samuels, *Journal for Psychoanalysis of Culture and Society*, 1 (2): 13–25.

Lanzerath, D., M. Rietschel, B. Heinrichs, and C. Schmäl (2013), *Incidental Findings: Scientific, Legal and Ethical Issues*, Köln: Deutscher Ärzte-Verlag.

Lehman, A. (2000), "Psychoanalysis and Genetics: Clinical Considerations and Practical Suggestions," in P. Mieli, J. Houis, and M. Stafford (eds), *Being Human: The Technological Extensions of the Body*, 201–10, New York: Marsilio Publications.

Malone, D. and H. Swindle (1999), *America's Condemned: Death Row Inmates in Their Own Words*, Kansas City: Andrews McMeel Publications.

Raine, A. (2013), *The Anatomy of Violence: The Biological Roots of Crime*, London: Allen Lane.

Third, A. (2010), "Imprisonment and Excessive Femininity: Reading Ulrike Meinhof's Brain," *Parallax*, 16 (4): 83–100.

Part Two

From Couch to Culture

1

Of Drives and Culture

Mladen Dolar

It would all seem that drives and culture stand at opposite ends, in an antagonistic relation, that they form a conflict that is structural, pertaining to the nature of the two entities, and thus never to be lifted or suppressed. Drives appear to be the enemies of culture. What one commonly assumes about the notion of drives--and I will not start by some textbook definitions, rather with common assumptions--stands on the side of the physiological, the somatic, the bodily, and it can be generally put under the heading of nature and thus "spontaneously" opposed to culture. Culture stands on the other side of the divide, and this is the most dramatic divide that exists. The old translation of Freud's term *der Trieb* by "instinct"--proposed by James Strachey and systematically used throughout the *Standard Edition*--is indicative of such an assumption. The drive would seem to stand for the instinctual, something outside the realm of culture, and culture would thus be called upon to mold these instinctual forces, make them manageable and pliable, tame them, and thus enlist them for cultural aims. We, the humans, are special by our culture, while the drives would seem to be something that we share with our animal substratum. If we look at the title of Freud's famous text that I will be considering here, *Das Unbehagen in der Kultur* (1929–30), *Civilization and Its Discontents*, one can quickly assume a script implied by this title and subtending it: We don't feel well in culture; there is a discontent, a malaise, a discomfort (the latter was, by the way, the English translation proposed by Freud himself), an unhappiness that sticks to our being-in-culture, a discontent that is necessary and structural, unavoidable, not to be done away with, it pertains to our cultural being as such. And if there is this perpetual unhappiness to which we are doomed as human beings (the first intended title was actually *Das Unglück in der Kultur*, the unhappiness in culture), this must be due to the way that culture imposes on our drives, on our natural inclinations, the way it restricts them, inflicts constraints upon them, a task which it can never quite fulfill, however much it tries, by ever-more sophisticated means. For the drives are recalcitrant, they strike back, they don't easily let themselves be imposed on, they don't readily give in to renunciation, and the price we must thus pay for our entry into culture is this constant discontent, a very high price to pay for the glory of our cultural achievements. Already in the early *Three Essays on the Theory of Sexuality* (1905), Freud maintained that there is "the inverse relation holding between civilization and the free development of sexuality" (Freud 1977: 168), thus himself giving ample backing to this kind of understanding. The idea is also expounded in "'Civilized' Sexual Morality and Modern Nervous Illness" (1908), where the very title already suggests and delivers this message.

In what follows I will try to dismantle this common assumption, and I can state from the outset that in psychoanalysis, everything depends on abandoning the very presuppositions of such an understanding, despite the fact that Freud might well seem to have endorsed it himself. I will proceed by following Freud's steps in the third section of *Civilization and Its Discontents*, which are simple and even in many ways commonsensical, yet they contain a number of side implications, abysses, and traps in their very self-evidence, jeopardizing the presuppositions that we start with.

"Das Leben, wie es uns auferlegt ist, ist zu schwer für uns," says Freud (1982: 207). "Life, as we find it, is too hard for us; it brings us too many pains, disappointments and impossible tasks" (1985: 262). Life is too much for us; there is more life than we can bear. "wie es uns auferlegt ist"—a more accurate translation would be "life such as it is imposed on us," implying that life is an imposition. There is a too-muchness of life, to use the expression proposed by Eric Santner, a constitutive too-muchness that we can never contain.[1] Life is not made by human measure. One cannot read such sentences without some bemusement and precaution, for nowhere else had Freud such a tendency to "coffee-house" philosophy, the sort of general wisdoms that are easily dispensed while sitting in cafés (and Vienna is notoriously the city of cafés), as in *Civilization*—there is a thin edge between the stringent theoretical pursuit and the questionable wisdoms about the nature of the world and the unhappy fate of humankind. As Freud himself put it:

> In none of my previous writings have I had so strong a feeling as now that what I am describing is common knowledge and that I am using up paper and ink… in order to expound things which are, in fact, self-evident. (1985: 308)

Hence, our task is how to disentangle, from within Freud's argument that can easily be seen as verging on the commonplace, something that goes profoundly against any self-evidence and commonsense.

If life is too hard for us, it is because the reality principle is at great odds with the pleasure principle that guides our psyche, and the reality principle is displayed in three basic forms: Nature, that we cannot fully master; our bodies, that are fragile, vulnerable, and mortal; and our fellow human beings with whom we cannot arrive at a coexistence, which would be free of conflicts and traumas. The first two sources cannot be removed, but the third one lies fully within our powers, it is a constellation that we have produced ourselves and hence we could order it and arrange it to our benefit. But here lies the source of our troubles: We seem to be unable to prevent suffering that we have imposed on ourselves, and if our coexistence with others is another name for culture and civilization, then we arrive at the paradox contained in the title, namely that the principle culprit for our misery (*das Elend*) is "our so called culture" (1985: 274).[2] That is, the main source of misery is what makes us human, the very instrument we have invented against suffering and against our dependence on nature.

> Human civilization, by which I mean all those respects in which human life has raised itself above its animal status and differs from the life of beasts—and I scorn [*ich verschmähe es*] to distinguish between culture and civilization. (*The Future of an Illusion*, 1985: 184)

The cure turns out to be worse than the disease. Every cultural progress produces ever more trouble, which is then supposed to be cured by ever more cultural progress. Culture appears to be an auto-referential project, which ultimately serves attending to troubles that it itself produces. If culture can be seen, by a rough approximation, as the attempt to master nature, then the paradox is that it itself produces something more intractable than the proverbial indomitable forces of nature.

Let me take up the basic traits of culture such as Freud enumerates and scrutinizes in the third section of *Civilization*. Freud has no high ambitions in this section; he is not trying to work out a definition of culture, but he is rather following a more modest question: What do we speak about when we speak of culture? He takes up a number of common assumptions that we make when using this notion and proposes a number of elementary traits. The list is a bit haphazard, not systematic; it could be extended, yet it presents some basic ideas about what we usually understand under the term "culture" (and I will follow Freud's lead in not distinguishing culture and civilization, although the distinction between the two is not trivial and has given rise to quite a bit of discussion). I will, in view of simplification and systematicity, consider six traits, in Freud's footsteps, and examine their relation to the enigma of the drives as their supposed other.

The first trait, the most obvious and seemingly self-evident, is that culture is based on progressive mastering of natural forces. Its starting point is the use of tools, in the beginning, by gaining control over fire and the construction of dwellings. This is the germ of a gigantic progress, the incredible increase of human powers, with the tool placed at its core: The tool figures as an elongation, extension of the human body, expansion of its limits. Machines prolong the muscles, microscopes and telescopes enhance the eyes, photography and gramophone stop and stack the time, the computer prolongs the brains, ships and planes conquer distances—the human body, equipped with these gadgets, is magnified and extended to enormous proportions. Science thus appears to be the realization of the fairy tale: We can indeed fly over mountains and seas, talk at great distance, see the invisible. Man becomes equal to god by his increasing omniscience and omnipotence. But he can only be compared to god as long as he has his extensions at hand, his auxiliary organs, says Freud, so in a famous phrase man has become *ein Prothesengott* (1985: 280; 1982: 222), a prosthetic god, that is, man is godlike only as long as he is endowed with prostheses. Our divinity resides in our prostheses, *Prothesen*, it depends on the bodily supplements, it is a divinity on crutches. Yet a man without prosthesis is not a man—if he is indeed "a tool-making animal" (the proposal that stems from Benjamin Franklin and that Marx was very fond of), then the prosthesis makes him a man at all.

This view of technology, even in this minimalistic (or rather massive) scope, already implicitly indicates a connection between technology and drives. A lot depends on how to conceive the drives, and Freud mostly proposed the model of energy that flows in one direction or the other, of a reservoir of libido, of a somatic pressure to be released, of energy that can be dammed up and discharged, etc. Let's call this the energetic model, where drives are seen as a free-flowing energy that seeks release. In Lacan's view this model was limited and rather misleading, so he proposed to conceive the drive in topological terms: not as a somatic pressure or an energy flow, but as something to be placed into the extension of the body, something that prolongs the body toward the outside yet doesn't quite fall into the externality nor does it remain internal. Neither inside nor outside, the drive is the creature of the edge and the transition, always pertaining to bodily orifices, that is, to the privileged points of transition between the inside and the outside (hence the oral drive, the anal drive, etc.), the points where the most dramatic epistemological line has to be drawn that relates a subject to an object—drives are thus placed in a zone in between subject and object. Thus Lacan proposed that drive should rather be conceived as an organ, a paradoxical organ (Freud already spoke of "an auxiliary organ"), a strange kind of organ, "situated in relation to the true organ" (Lacan 1979: 196), but nevertheless an "ungraspable organ,… in short, a false organ" (Lacan 1979: 196), "… whose characteristic is not to exist, but which is nevertheless an organ" (Lacan 1979: 197–8), "an unreal [*irréel*] organ… Unreal is not imaginary. The unreal is defined by articulating itself on the real in a way that eludes us, and it is precisely this that requires that its representation should be mythical" (Lacan 1979: 205).

Elaborating on the idea that drive is an organ, Lacan produced his own myth about the drive, something of a parody of the Platonic myth of the missing halves: The missing half that would complement a human being (human being as sexed) and make him or her whole would be a lamella, "something extra-flat, which moves like the amoeba… it goes everywhere… it survives any division… it can run around…. And it is of this that all the forms of the *objet a*… are the representatives, the equivalents" (Lacan 1979: 197–8).

So in order to imagine the object of the drive, one has to conceive an organ which is lost and missing, but which nevertheless prolongs and extends the body, being molded by the orifices and the borders of our body, the transition between the inside and the outside (and what Lacan called "object *a*" stems precisely from that topological location in all its forms), infinitely pliable, yet never fitting and never quite graspable, except through the "tour of the drive."

I cannot dwell on this any further; all I want to point out is a hidden implication that one can glimpse in Freud's description of the tool as prosthesis. The tool always steps into the place of the missing organ, as an expansion and extension of the body, and in this topological location, it inevitably becomes the object of the investment of the drives. The drive intervenes, as it were, in the gap between the body and its prosthesis, it is itself prosthetic in its nature. The missing and lacking organ is as if made present in the tool, and the tool is secretly endowed with the nature of a lamella, which denaturalizes every natural relationship. It sublates nature, thereby gaining the quality of a blind driving force, which can appropriate everything, regardless of the benefit, driven by its own expanding force and pursuing its own agenda.

Freud speaks a few times somewhat enigmatically about a *Wisstrieb*, a drive for knowledge, but maybe one can see in science and technology as its extension a sort of paradoxical embodiment of the blind nature of the drive.

Natural forces are blind, as one says, but the forces that tame nature may turn out to be equally blind. Technology can never be caught into a homeostasis, synergetically working for our best advantage—hence, among other things, all the ecological problems. What drives science? The thirst for knowledge? The endeavor for the benefit of mankind, well-being, making life easier and more livable, the effort to alleviate that in life which is too hard for man to tackle, its too-muchness? It is clear that within all these reasons something else is at stake and that the high goals—progress of knowledge, usefulness to humanity—may well function, at some point, as a rationalization, an excuse, a stand-in reason, an *ersatz* justification for something that cannot be quite justified in these terms. In science and its progress, in the progressive technological mastering of nature, there lurks an automatism that doesn't heed utility, benefit, welfare, advantage, and pays no attention to ethical norms—hence the necessity of ethical committees designed to bridle its excesses and to remind us of the true values (just as throughout history one constantly attempted to bridle, with ethical norms, the excesses of sexuality—the analogy is strange, but maybe not unjustified). The paradox is that what is designed to tame nature (and the drives) itself behaves as a drive that one cannot tame. The tools as the extensions of the body take over the body, rather like drives driving the body that they merely prolong.

Let me end this first point with a quote by Slavoj Žižek making a similar point:

> Is not the paradigmatic case of such an "acephalic" knowledge provided by modern science which exemplifies the "blind insistence" of the (death) drive? Modern science follows its path (in microbiology manipulating genes, in particle physics etc.) heedless of the cost—satisfaction is here provided… not by any moral or communal goals scientific knowledge is supposed to serve. All the "ethical committees" which abound today and attempt to establish rules for the proper conduct…—are they ultimately not desperate attempts to re-inscribe this inexorable drive-progress of science which knows of no inherent limitation… within confines of human goals, to provide it with a "human face", a limitation?… Any limitation like this is utterly foreign to the inherent logic of science. (Žižek 1997: 149)

If the first trait of culture is placed under the heading of utility, with the benefits of mastering nature and improving our lives with technological gadgets, then **the second trait** is placed under the heading of the futile. The true indications of culture, says Freud, are to be sought above all in something that is completely useless, irreducible to the function of survival and the taming of nature. Culture manifests itself in something that doesn't serve any purpose, in an ornament, adornment, a supplement, in something merely beautiful for its own sake, without a function (one can be reminded of Kant's "purposefulness without a purpose"). From embellishments and flower-beds that adorn our living space, to jewelry, bracelets, earrings, make-up that supplement the natural bodily beauty (again, the prostheses?) to finally the great works of art. Only when we occupy ourselves with the useless, when we waste time and energy ("when friends converse and waste their time together," in Shakespeare's words), are we truly in culture. Cultural functions are precisely those that are irreducible to the economy of survival and the increase of power, calculation, and progress. One needs *otium* for culture, free time and exemption from work, waste. If one says "the culture of food" or "the culture of clothing," then one means precisely those traits that are beyond what is necessary for survival, a frivolous addition, but at the same time highly codified (one can recall the entire opus of Claude Lévi-Strauss in this respect). The moment of expenditure, of the non-functional, of waste, which defies the logic of self-preservation and survival, is the true breeding ground of culture. (One can recall Georges Bataille, whose reflections massively turn around the fact that culture is built around pure expenditure, spending for nothing, sacrifice, the excess which transgresses economy.)

What is the function of what has no function? The telltale sign of culture resides perhaps in the fact that what is useless is at the same time most highly valued. Only in the futile and the nonfunctional can the human being be on his or her own—hence the philosophical and sociological speculations about the nature of the game, from Huizinga to Roger Caillois, to name the most important, the game as a frivolous and futile pastime, set apart from the satisfaction of needs. It's only there that he or she displays the elevation over animal nature, and this is where he or she appears to be more than an animal, which happens to be more successful than other animals in the skills of survival. And if we could detect the dimension of the object of drive in tools and technology, then we can detect its obverse side in the supplement, the high valuation of the futile. Isn't the object of the drive by its nature an addition, a supplement, a *parergon* (to use another Kantian term)—an ornamental accessory and embellishment, literally *para ergon*, beyond work,[3] an excessive object, an objectal excess?

The two first traits form a paradoxical couple: on the one hand, culture as the maximization of utility, and on the other hand, culture as uselessness, pure expenditure. Is culture something that serves best or something that doesn't serve at all? Utility or futility? The maximum purpose or no purpose at all? But purpose for what, in view of what?

The third trait of culture is in a way connected to the second one, namely the endeavor for order and cleanliness. Dirt is the sign of barbarism, cleanliness the sign of cultural progress. The simple yardstick of civilization can be the use of soap, in Freud's words, the bathroom being the true sanctuary of civilization, its temple, far more important than the so-called cultural institutions. Culture begins with hygiene. "Dirtiness of any kind seems to us incompatible with civilization" (1985: 281). Cleanliness is intriguing insofar as, here again, there is something other at stake than the function of survival. It is of course true that it greatly improves health and enhances the chances of survival, yet animals on the whole do very well without it and the knowledge about its blessings is of rather recent date. Hygiene is in some ways just as dysfunctional as the ornament, and it was not implemented primarily on the basis of knowledge about its benefits for health. The more decisive part is its libidinal investment—the link between filth and the body in its natural functions, or more pointedly, between filth and enjoyment. Purity is the path of elevation beyond enjoyment, the path of purification, *askesis*, the rise above the body, the liberation from the flesh, but producing another kind of enjoyment as its side-effect that sustains this elevation beyond enjoyment, a surplus enjoyment in the very renunciation of the bodily enjoyment. Cleanliness is linked to purification as the metaphor of spirit elevated over carnality. So the first act of culture is the control over the excremental function, its *réglementation*, regulation, its confinement to a particular place and time, to a schedule, and to a place apart. "Is this child clean?" To every infant who has ever crossed the threshold of a kindergarten, it is crystal clear what is the first stage of culture, what constitutes the entry ticket into civilization, and what divides the human from the sub-human. For Freud the discipline of bodily functions in the anal stage is the very model of every discipline, and each transgression of this prohibition evokes "dirty enjoyment" and the banned link between filth and enjoyment. Animals have no such problems; they don't find excrements repulsive or odious. The first prohibition that the child must be submitted to is the prohibition

> against getting pleasure from anal activity and its products [which] has decisive effect on his whole development. This must be the first occasion on which the infant has a glimpse of an environment hostile to his instinctual impulses, on which he learns to separate his own entity from this alien one and on which he carries out the first "repression" of his possibilities for pleasure. From that time on, what is anal remains the symbol of everything that is to be repudiated and excluded from life. (Freud 1977: 104)

As an aside: when Lacan was touring American universities in 1975, he had a lecture at the MIT, where he brought up, to the consternation of his audience, the question of elephant shit—there must be masses of it, yet it doesn't seem to present any problem, whereas for us even the tiniest amount is a ponderous problem. Hence his line (which he repeated on several occasions): *Cloaque, c'est la civilization*. Civilization is cloaca, shit management.[4]

The endeavor for cleanliness and purification stands in a close connection with striving for order, although the latter presents slightly different kind of issues, so that it can be singled out as an independent **fourth trait** of culture. Order imposed by culture tends to take, in its initial gesture, the natural cycle as its model—as opposed to cleanliness, which is inherently "unnatural." Its pattern and support can be provided by the regularity of astronomical cycles, the rhythm of day and night, the seasons, the movement of celestial bodies returning to the same place, providing the model for the calendar as the elementary disposition of ordering and partitioning time. Some of the oldest monuments of civilization (from pyramids to Stonehenge) were erected on the basis of an astronomic pattern, with a view of culture to be attuned to celestial order. Order enables the economy of time and space, the economic use of the one and the other. Yet again, its functional use rather disguises than reveals its libidinal impact—what is at stake, beyond functionality, is an excess which manifests "the compulsion to repeat," and this is precisely the mechanism in which Freud sees the basic property of drives. "Order is a kind of compulsion to repeat… " (1985: 282). Drives are endowed with a vector, which compels them to return to the same place, the place of the crime, that is, the place of satisfaction, a satisfaction beyond use and need, and this is what epitomizes the object of the drive. There is a blind automatism built into the drive, which entails repetition, insists as repetition, the repetition of what procures pleasure (and ultimately, enigmatically, also the repetition of something which is "beyond the pleasure principle"—that was the problem that Freud's most remarkable text of that name (1920) had to deal with). Order is tightly connected to automatism, regularity, compulsion (*Zwang*), there is always more in the insistence of order than mere utility, and this excess of libidinal investment makes it possible for order to be implemented at all and to make it acceptable. Utility does not explain cultural compulsion and repetition; something else must be at work besides.[5]

The further trait of culture--**the fifth trait** by our count--is the high valuation of spirituality, of ideas and ideals. The leading role ascribed to ideas in human life is the sign and the measure of civilization, that is, the high valuation of everything that raises us beyond the survival function. And here again one can quickly see the link with the drives—precisely with one of the fundamental "vicissitudes of the drives" that Freud described as sublimation, the inherent trait of the drive that renders possible the proclivity of the drives to be satisfied with proxies and stand-ins, with ersatz satisfaction, thus opening at the outset a leeway where the intellectual, spiritual, scientific, religious, artistic pursuits could spectacularly sneak in.

Freud posits an equation between sublimation and desexualization, for example, in 1908: "This capacity to exchange its originally sexual aim for another one, which is no longer sexual but which is psychically related to the first aim, is called the capacity for sublimation" (1985: 39). The sexual drive has the curious ability "to displace its aim without materially diminishing in intensity" (1985: 39). What more is, and this is really astounding, this can happen "*without* involving repression" ("On Narcissism: An Introduction" (1914), Freud 1984: 89). There is a glaring paradox: One would think that the deflection of the aim from its original purpose, from a sexual goal, comes with a high price, but not at all—sublimation averts the initial sexual aim without repression, and it foists a surrogate for the real thing without imposing repression and without diminishing intensity. Not something one would expect Freud to say. Already in the *Three Essays*, which introduced the notion of the drive, and then in the meta-psychological paper on the vicissitudes of the drives (1915, Freud 1984: 113–8), one can see that the drive essentially consists in a roundabout, in the capacity for substitution, in a displacement from the direct satisfaction to indirect ones. To follow this basic insight, drives are not simply a primary given; they rather appear as intruders, which denaturalize the supposed natural course of the satisfaction of needs and thwart it by the slide toward surrogates. They emerge only at the point of a slide of a supposedly natural course, being substitutive at their very origin (hence Freud's theory of *Anlehnung*, the drives emerging by "leaning on," taking support in, natural satisfaction of needs, what Strachey translated by the "anaclyctic" nature of drives). Drives, instead of being indomitable giants, which always force their way to satisfaction, thus rather appear to be easily tamed, lured by stand-ins, fed by ersatz, prone to sublimation, to deflection from the true satisfaction, but this doesn't make them any less indomitable nor this satisfaction any less real. Could one coin an adage "Love your surrogate as yourself"? So with sublimation as "desexualization" it would rather seem that already "sexuality," in any common sense of the word, was itself retroactively thoroughly "desexualized" by Freud, bereft of its natural givenness and made dependent on a substitution.

Last but not least--and this is the last, **the sixth trait** of culture--there is the regulation of social relations in a way that enables the coexistence in a family, a society, a state. In the hypothetical natural state, the decisive factor was the supremacy of physical power, but the origin of society requires the insight that community is stronger than the individual. The first step of civilization is the supremacy of the social over the individual, so that all individuals have to accept a mutual limitation. Hence the idea of law and justice, equally valid for everyone and which shouldn't be transgressed in favor of any particular individual. If everyone is equally submitted to the law, then everyone has to accept the renunciation of the drives. An individual can ultimately be free only outside of society and culture--hence the model of a free individual is the primal father--while the realm of culture is the realm of restriction, the balance between the demands for individual freedom and autonomy and, on the other hand, the demands of society, the heteronomy.

Thus we arrive at, or come back to, the central problem, that culture appears as the renunciation of the satisfaction of the drives. Freud uses a series of expressions, which all point in the same direction, exhibiting at the same time a terminological uncertainty. *Triebverzicht*—renunciation of the drives; *Nichtbefriedigung*—non-satisfaction, dissatisfaction; *Unterdrückung*—suppression; *Verdrängung*—repression (Freud adds a question mark: "by suppression, repression or some other means?" (1985: 286)); "*Kulturversagung*," in quotation marks—cultural renunciation, a term that is (unwittingly?) ambiguous, for it can mean that we have to renounce in favor of culture, or that culture itself falls short, *versagt*, it fails to provide satisfaction. A bit later Freud speaks of *Triebeinschränkung*, inherent limitation of the drives; and finally there is the constant use of the adjective *zielgehemmt*, namely the inhibition of the drive on the way to its goal (Freud 1982: 226-8).[6] But the drive that doesn't attain its goal nevertheless reaches its aim (to use Lacan's helpful distinction); it gets its satisfaction on the way to satisfaction, it gets its bit in the very dissatisfaction, it is satisfied whether one wants it or not, and it reaches its *Ziel* through being *zielgehemmt*. In the renunciation, in the inhibition imposed by society on the individual, something is produced that keeps the drive going, something that drives the drive and which is its true object. This surplus is what sustains cultural and social coexistence as well as marks it with an impossibility.

Thus we can see that the result of Freud's attempt to list the basic traits of culture is that it paradoxically coincides with the list of the basic traits of the drive. "Six fundamental traits of culture" can be read as the "six fundamental traits of the drive."

1. Mastering of nature, whose tool is precisely the tool, can be seen as the parallel to the fact that the tool as the prosthesis prolongs the body and is placed in the "grey zone," which reaches beyond the body without being simply external, the zone where the drive extends over the body and turns around the non-bodily organ, where the body extends over its physical limits.
2. The ornament, the *parergon*, the non-functional supplement, the addition, shows the object of the drive from the reverse side, as a useless appendage, the object of enjoyment in the place of pure expenditure.
3. Cleanliness as the yardstick of culture points to the anal drive, the disciplining of anality, the way where the (anal) drive doesn't start from the bodily needs but takes the demand of the Other as its object.
4. Order points to the compulsion to repeat as the basic matrix of the drive, *Wiederholungszwang*.
5. Spiritual elevation, the high valuation of ideas, points to sublimation, the inherent substitutive nature of the drive, its slide to the indirect *ersatz* satisfaction.
6. The social nature of culture points to renunciation and inhibition in relation to the supposed goal. The drive is necessarily inhibited and deviated in culture, yet it forces its satisfaction by this very way.

So what follows from there? If the unconscious is structured like a language—Lacan's famous dictum—are drives structured like culture? Do they get the basic traits from their opponent, which is supposed to be there to restrict them and to mold them? What are they "in themselves," if we could consider them apart from this molding? Do they have an independent existence as a separate realm? Do they get their satisfaction from what was supposed to oppress them?

There is a paradox at the core of this. The cultural instances are supposed to restrict sexuality, and Freud indeed describes the progress of culture as the progress of growing restriction, constraint, displacement, and channeling of sexual drives. Yet, is sexuality restricted by something that is completely alien to it, by an external oppressor? Do the drives rather form a strange alliance, a compromise with what was supposed to oppress them, willingly espousing surrogates? Maybe we were looking at the picture from a wrong perspective. "Sometimes one seems to perceive that it is not only the pressure of civilization but something in the essence of the [sexual] function itself [*etwas am Wesen der Funktion selbst*] which denies us full satisfaction and urges us along other paths. This may be wrong; it is hard to decide" (1985: 295; 1982: 235). This seems to be a very strange idea—there is something in sexuality itself that resists its full satisfaction? This strange idea is not new. Freud gave it a voice already seventeen years earlier, in "On the Universal Tendency to Debasement in the Sphere of Love" (1912): "It is my belief that, however strange it may sound, we must reckon with the possibility that something in the nature of the sexual drive itself is unfavorable to the realization of complete satisfaction" (1977: 162). Freud, in this paper, goes on to give the humorous example of the happy relation between the drunkard and his bottle—the drunkard has no need to go to some faraway country where the wine is more expensive or the use of alcohol is prohibited. It seems that the relation of drunkard to the bottle is pure harmony, the model of a happy marriage, as opposed to the "gender trouble" we are doomed to, the trouble that may mysteriously stem from sexuality itself, not from its repression, from something in sexuality that resists straight satisfaction on its own grounds, not because of external intervention and oppression, so that restriction would then rather appear as an externalization, a consequence of an internal impasse, not the cause of conflict, but its result.

But how to conceive the nature of this conflict, which at the outset seemed to be the conflict between the drives and the culture imposing restrictions on them, but which turned out to be far more convoluted, so that the restrictions turn out to be the extrapolation of something that is ridden with impasses in itself? Drives and culture thus appear to be inseparable, not on opposite banks, yet nevertheless structured and driven by a conflict that cannot simply be played out between the two, but seems transversal, affecting both. And to start with, how many drives are there?

Freud famously proposed an all-pervasive conflict between two kinds of drives, which in their antagonistic relation subtend all cultural formations, in a strife that has no end in sight. There is, on the one hand, the Eros, which is the force of unification, union, and integration. In one part of the argument he speaks about the deflection of the libido from its immediate sexual aims, which can then form the ties of friendship, neighborly love, groups, social formations, nation, state, humanity, the force of cohesion, which, along with the mechanism of sublimation, forms the edifice of culture, providing its unifying glue. There is on the other side the death drive, *Thanatos*, the force of disintegration, negativity, aggression, dissolution, destruction, which strives in the opposite direction and prevents any unity, undermining union by its thrust to separation.[7] Thus one can ultimately regard all culture as "the struggle between Eros and Death, between the drive of life and the drive of destruction, as it works itself out in the human species" (1985: 314). Eros would thus be the building force of culture, and death drive would be its opponent, undermining and undoing the ties of cohesion, so that the apparent conflict between culture and drives is thereby transposed into the conflict between two kinds of drives, one promoting cultural goals and one undoing them. This is the spirit in which the famous closing page is written: "Thus I have not the courage to rise up before my fellow-men as a prophet, and I bow to their reproach that I can offer them no consolation" (1985: 339). The most fateful issue of culture is thus how to master and subdue "the drive of aggression and self-destruction", since technology has advanced to the point that humanity can annihilate itself ("exterminating one another to the last man"). But Freud is helpless and has no answer. "And now it is to be expected that the other of the two 'Heavenly Powers', eternal Eros, will make an effort to assert himself in the struggle with his equally immortal adversary. But who can foresee with what success and with what result?" (1985: 340). This is the last sentence of this work, and as the editors' note tells us: "The final sentence was added in 1931 [in the second edition two years after first publication]—when the menace of Hitler was already beginning to be apparent."

So in this eternal struggle the best we can do is to hope that the balance will be swayed on the good side, the side of Eros; all we can do is to keep our fingers crossed for the better opponent in an endless strife, strife as old as humanity, knowing full well that the other opponent is equally mighty and ultimately unbeatable.

But one can easily see that this solution is far from being satisfactory. Doesn't the dualism of the drives, posited as this eternal quasi-cosmic struggle of two "heavenly powers," rather simplify that paradox and avoid its true sting? Freud himself spoke a number of times about the psychic mechanism of dealing with a contradiction by dividing it into the good part and the bad part, say the image of the good father and the bad father, keeping the two separate, side by side, instead of addressing the complexity of their conflictual nexus. The story of the eternal struggle is suspiciously similar to the countless Manichean mythical accounts of the eternal strife between the forces of light and the forces of darkness, and Freud himself, in "Analysis Terminable and Interminable" (1937), sang great praise for a quasi-mythical reference to Empedocles, one of the greatest Greek naturalists of his time, but also the author of the mythical account about the strife between *philia* and *neikos*, forces of love and forces of disintegration. "Empedocles comes so close to the psychoanalytic theory of the drives that one could maintain that they are identical, if it wasn't for the difference that the Greek's theory is a cosmic fantasy while our theory pretends to have biological validity" (Freud 1975: 385). Just as in *Beyond the Pleasure Principle*, Freud had to have recourse to the Platonic myth of the missing halves as the best account of the origin of sexuality. Where would that thin difference lie? Perhaps one should then take seriously Freud's assertion, in the *New Introductory Lectures on Psychoanalysis* (1932), that "the theory of the drives is so to say our mythology. Drives are mythical entities, magnificent in their indefiniteness. In our work we cannot disregard them, yet we are never sure that we are seeing them clearly" (Freud 1973: 127). Mythical creatures, never to be seen clearly nor scientifically proven or provable, would thus entail a mythical account as the best we can do to talk about them at all. Can this be an ultimate answer, or rather an admission of defeat?

How many drives are there? When Freud introduced the notion of the drive and libido in the *Three Essays* (1905), a quarter of a century earlier, it was presented in a completely different light than at the end of *Civilization*. The reader of *Three Essays* would be completely confounded to find out that the fragmented, partial, polymorphous nature of libido in the first book would turn into the cultural hero of unification and love in the second, to the point of presenting our best hope for the salvation of culture, endowed with a high cultural mission, difficult to tell apart from the traditional praise of the forces of love. If the first book made a scandal (one of the biggest early scandals inaugurating psychoanalysis), then precisely for presenting an image that was completely at odds with the traditional views of sexuality and love: A libido depicted by deviations and aberrations, *Abweichungen* and *Abirrungen*, by autoeroticism, polymorphous perversion, anarchy, fetishism, partial objects—objects partial in themselves, not just part of objects, and hence a libido that is "partial" in this way, never to be totalized, never to be seized and encompassed by One, as far removed from the force of unity as possible.

Freud tellingly started his argument in the *Three Essays* by considering sexual aberrations, *Abirrungen*, and then proceeded to consider sexual *Abweichungen*, deviations regarding the sexual object and the sexual goal. There is something in sexuality as such that is defined, for Freud, by deviation and aberration, or in another word, by a declination, a *clinamen* from the path of natural causality and the satisfaction of physiological needs. There is a deviation in the very concept of sexuality, in the very concept of the drive, which, to put it in a nutshell, cannot be grasped independently of its deviation. There is the famous adage by Brecht, at the end of *The Threepenny Opera*: "What is a bank robbery in comparison with the establishment of a bank?" What are all the petty thieves in comparison with a systematic, legalized, and long-term robbery accomplished by banks? By analogy (I know, a strange analogy), one could say that Freud's treatment of deviations and perversions in that book presents the following argument: What are all these perversions, deviations from the usual sexual object or goal, in comparison with sexuality as such, which is in itself nothing but a massive deviation, more spectacular than any perverse deviations? Aberrations and deviations are not placed at the beginning of the argument in order to lead us to the consideration of "normal sexuality," but in order to show that "normal sexuality" is itself based on an aberration and a deviation.

The old idea of *clinamen*, stemming from Epicurus and Lucretius, from the early origins of materialism in the history of thought, the idea of a departure from a straight path and from the supposed natural causality, a swerve that the universe may hold at its origin and its core, is perhaps a useful tool to think about this. *Clinamen* presents not a principle or a substance as the point of departure or origin, but precisely the very departure from a principle, a swerve. The drive is such a *clinamen* of human nature.[8]

So how many drives are there? I made this excursion into the *Three Essays*, the originating point of Freud's theory of drives, to arrive at a simple point: The drive, libido, is not a One, it is not a substance, it possesses the key quality of the drive by the very impossibility to be substantialized and totalized. It is not a substance that one could ever delimit and localize, say by positing sexuality as the firm determining force, a substratum that lies under all seemingly higher endeavors, a universal answer—it consists precisely in the very impossibility of such a delimitation or localization, it is a universal question rather than an answer. It is neither reducible to biological needs and pressures nor separable from them, occurring only in their bosom, nor can it be seized independently. No doubt Freud's less than satisfactory dualistic account can be criticized precisely because he thus turned the drives into two opposing substances or principles. The drive is neither One (and this was Jung's idea of turning libido and the drives into a unified notion of life energy) nor a Two, Eros and Thanatos, the positive and the negative, the binding and the unbinding, in eternal dualism. Nor is it simply a multiple heterogeneity, "multiplicities of multiplicities," in Badiou's parlance—to recur to multiplicity is usually rather a way to avoid the tensions and contradictions by relegating them to multiplicity, thus avoiding the break and the cut (the negative one, as it were) that subtends it.

But this brings us to the core of the problem. If the nature of the drive consists in deviation and substitution, if the symbolic is the obverse side of this deviation and substitution, then the drive shares from its "origin," its deviating origin, the ground with culture. The culture molds basically not nature or instinct, but something that it produces itself. Or rather, both culture and the drives share the same lack of origin, which is placed in something that could be seen as a deviation to start with. What follows is that we are never dealing with the problem of having a natural substratum that culture would then come to restrict, but rather that we are always dealing with their interface, the interface that comes first, as it were, the field of tensions and contradictions that "precedes" or dislocates the neat division into nature and culture. Or in other words, we don't have two separate, independent, and opposed areas, neatly localized and delimited, which would come into conflict, with an always unsatisfactory outcome, but rather a field of tensions and overlaps, an interface where inter "precedes" the two faces, and the neat opposition between nature and culture, drives and culture, is precisely a way to avoid this paradox, or to repress it or to circumvent it or to obfuscate it. "Drives are the representatives of the somatic in the psychic"—this is Freud's recurrent formulation from which it follows that they are precisely an interface, but it is wrong to assume, as we spontaneously do, that there are the constituted independent areas of somatic and psychic, nature and culture, prior to that interface.

The history of psychoanalysis has always oscillated between the two poles of naturalization and culturalization. There was the strong tendency, already in Freud, to pin it to sciences of nature, in the hope of finding the chemical and physiological grounding for what it describes (Freud sometimes even presented psychoanalysis as a provisional science valid for the time being only until the true natural basis can be discovered in the biological and the chemical; an interim science in suspense). Nowadays this is what drives the attempts to make it compatible with cognitive sciences. On the other hand, psychoanalysis has largely made its career as a theory of culture, in humanities and social sciences, where it is mostly taught in universities, Freud being mostly praised as a cultural hero in the *Zeitgeist*.[9] But there is something that gets lost and obfuscated in both these receptions and accounts, a point where neither nature nor culture can be totalized and neatly opposed, where they both reach beyond themselves into their other, the blind spot of their opposition, where both nature and culture appear as non-all, not fully constituted, held together by their impossible overlap. We cannot simply oppose two massive totalities of nature and culture, for the Freudian notion of the drive can be seen as the concept whose aim is ultimately to de-totalize the two, to undermine this very opposition and its self-evidence.

Notes

1. "Psychoanalysis differs from other approaches to human being by attending to the constitutive 'too muchness' that characterizes the psyche; the human mind is, we might say, defined by the fact that it includes more reality than it can contain, is the bearer of an excess, a too much of pressure that is not merely physiological" (Santner 2001: 8).
2. "This contention holds that what we call our civilization is largely responsible for our misery, and that we should be much happier if we gave it up and returned to primitive conditions" (Santner 2001: 274).
3. Cf. Derrida, who made a big case of Kant's reflections on *parergon* in *The Truth in Painting* (Derrida 1987).
4. "Excrements perhaps come from the interior, but the human characteristic is that man doesn't know what to do with his excrements. Civilization is the excrement [*le déchet*], *cloaca maxima*" (Lacan 1976: 61).
5. "Aber der Nutzen erklärt uns das Streben nicht ganz; es muss etwas anderes im Spiele sein" (Freud 1982: 224).
6. "Here we can clear up the mystery of the *zielgehemmt*, of that form that the drive may assume, in attaining its satisfaction without attaining its goal...... When you entrust someone with a mission, the aim is not what he brings back, but the itinerary he must take. The aim is the way taken. The French word *le but* may be translated by another word in English, goal.... If the drive may be satisfied without attaining what... would be the satisfaction of its end..., it is because... its aim is simply this return into circuit" (Lacan 1979: 179–80).
7. "[C]ivilization is a process in the service of Eros, whose purpose is to combine single human individuals, and after that families, then races, peoples and nations, into one great unit, the unity of mankind.... These collections of men are to be libidinally bound to one another. Necessity alone, the advantages of work in common, will not hold them together. But man's natural aggressive drive, the hostility of each against all and of all against each, opposes this program of civilization. This aggressive drive is the derivative and the main representative of the death drive which we have found alongside of Eros and which shares world-dominion with it" (1985: 313–14).
8. Lacan, in a felicitous pun, implied a relation between clinics and *clinamen*: "clinical relations (clinical, the analyzand is on a couch [indeed *reclining*, one can add], there is the question of a certain *clinamen*, cf. Lucretius...)" (Lacan 1976: 58). On the question of *clinamen* and psychoanalysis, cf. Dolar 2013.
9. I must refer, concerning this central point, to the brilliant work by Alenka Zupančič (2017), which also served as one of the major inspirations of this chapter.

References

Derrida, J. (1987), *The Truth in Painting*, Chicago: The University of Chicago Press.

Dolar, M. (2013), "Tyche, clinamen, den," *Continental Philosophy Review*, 46: 223–39.

Freud, S. (1973), *New Introductory Lectures on Psychoanalysis*, Harmondsworth: Penguin (The Freud Pelican Library, vol. 2)

Freud, S. (1975), *Schriften zur Behandlungstechnik*, Frankfurt am Main: Fischer.

Freud, S. (1977), *On Sexuality*, Harmondsworth: Penguin (The Pelican Freud Library, vol. 7).

Freud, S. (1982), *Fragen der Gesellschaft, Ursprünge der Religion*, Frankfurt am Main: Fischer.

Freud, S. (1984), *On Metapsychology*, Harmondsworth: Penguin (The Pelican Freud Library, vol. 11).

Freud, S. (1985), *Civilization, Society and Religion*, Harmondsworth: Penguin (The Pelican Freud Library, vol. 12).

Lacan, J. (1976), "Conférences et entretiens dans des universités nord-américaines," *Scilicet*, 6 (7): 5–63.

Lacan, J. (1979), *The Four Fundamental Concepts of Psychoanalysis*, Harmondsworth: Penguin.

Santner, E. (2001), *On the Psychotheology of Everyday Life*, Chicago: The University of Chicago Press.

Žižek, S. (1997), "Desire: Drive = Truth: Knowledge," *Umbr(a)*, 1. Available online: http://www.lacan.com/zizek-desire.htm (accessed February 8, 2019).

Zupančič, A. (2017), *What Is Sex?* Boston: MIT Press.

2

Lars von Trier's *Nymphomaniac*. Boredom and Knowledge as Defense. The Discourse of the University and the Discourse of the Hysteric

Kirsten Hyldgaard

When I read the following passages in Pauline Kael's "Trash, Art, and the Movies" from *Going Steady*, I immediately thought of Lars von Trier's notorious schoolmaster attitude.

> Movie audiences will take a lot of garbage, but it's pretty hard to make us queue up for pedagogy.
>
> Keeping in mind that simple, good distinction that all art is entertainment but not all entertainment is art, it might be a good idea to keep in mind also that if a movie is said to be a work of art and you don't enjoy it, the fault may be in you, but it's probably in the movie.
>
> (Kael 1971)

Von Trier does not make movies in order to entertain us or boost our morale. In an interview, he has stated that he makes movies for an audience that is dumber than he (Thorsen 2010: 213). Nor are his movies merely an exploration of the possibilities of the medium; after all, many highly entertaining movies are also reflections on their genre and particular techniques. Von Trier lectures the audience: What is a movie? What does it do to us? We are queuing up for pedagogy. Apparently, it is not enough for von Trier to be able to control cinematic techniques; this is something mastered by any great director, scriptwriter, or producer. He always makes a point of showing us, often at the very end of the movie, that we have been manipulated. The great bells tolling in heaven in *Breaking the Waves* (1996), offering a true God's eye perspective, is one example; the final scene of *Nymphomaniac* (2013) is the other obvious example. Von Trier is messing with the audience. Therefore, not surprisingly, many of us need to come up with a defense, not least through a certain reluctance to go to see his movies.

My contention in the following is that both boredom and knowledge can serve as defense. The first concerns the audience's response or, to be exact, my own experience of excruciating boredom when I watched the four-and-a-half-hour-long *Nymphomaniac* for the first time. The second concerns the principal character Seligman's (Stellan Skarsgård) way of listening, speaking, and reacting to Joe's (Charlotte Gainsbourg) storytelling. It concerns the relation between Lacan's (1991: 31) "discourse of the university" and "the discourse of the hysteric," exploring how the discourse of the university can serve the purpose of "not wanting to know" and how the discourse of the hysteric is the discourse of provocation.

Boredom

I was bored when watching *Nymphomaniac*. However, the day after, I dutifully sat down to write a paper for a conference on "Lars von Trier, Sexuality, and Psychoanalysis" (2014), and one painful scene after the other showed up in my memory. I had been twisting and turning in the theater seat, with only professional discipline drawing me back after the intermission, but thinking about and working through the experience was anything but boring. This experience, full of contradictions, forced me to think about the phenomenon of boredom as defense, the psychoanalytic concept that presupposes an unconscious conflict. In the following, I have also sought and found help in Heidegger's phenomenological description of boredom as mood (1992).

When you speak about boredom and especially when you speak about being bored by something specific—a movie, a book, another human being, the company in general—it implies a touch of arrogance, an assumption that the object or the other is the cause of our boredom. My contention is that this arrogance is unfounded, that the subject is implicated in being bored. We are, so to speak, responsible for our own boredom. We cannot just dismiss the problem by dismissing the object, by escaping, by leaving it behind. The question is in what sense the subject is implicated. Many years ago, I read a statement by a psychoanalyst that has stuck in my mind ever since: When an analyst is bored, it is a symptom of resistance, a defense against being implicated in the desire of the analysand. This generalization might seem gratuitous; after all, anything could be labelled a defense and as resistance. In the following, however, I will defend this anonymous psychoanalyst's contention by interpreting knowledge in the capacity of "agent" in the discourse of the university as serving the same purpose. "Defense" is what ties together the question of boredom and Lacan's "discourse of the university."

I was bored, but, keeping in mind Pauline Kael's words at the beginning of this chapter, does that make *Nymphomaniac* a bad movie? It raises the question whether von Trier's work qualifies as pretentious pseudo-art. Has a charlatan duped us? There is no need to keep the reader in suspense about my position on this matter: *Nymphomaniac is* art. And art is here defined as a way of thinking in the material. In the technically multifaceted movie, thinking is going on; it is what transcends simple entertainment, decoration, or any political, moral, or ideological purpose, and it is what transcends any explicit intentions of the "auteur." However, not only is thinking going on in von Trier's movies; he also forces us to think; he educates us like a schoolmaster.

The movie testifies to a curious contrast between the so-called nymphomania, which is supposed to be a standard masculine fantasy, and the fact that the movie allows little, if any, pleasure. Rather, the movie shows involuntary enjoyment. *Nymphomaniac* is devoid of Hollywood sex. It shows a kind of enjoyment that is beyond the homeostatic pleasure principle.

Knowledge

First a brief synopsis of the movie. It features two main characters, a man and a woman: the scholar and virgin, Seligman, and the sexually promiscuous Joe. Seligman finds Joe beaten up in a dark alley, picks her up, puts her to bed. While she recovers, she tells him the story of her life in eight chapters. A dynamic relationship is established between, on the one hand, the virginal, encyclopedic subject of knowledge, the compassionate, understanding, male humanist and, on the other, the decadent, female nihilist.

Seligman listens; he strives to understand Joe's story. We, the movie's audience, likewise strive to understand and find meaning in Joe's sexual activities. By "understand," I mean that we try, many of us in vain, to identify with Joe. However, it is my contention that we identify with the virginal scholar who lends her a compassionate ear, the humanist subject who considers nothing human to be alien to him. This is pointed out to us in the movie's final scene.

Throughout the movie, a dynamic conflict is established between, on the one hand, Seligman's desire to listen to a story that provokes and defies understanding, and, on the other hand, a defense against this very desire. When Joe's story becomes too much for Seligman, when he does not want to know, he breaks into a lecture about a random topic: fly-fishing, the difference between the Roman Catholic Church and the Russian Orthodox Church, various mathematical issues. Joe succinctly punctuates one of his lectures: "That was one of your weakest digressions."

When in a position of knowledge, when you assume that you know, you do not need to listen. You can proceed to "treat" the other: prescribe a therapy or volunteer your well-meaning advice. When you are the one who is supposed to know, you have a license to speak; you are relieved from listening, from risking that your lack (of knowledge) is exposed. Seligman, in his capacity as an agent of knowledge, satisfies no one. The "other" of his discourse is the "a," the notation for the cause of desire, the "surplus enjoyment"; that is, Seligman can "go on and on" and never reach the point—like any lecturer in his or her field of expertise.

In the discourse of the university, we find the split subject at the place of production. Seligman's educated, lecturing position of knowledge only provokes Joe's dissatisfaction, and she, in response, addresses and even provokes the master signifier through her seemingly autobiographical stories; she also takes her cues from random elements in the room and the situation in general. Joe responds in the manner of the good hysteric, where the split subject is in the position of the agent, and addresses and even provokes the master signifier, that is, the precondition for Seligman's benevolent, patronizing attitude and his supposition that nothing can defy knowledge and understanding.

Boredom according to Heidegger

Now, one thing is the relation between the two characters' ways of speaking; another question is why this had the effect of boredom on at least some of us. Usually we experience boredom as oozing out of the object: the book, the movie, the other. However, even though boredom seems to be caused by and be the very essence of the object, it is somehow related to the subject when it sneaks up on us, even overwhelms us (Heidegger 1992: 124–6). To say that a movie is boring is not the same as to say that it is poorly crafted. A poorly crafted movie is annoying, irritating, a waste of our time. Finding the images and scenarios displayed on the screen repulsive—for instance, violent and abusive pornographic scenarios—is different from being bored by this movie's sadomasochistic scenarios. Boredom is, above all, different from something just being irrelevant. According to Heidegger, it is exactly because something or someone is *not* irrelevant to us that it can be boring. Boredom can overwhelm us *because* we expect something from the object or the situation that it does not give us. This applies to *Nymphomaniac*'s sex scenes. Defying the conventional distinction between feature films and porn movies, *Nymphomaniac* shows an abundance of genitals, and the simple question is whether it is humanly possible to be indifferent toward genitalia. We can have all sorts of different reactions—intense, obsessed interest or equally intense repulsion—or the other's genitals can provoke heightened anxiety, but is indifference possible?

Heidegger uses the word *versagen* (renounce); something is said (*sagen*), announced, that is then renounced. We do not listen to it; we do not have ears for it; we ignore it. We pass the time or are struck by an almost irresistible urge to take flight from the cinema in order not to hear what is being announced in boredom. It is even an *Überschreien*, an outshouting of what is being said. Heidegger asks whether we do not have the guts to hear what we, after all, already know (1992: 117–18).

Now, this must ring a bell for anyone familiar with psychoanalysis. The unconscious is not just about ideas and fantasies that are not "conscious," whatever this concept may refer to. The unconscious is fundamentally about knowledge. It concerns knowledge as far as the subject's enjoyment is concerned, a knowledge that the subject cannot recognize as his or her enjoyment. This unconscious knowledge is "not me." We try to avoid boredom; we pass the time by being terribly busy or by common socializing. However, we "know" with a strange kind of knowledge, Heidegger claims (Heidegger 1992: 118); the kind of knowledge that psychoanalysis calls unconscious knowledge. Authentic boredom, that is, the kind of boredom that we cannot take flight from bypassing the time, overwhelms us and forces us to listen. When we are authentically bored, we are subject to a superior force that the singular subject cannot control or avoid (Heidegger 1992: 209).

What is it that we do not want to hear? To simplify a long argument made by Heidegger: Boredom, like any kind of mood (*Stimmung*), both uncovers Being as a whole and shields us against the anxiety-provoking Nothing (with a capital N) (1981: 31). Moods conceal Nothing; that is, the foundation of Being (as a whole) is Nothing. There is no transcendental signified, no Other to the Other. Moods do tell us something, but at the same time, they conceal something— not just boredom, all kinds of moods. What they conceal is that existence has no foundation. However, for Heidegger, as in psychoanalysis, anxiety has a special status among moods: Only anxiety can confront us with Nothing, the fundamental lack. There is a point to this very brief outline of Heidegger's 150-

page phenomenological description of boredom, as it can provide a backdrop for my analysis of the final scene of the movie, the final act of abuse.

For Lacan, anxiety is the only mood that does not lie—hatred can conceal love, and vice versa, and excessive joy can cover up a deep melancholia. Moods or affects also conceal and lie in psychoanalysis—except anxiety, the mood of all moods. In this sense, you can translate boredom into psychoanalytical terminology and contend that a concrete case of boredom, like watching *Nymphomaniac*, is a defense against existential anxiety.

However, the congeniality between Heidegger and Lacan needs reservations. According to Lacan, the object of anxiety is not the classical Nothing of existential philosophy; rather, it is the overwhelming proximity of the Other. When the desire of the Other overwhelms us, we must defend ourselves. My contention is that withdrawing into boredom, withdrawing our cathexis from the movie, leaving us cold and disinterested, serves the purpose of defense. We are bored when we defend ourselves against the desire of the Other, when we cannot or do not want to know of the Other's desire, the Other's way of enjoying himself or herself.

Therefore, I must grant the aforementioned anonymous psychoanalyst's sweeping statement some validity. While preparing my conference paper, I was reminded of one scene after the other, all of which were anything but boring. Working on the conference paper convinced me that there is something to it when it is said that boredom is caused not just by the object but also by the subject in a psychoanalytical sense, that is, a subject that cannot be thought of without the desire of the Other. In Heidegger's work, mood is a *Zwitterwesen* ("something in-between," 1992: 132); that is, mood exists "before" the distinction between subjects and objects. The same applies to Lacan's concept of the subject: it is something in-between, an unsettled matter, a difference, defined as a question both of the desire of the Other and of the reciprocal relationship between the signifier and the subject; "a signifier represents a subject for another signifier."

Somehow, forced by circumstances, in this case having to write a paper for a conference, boredom evaporated. Working through the experience made it bearable *not* to understand, *not* to be able to identify with the desire of the Other, *not* to shield myself (as Seligman does) from the Other's—that is, Joe's (and Lars von Trier's)—hysterical provocation of Seligman (and the audience). It became possible to bear the Other's enigmatic desire, the Other's otherness; that is, not to be able to understand and identify with Joe's story. *Not* to understand is the prerequisite for analysis, and analysis in the psychoanalytical sense is not about reaching an understanding.

Knowledge according to hysterics and obsessionals

Not only boredom but also knowledge can serve as a defense. Seemingly, knowledge is something we cannot get enough of: a blessing, an unequivocal advantage in all situations. *Nymphomaniac* questions this as a self-evident truth, suggesting that knowledge can also be in the service of repression, of resistance.

Reportedly, one of the most difficult aspects of an analyst's practice is to abstain from a position of knowledge, from being the agent of knowledge (the "S_2" of "the university discourse"). Being in a position as someone who knows can be an almost irresistible temptation. Why? Because when you lecture, explain, and give advice, you do not have to listen to the Other.

This phenomenon is common in the academic world. The representative of encyclopedic knowledge; Mr. know-all; he who lectures, explains, instructs; the obsessional that never asks a question, neither of himself nor of the Other; he who never articulates but always conceals any lack of knowledge—that is, he who conceals desire. Knowledge is a means to yield to desire. The particular other is never in the position of the Other. The particular other never represents an enigma or someone who knows something the obsessional does not know. The representative of encyclopedic knowledge speaks *to* you, not *with* you. You are silenced, even put to sleep, by already given knowledge. Your desire is not allowed to circulate; lack is never allowed into circulation.

Obsessionals are experts as far as endless lecturing is concerned; their speech can have a curious sleep-inducing effect. You are not allowed to stay awake, pay attention, doubt, wonder, not understand; that is, you are not allowed to articulate something that risks provoking the lack of the Other. This stands in complete contrast to hysterics, who cannot stop themselves from asking questions, provoking the lack of the Other: this ongoing, never-ending doubt regarding the foundation of everything and anything, whereby any effort to satisfy the particular other just provokes the hysteric to shower you with more questions. Hysterical discourse assumes that the Other knows and, by this very assumption, provokes the lack of the big Other—of authority, of being a representative of knowledge. But this puncturing of authority is the condition for the production of new knowledge. In the hysterical discourse, knowledge is situated at the place of production. Not knowing while at the same time questioning assumed knowledge produces new knowledge. To the hysteric, any well-meaning and seemingly competent effort to fill up the lack of knowledge is only a source of dissatisfaction. As a teacher, as a professor, you are castrated.

Lars von Trier is notorious for obsessing about rules and regulations, creating obstacles for himself, and submitting meticulously to this Other that he himself has brought into existence (cf. the notorious Dogme 95 rules)—like any good obsessional who is obliged to submit to rules that no particular other has demanded of him, rules that are meaningless to anyone else. The obsessional's speech, as Freud has taught us, is only a "dialect" of hysteria. This is evident in the fact that von Trier makes up his own rules, like any good obsessional, only to then, like a good hysteric and in the manner of Joe's provocative nihilism, flaunt conventions: both cinematic convention and the humanist hypocrisy of educated society. Like any so-called control freak, he meticulously obeys the obstacles, rules, and regulations that he himself has stipulated *and* he provokes and transgresses incessantly any rules and regulations of conventional cinema. He both addresses and exposes the hidden master signifier of movie making and exposes the hypocrisy of humanism and educated society.

The final scene—a question of identification

The movie's form raises the question of the relation between art and pedagogy, art and didactics. This is obviously not unheard of: Brecht and his technique of *Verfremdung* (alienation) spring to mind. But then the puppeteer, von Trier, strikes back: despite the all-pervasive technique of *Verfremdung*, which should prevent us from immediate, naïve emotional identification and promote reflection, the ending shows us that we have been identifying with Seligman. After Seligman has tucked Joe in and left the room, he returns without pants and tries to penetrate Joe, justifying his actions with the rhetorical question that, since she has had so many men, why not him? The gun, presented earlier in the film, comes in handy, in line with dramatic convention: we hear Seligman get shot and Joe run down the stairs.

At this point, those of us who had sat through the film for four and a half hours gasped in unison. We were reduced to being the naïve movie audience that, as legend has it, at the dawn of cinema took flight from the movie theater when witnessing a train arriving at a station. Watching the final scene of unexpected abuse, I realized that I had identified with Seligman, this know-it-all, this understanding, compassionate humanist with his encyclopedic knowledge. As far as form is concerned, von Trier reduces the educated academics and intellectuals to a naïve movie audience. By demonstratively using these outdated, even obsolete techniques of *Verfremdung*, von Trier flatters us; he seduces us, ensnares us with a knowing wink; we are among the select few, joining the ranks of the educated. And then he makes a fool of both us and the technique of *Verfremdung*—just as the church bells at the end of *Breaking the Waves* made a fool of those of us who had spent that movie on an emotional rollercoaster, gasping and weeping.

We identify with the Good Samaritan, with the considerate gentleman who rescues a damsel in distress without expecting anything in return, and then von Trier reminds us that there is no such thing as a free lunch. Common escapism had been at play after all, precisely because of our identification with Seligman. It is first and foremost the incarnation of humanism and rationality, the kind of humanism to which nothing human is alien, that is stripped bare; moreover, a blow is dealt to the analytically guarded, aloof, and withdrawn. The final scene is merciless. It sets the stage for the traditional sentimental wrap-up, showing that good people exist after all, and so does the power of friendship, especially friendship between men and women. But then we get an ending that flaunts the banal sentimentality of convention. We stare right into the Nothing, the Nothing that constitutes the foundation of existence. To repeat, even though von Trier demonstratively uses techniques of *Verfremdung*, the ending shows that we—all the well-educated, the academics, the intellectuals—have been identifying with Seligman despite the use of this *Verfremdung* that should have protected us against naïve identification. The ending makes fun of *Verfremdung*, maybe even ridicules it; it is almost a negation of *Verfremdung*. And what might von Trier's point be? No matter what, identification is a condition for watching a movie, even when we think of ourselves as cool and detached analysts that, of course, do not just surrender ourselves without reflection to immediate identification with the plot and fantasies on screen. The movie shows us that this withdrawn position is an illusion. The godlike view from nowhere, the godlike analytic perspective, is nothing but an illusion. Von Trier tells us that the big Other does not exist in this nihilistic universe, where no hope is left. This is exactly what we expected, those of us who were watching the film without anticipating the possibility of the last act of abuse.

If this is not a valid interpretation of the movie's final scene, what is? Is the final scene a case of a lack of poetic justice? A meaningless breach of contract in the form of a random plot twist that makes no sense, that is, that could not be anticipated?

Von Trier's *Nymphomaniac* is without any doubt the most nihilistic movie I have ever seen. Those of us who were bored had good reasons to be so. Our boredom was not due to a failure to properly understand von Trier's message. It was not a question of lack of sensibility or understanding for great, sophisticated art. We merely demonstrated an all-too-human defense against Nothing: against nothingness, godlessness, and the fact that the Other does not exist.

References

Heidegger, M. (1981), *Was ist Metaphysik?* Frankfurt am Main: Vittorio Klostermann.

Heidegger, M. (1992), *Die Grundbegriffe der Metaphysik. Gesamtausgabe. Band 29/30*, Frankfurt am Main: Vittorio Klostermann.

Kael, P. (1971), "Trash, Art, and the Movies," in *Going Steady*, Boston, MA: Bantam Books.

Lacan, J. (1991), *Le séminaire. Livre XVII. L'envers de la psychanalyse*, Paris: Seuil.

Nymphomaniac (2013), [Film] Dir. Lars von Trier, Denmark: Zentropa.

Thorsen, N. (2010), *Geniet. Lars von Triers liv, film og fobier*, København: Politikens Forlag.

3

Courtly Capitalism

Center for Wild Analysis

Why Analyze Pretty Woman?

Pretty Woman,[1] Gary Marshall's blockbuster from 1990, won Julia Roberts a Golden Globe award and elevated her as well as her fellow actor, Richard Gere, into the spheres of Hollywood superstardom. The film is a simple story about a rich businessman (Edward Lewis, played by Richard Gere) who accidentally encounters a prostitute (Vivian Ward, played by Julia Roberts) at Hollywood Boulevard in Los Angeles. They end up in the same hotel suite, and after a series of mild interruptions, they fall in love. As the film progresses, the unlikely couple manages to overcome various social and psychological obstacles, and just like in a fairy tale, the ending sees them united to live happily ever after.

On the face of it, *Pretty Woman* is a romantic comedy like endless others. It tells a well-known story, and it makes use of a large amount of well-known clichés and effects. Analyzing the film could seem to have to consist in explicating what makes it entertaining and recognizable: "Aha, this is another version of the Pygmalion; this or that element obviously draws inspiration from fairy tales or from Disney movies, etc." Yet this is exactly why we need to look closer. If we start to decipher the details of this film, we encounter some much more interesting features that tell a significant story about the age it appeared in. It is more than just a well-crafted romantic tale; it is a piece of ideology, or perhaps even more precisely: The film should be read as a *myth* about two things that hold a central place in Western culture—money and love. The film attempts to stabilize the relationship between these two, and in many ways, it does so very successfully. Yet in the very process of its doing so—its "myth-work"—it also reveals ambiguities and paradoxes that may be taken as symptomatic for the culture in which the narrative is at work. Therefore, it should be read "to the letter," as Lacan famously advised.[2]

The myth of the myth… and the myth

In order to analyze *Pretty Woman* as a myth, we take inspiration from Alenka Zupančič's reading of Plato's famous "sphere theory" of love from the *Symposium*. In *The Odd One In*, Zupančič shows how Plato's myth is much more complex, and in a sense much more Lacanian, than most of us would think at first glance (Zupančič 2008: 185–92). What people tend to remember about the myth is the story of love as the perfect union of two halves, whereas the literal myth contains much more disturbing elements, such as the gods cutting off sexual organs and repositioning them on the body, creating a union not of two halves that were perfect for each other and meant to be, but of a whole list of strange parts (some of them bodies without organs, some of them organs without bodies).

Zupančič's discussion of the myth of the missing halves identifies a structure that may pertain to myths in general, namely a dual structure. On the one hand, we have the literal myths themselves: the narrated stories with all their enigmas and details and curious developments. On the other hand, we have the myths of the myths: The ways in which myths tend to become received as conveying a very clear and unified meaning.

Two things should be noted in this regard. First of all, the "myth of the myth" is a reduction of the "literal myth." It is a simplification. Secondly, the myth of the myth must be part of the myth; it is not simply an external structure that has been forcibly imposed on an originally free mythical construction. This myth of the myth is the myth's own rationalization of itself, so to speak, in the same way that Freud notes that dreams tend to rationalize themselves in the so-called "secondary revision." The myth tells this "rational" story itself, it is there to be found, and it usually becomes the predominant conception of the myth, the general cultural recollection of what the myth was about. Simultaneously, however, there is another story, which tends to be left out of the picture, and which might contradict some or all of the "official" version. Every myth distributes consistency (the fantasmatic myth of the myth) and inconsistency (the literal myth), and the task is to measure the way that it does this. What is it that the myth attempts to think? Where does it stop, and where does it say more than it thought it did?

The myth of *Pretty Woman*

Making the move from the *Symposium* to *Pretty Woman*, it should be relatively easy to point out the myth of the myth. *Pretty Woman* provides us with the prototype of a so-called romantic comedy. Two lovers from different worlds meet, move through a series of obstacles, and unite in the end. It is as a story with this specific narrative that the film has subsequently become famous. Viewed from this angle, the film provides us with a most basic ideological structure. When a man and a woman meet, it has the possibility of bringing social status to the woman and a more genuine content to the life of the man. As such, the myth in *Pretty Woman* already borrows its structure from a whole history of previous love-narratives, perhaps going back to Aristophanes himself. In other reiterations, love can be the turning point of "taming the shrew" or overcoming "pride and prejudice," it can also serve as the backdrop of *Educating Rita*, or set up a union of New York high life and the Australian outback, as it did in *Crocodile Dundee* (which incidentally shares one of the theme songs of *Pretty Woman*: Iggy Pop's *Real Wild Child*).

We should be careful here to detect what the myth of the myth covers up. Here, we find something surprising. The official approach to the film would have it that the driver of the film is Vivian's problems, caught as she is in prostitution, and her "lucky punch" to run into a generous (and wealthy) man, who is able to see her true qualities. There is, however, something way too easy about this solution, which not even satisfies our spontaneous understanding of the film. It would simply be the story of a Good Samaritan, Edward, and the lucky object of his interest. It would be the story of some kind of a miracle, the story of how one person, Vivian, was destined to a better life. What the literal myth of *Pretty Woman* engages us in, however, is rather another, much more serious, set of obstacles: The film in fact begins with Edward's problems, the problems of an immensely successful businessman who is bored with his life, possibly even with his money and his profession. To him, Vivian's charm and childish approach to the world become a way out, a beacon of light in the gray world of financial capitalism. What the film tackles is not simply the problems of the poor and the exploited, pointing to a miraculous solution, but—through Edward—the problems of the very system of exploitation itself. It is with these ambitions that we have to read the film. Not simply as a romantic comedy with a miraculous romantic solution, but as a heavy piece of thought about the current status of financial capitalism and its future.

First of all, there is Edward, the businessman. One could say that Edward has it all, except a reason to have it; that is, his life contains everything a man could want, but he does not know what to do with it. He is the perfect embodiment of the "last man" in the tragic, impotent version rendered by Francis Fukuyama (1992) who melancholically admitted that after the end of history and the ultimate victory of liberal democracy and capitalism, there was not much left to do but some petty bargaining and a little bit of golf and wine drinking ("and a lot of poison in the end," as Nietzsche himself said (2003: 12)).

Then there is the prostitute Vivian Ward, who in several respects stands as a kind of opposite or a complement (and a supplement) to the figure of Edward Lewis. Whereas Lewis lacks the classical qualities of a worker—the ability to engage his body in work, to handle tools and vehicles—Vivian has got precisely that (already at their first encounter, she shows remarkable skills as a driver and mechanic). And whereas Edward is emotionally "dead," unable to passionately enjoy life, Vivian Ward is constantly laughing, making fun, singing in the bathtub, and watching old television series with a childish enthusiasm. Following this perspective, the movie also clearly depicts Lewis as the adult while Vivian is the amused child. As the film develops, the two partners swap qualities, so that Lewis gradually unlocks "his inner child" and adopts a happier, more creative approach to life, whereas Vivian in turn receives a place in the world of adulthood, the world of business, as she is (humoristically) crowned "chairman of the Edward Lewis scholarship foundation."

In Lacanian terms, Edward is all "symbolic." In fact he is an incarnation of the symbolic, a father-name or a phallus who by his very presence serves to hold together a certain social fabric. But in order to maintain a libidinal dynamic, in order to be a subject at all, he needs a point of reference in the real, an object *a*, which is what Vivian brings to his life. She is the Real, the wild, and the child all in one figure. So, what happens when the film connects the phallus with the object *a*?

The money shot

As the film progresses, we learn that there are a lot of particular things Vivian can do for Edward. But in the perspective of the movie as myth, it could be claimed that she not only saves a man in a suit; she is actually designed to provide an answer to the problems of financial capitalism itself. The opening shot of the movie has already indicated this. From the black screen of opening credits, the very first shot takes us up close, to a shot of a hand holding a coin. As fingers move, the coin disappears, then emerges again, then disappears again. It turns out that we are at an afternoon party among upper-class Americans, where a circle of women are looking at a male magician performing coin tricks. The underlying problem, indicated in this initial scene, concerns the status of money itself: How do they exist? How do they grow, disappear, reemerge? And if they are indeed as volatile as the magician's fingers may suggest, how do we find a stable place for them in our lives? How, indeed, do we handle a thing as strange as money?

Returning to the relationship between Edward and Vivian, it is precisely *through* Vivian that Edward's money becomes genuinely visible and attains a kind of stability, first and foremost by him teaching her to spend it (before she enters the picture, it seems like money only exists elusively in the background, in endless amounts, apparently generated by his use of the telephone). And inversely, it is through Vivian that *he* finally learns how to spend it in the right way. The central scenes of the movie all concern this particular transformation of Vivian from "streetwise" hooker to sublime consumer. Three times Vivian tries to go shopping, first failing, then succeeding, and finally, succeeding to the fullest degree.

In the third shopping scene, Vivian's transformation is underlined by the Roy Orbison song "Pretty Woman," which fades in during the scene's montage. It serves to underscore the fact that the woman who was first a "wild child" (underlined by the Iggy Pop song) and then a "wild woman" (underlined by Natalie Cole) has now finally become a respectable "Pretty Woman." Moreover, this third shopping scene contains nothing less than a theory of money, a mythical solution to the problem of money, as the dialogue reveals when put under scrutiny.

In a short exchange between Mr. Hollister (the shop manager) and Edward Lewis, Lewis declares that he will be spending "an obscene amount of money." Logically, of course, this concept presupposes that there must be a way of spending that is not obscene—what we might call the normal-pathological spending of money. Lewis does not explain what that would mean, but it is clearly something that he is both ready and able to exceed. (One should probably think of what common people do when they buy things they need in normal shops at more or less normal prices.) The obscene amount of money thus relates to a kind of excess, a conspicuous consumption that goes beyond one's actual needs. It relates to a "spending too much." But more than this, Mr. Hollister later returns to Lewis to clarify more specifically, whether he means a "profane" or a "really offensive" amount. Curiously, the term "obscene" is not enough; a further distinction must be made. Before we can analyze the way in which these obscene amounts of money meet the body of Vivian Ward, we should unpack the tripartition between nonobscene, profanely obscene, and really offensively obscene, which follows from the exchange between Hollister and Lewis.

This tripartition in the realm of consumption, that is, in the ways of spending money, mirrors a tripartition in the realm of production, that is, in a Marxist perspective, on the side of the forms of value production that make possible certain kinds of relations to money. On the level of "normal," everyday nonobscene spending, we are guided by a fantasy of a balanced relation between commodities and money. We work and exchange our work for other kinds of work, using money merely as an intermediary—the "general equivalent," as Marx called it. Twenty yards of linen can be sold for ten shilling, which in turn can be exchanged for one shirt. This relation between commodities and money is expressed in the relation C-M-C: Commodities are exchanged for other commodities by means of the general equivalent.

The obscenity of money, however, is lurking just beneath the surface. In particular, money becomes obscene, when there is too much of it in some sense. "Flashing" one's money is a good example; bragging by spending money is a profanely obscene form of consumption. A typical *nouveau riche* businessman would probably spend a "profanely obscene" amount of money in Mr. Hollister's shop—too proud of his money, and with an urge to flash it and make a bitchy point out of the precise amount that he is willing to spend. On the side of production, this would be mirrored by the capitalist form of production that generates a surplus in the form of profit, which Marx famously analyzed in *Capital* (Marx 1867). The capitalist spends his money on a commodity (labor force) that, while being used, generates more value than it was bought for, which may be summarized in the sequence: M-C-M+. The surplus value generated by labor creates the basis of the excess spending that the capitalist can then allow himself in a profanely obscene way.

In a capitalist society, the normal state of affairs is of course that of surplus value production. Therefore, the nonpathological way of relating to money is literally an ideological fantasy. We maintain this fantasy, however, through an elaborate network of everyday practices. We often do not even notice the money circulating between us. We have "objective rituals" for the handling of money. When we pay for groceries, there is no question about how or where money should change hands; the exchange takes place discretely and with as little inconvenience as possible. We use technology to make routine economic transactions easier, from apps on the phone to "touch-free" credit cards, which communicate with cash registers by themselves. These and other rituals could be seen as defense mechanisms against the profane obscenity of money.

We encounter the profanely obscene money, however, when the excess of money is there, plain to see. In this case, something that ought to have been held concealed or implicit—that is, wealth—is displayed all too blatantly. Money becomes obscene in the profane sense by dragging the otherwise "sacred object," the thing that should have been discrete, implicit, or hidden, out into the open. This is also the way in which the "potlatch-character" of social gift-exchanges can become obscene rather than a token of good friendship, say if you show up at a Christmas dinner bringing everyone gifts that are double the value of what they have bought for you. Sooner or later, things become awkward, and the ritual that should have been about giving, caring, and showing friendship starts to become something else. (If someone brags too openly, questions might begin to appear as to the justification of their wealth in the first place: "How has he deserved this much money, when everybody knows that we are really working more than him?")

The really offensively obscene amount of money must logically exceed the profanely obscene amount of money, and on the side of production, it must (by analogy) somehow exceed the logic of capital in the M-C-M+ circulation. This excess (of the excess) could be found in the kind of money that is not even (or only) based on the unfair exploitation of the worker but on the generation of money out of nothing, or more precisely, the generation of money from money itself. What capitalism has made possible is a global flow of money that has become so far separated from its material basis that it rather seems to appear out of the blue (like the coins in the magician's hands in the opening scene of *Pretty Woman*). In contemporary financial capitalism, it is money itself that is put to work, and thus we find an expansion of the circular logic of money generation in capitalism that could be expressed as M-M-M+. Money is exchanged for money in order to get money, and (almost miraculously) from this process, more money is generated.

True wealth is not generated by those who establish factories and exploit their workers by paying them less than the value of what they produce, but those who find ways of extracting surplus from the very circulation of capital itself: from fractional reserve banking, currency speculation, to automatized trade of stocks through algorithms. In late twentieth-century America, the real wealth is generated in systems so abstract that the best way to become wealthy is not by knowing "how the market works," that is, how one produces, sells, and buys stuff, but how the mechanisms supposedly facilitating the market work: interest rates, amortization, stocks, taxes, etc. This is what Edward Lewis knows. Although he does engage with "actual businesses" in the sense that he seems to be buying and "liquidating" companies, he represents the premonition of pure speculation—of the ability to create money without any relation to actual production or actual workers, etc. This is what it means that he has a really offensively obscene amount of money at his disposal.

Really offensive money is the miraculous kind of money. It is the kind of money one has access to, when one has control over the means of production not only of goods but of money itself. It is only there as the pure excess. In *Organs without Bodies* Slavoj Žižek notices a striking feature of the coronation scene in Sergei Eisenstein's *Ivan the Terrible*:

> [W]hen the two (for the time being) closest friends of Ivan pour golden coins from the large plates onto his newly anointed head, this veritable rain of gold cannot but surprise the spectator by its magically excessive character—even after we see the two plates almost empty, we cut to Ivan's head on which golden coins "nonrealistically" continue to pour in a continuing flow. (Žižek 2004: 3)

In terms of the theory of money, we encounter in *Pretty Woman*, this unending flow of money is the best image of really offensive obscene amounts of money one could give. But it is important to notice that it is an image that only works by keeping the Thing itself off-screen—the impossible space from which the unlimited flow of money originates literally cannot be shown. Whenever the camera returns to show the plates, they contain a certain amount of coins that is in no way unrealistic. The excess of this money is only visible when we see the effect: that it continues to flow long after it ought to have stopped.

Would it be too much to claim that this precisely is the reason why really offensively obscene money must be handled with the greatest care? It is the presence of really offensive money that we sense when we are confronted with leaks from tax havens like Luxembourg, Switzerland, or Panama. But we always only see them in glimpses and at a distance. In other words, if you own the very means of the production of money, you should be very careful not to show the public too much of your wealth, or better yet, you should find a way to sublimate the very obscenity itself—turn it into a quality that does not immediately appear as obscene.

Here, we should notice how Edward invents a first solution in the shop, a first version of a machine for his money-laundering. Edward "installs" Vivian in the shop and then he receives a phone call and leaves. So it is as if Vivian calls forth the obscene side of Edward's world, and at the same time, she is left there to live it. There is already some cruel, "sublime" mechanism at work in this setup: Vivian being forced to stay in the shop, with Orbison's tune repeated in an endless loop, working hard to keep spending Edward's self-generating money.

Courtly capitalism

Really offensive money is the kind of money we cannot possibly hope to have a ritualized, and thus fantasmatic, that is, in some way normal, relationship to. Really offensive money is the kind of money that renders the whole system of normally functioning fantasmatic money and profanely obscene money strangely obsolete. Once we truly witness the *real* of really offensive money, it is strikingly difficult if not genuinely impossible to make sense of "normal" money. As if our carefully laid-out rituals seem to falter here. What is needed to make the confrontation with really offensive amounts of money less catastrophic is something other than a ritual. The film identifies this as sublimation. This is the romantic solution to the deadlock of financial capitalism, and we shall see how it functions.

At the very end of the film, Vivian raises the stakes of their encounter considerably. She wants to be saved. She wants Edward to be her savior. "I want the fairy tale," she declares. As the end of their week together was approaching, Edward had suggested something rather more pragmatic to her: "I've arranged for you to have an apartment, to have a car, a wide variety of stores guaranteed to suck up to you anytime you want to go shopping." What Edward was doing here could very well be described as one last effort to handle their relation within the realm of profane obscene money. But Vivian refuses this solution. She makes this quite clear as she explicates what he is really suggesting: "You're gonna leave some money by the bed when you pass through town?," and they part ways in a melancholic state.

The whole affair ends up someplace else. It is as if Edward at the end has an epiphany and decides to engage in the fairy tale after all. He drives his limo to her flat, climbs the fire-escape stairs to the very top (even though he is afraid of heights), and asks, "So what happened after he [the proverbial white knight of the fairy tales] climbed up the tower and rescued her?" Ward answers: "She rescues him right back." At the level of the myth of the myth, this scene would be the apex of the narrative of romantic love: The opposites finally meet, the wound is healed, love takes place, and the Aristophanic halves are joined into a whole.

Taking the viewpoint of the literal myth, however, and in particular the problem it presents, of handling the obscenity of really offensive amounts of money, we can see that something else is at stake. What is clear from this vantage point is that *it is Edward* and not Vivian who is still in need of a specific fairy tale. What he needs is for her to take up a very specific position.

Instead of being placed somewhere in the realm of normal ritualized interactions, she, in the end, is raised to the dignity of the Thing, which precisely would be the formula of sublimation, Lacan was working with in *Seminar VII*. Vivian ends up as a sublime object, a princess, a Lady, something that not only wants a fairy tale, and gets it, but *is* a fairy tale character, and a very curious one that integrates the obscene with a Madonna-like sublimity. The final scene marks the coronation, but it would not have been possible without the shopping scene. It was here that Edward poured his dirty money into her and installed her as the caretaker of the excess: simultaneously a Lady, the most graceful and ideal of beings, and a manager of the obscene.

In *Seminar VII* Lacan famously analyzed the poetic tradition of courtly love (*L'amour courtois*). When we argue that *Pretty Woman* gives us an image of courtly capitalism, this is of course where we find our inspiration. Courtly love was a tradition of unhappy love, in which the troubadour poets wrote songs of longing for the Lady—the object, which was posited as something out of reach. As Lacan puts it:

> It is impossible to serenade one's Lady in her poetic role in the absence of the given that she is surrounded and isolated by a barrier. (Lacan 1992: 149)

Given that *Pretty Woman*, at least at the level of the myth of the myth, is a film about overcoming barriers—barriers between the rich and the poor, between refined and base, between man and woman—it may seem like a strange conclusion to draw that it ends in a story of courtly love. But we believe that it is only at the level of the myth of the myth that the film is about overcoming barriers.

What must be highlighted here is precisely the ambiguous status of the Thing in Lacanian theory. In courtly love, the woman is raised to the dignity of the Thing, but what this elevation conceals is the obscene desire circulating around this Thing. This would be the way to read Vivian as a Lady: She is now in the place of the highest of ideals, the princess of modern capitalism, but her new job is really not so flattering: to handle the dirty excesses of Edward's obscene money. If Vivian is the Thing, she must simultaneously become out of reach. Edward will never be able to buy her—this is the very premise of the fairy tale they engage in. But still, putting Vivian in this place of the unbuyable precisely becomes a machine for continuing to amass the money that cannot buy her. It is as if the Lady and the offensively obscene money somehow work at the same level. Only a Lady can trump such money. Or only a Lady, a sublime object, with her own inaccessible secret of *jouissance*, can stabilize the situation of obscene money.

The ass as Thing

The adventure of one object in particular underlines the link between Vivian Ward and courtly love. This object is her ass. Throughout the film, it takes center stage, beginning with the very first shot that displays it in highly stylized pictures. It portrays her almost naked body as a divinely beautiful body, as if untouched and untouchable, while at the same, it is displayed with our knowledge (that we already have or very soon after acquire) that it must have been the object of the most perverse of desires. (Just before this scene, we see a sign saying "HOTEL," where only the light in the letters "HO" shines.) The ass embodies the paradoxical coincidence of the Madonna and the Whore in *Pretty Woman*, and it continues to return to the same place throughout the film. When she meets Edward, she leans it against the car door, while he considers her prize; in the suite, she sits on his papers, places it on the morning table (instead of on one of the many chairs that are available, as he points out), and so on. Her ass constantly gets in the way.

If Julia Robert's role as Vivian Ward is the key part of the film, her ass is really the key "body part" of it. It thus comes as no surprise that Vivian's ass is not portrayed by any old ass. It is indeed portrayed by a very famous "butt double." Namely Shelley Michelle, who has been described as "a body double and ass model *extraordinaire*," and who has also replaced the likes of Kim Basinger, Madonna, and Sandra Bullock on screen.

Vivian's ass thereby shares another important trait with the figure of the Lady in courtly love poetry. Lacan argues that because of the depersonalization of the Lady, which follows from the fact that her defining characteristic is inaccessibility, it is almost as if there only ever was *one* Lady: "all the poets seem to be addressing the same person." The Lady in courtly love is always the same, just like Vivian merges into the Lady by losing her character, and just like her ass is literally the same ass as the one of a number of other iconic Hollywood figures.

In this way, we begin to fathom how the Pretty Woman is very much like the Lady of courtly love. She (Lady Vivian) is the ultimate fantasy: a screen which at one and the same time cultivates desire and keeps it at a safe distance.

And then there is one final parallel available to us. Lacan points out that a specific poem by "one of the most subtle and polished of the troubadours," Arnauld Daniel, is worthy of our interest, because it "breaches the boundaries of pornography to the point of scatology." He explains:

> The poem is concerned with a case that seems to be presented as a question to be resolved in terms of the moral casuistry of courtly love. The case involves a Lady, called Domna Ena in the poem, who orders her knight to put his mouth to her trumpet—an expression that is quite unambiguous in the text. (Lacan 1992 161–2)

The poem is not only unambiguous but enormously explicit as well, and Lacan uses it to illustrate a reversal that takes place with regard to the Thing that is elevated to a status of sublimity, out of reach: "That Thing," as he says, "whose function certain of you perceived in the relation to sublimation, is in a way unveiled with a cruel and insistent power" (Lacan 1992: 163). The Thing is the epitome of one's longing and desire, but also so powerful and intense that one is better off by keeping it at a distance, and that is precisely what is made possible by elevating the Lady.

In the realm of *Pretty Woman*, the link between Vivian herself and her ass could perhaps be said to account for a similar reversal. The sublimation involved in the making of a Lady—elevating Vivian Ward to the dignity of the Thing—is exactly what Edward Lewis needed. What Vivian offers is a way of keeping a proper distance, and thus a way of living with, the most dirty of all things: "Really offensive amounts of money."

Courtly capitalism is thus not simply the same as what has been called philanthrocapitalism or ethical capitalism. It adds a Thing or a sublime dimension to capitalism, which incorporates the very dimension of obscenity in the ambiguous figure of the Lady. With *Pretty Woman*, we have moved from the moral tales of honest capitalists doing hard work and making profits for the benefit of all of society to the myth of courtly capitalism. In a situation with really offensive money around, capitalism needs an additional myth to the one Marx called the original, capitalist accumulation. Obscenity can no longer be ignored. Therefore, it must be sublimated.

Notes

1 *Pretty Woman*, screenwriter: J. F. Lawton, dir.: Gary Marshall, 1990, Touchstone Pictures.
2 In one of his early lectures (from 1953), Lacan himself advised analysts to look for "The Neurotic's Individual Myth" (see Lacan 1979).

References

Fukuyama, F. (1992), *The End of History and the Last Man*, New York: Free Press.
Lacan, J. (1979), "The Neurotic's Individual Myth," trans. Martha Noel Evans, *The Psychoanalytic Quarterly*, 48 (3): 405–25.
Lacan, J. (1992), *The Ethics of Psychoanalysis*, New York and London: W. W. Norton.
Marx, K. (1867), *Capital, Volume 1*. Available online: https://www.marxists.org/archive/marx/works/download/pdf/Capital-Volume-I.pdf (accessed February 8, 2019).
Nietzsche, F. (2003), *Thus Spake Zarathustra*, New York: Algora Publishing.
Žižek, S. (2004), *Organs without Bodies*, New York and London: Routledge.
Zupančič, A. (2008), *The Odd One In: On Comedy*, Cambridge and London: MIT Press.

4

Is There a Way out of the Capitalist Discourse?

René Rasmussen

In today's society, with the dominance of the free market, consumerism constitutes one of the main discourses. Some would say this is a neoliberalist discourse (Bauman 2005; Laval 2007). Although many considerations of neoliberalist discourse are important, this text will focus on Lacan's ideas about capitalist discourse, which concern the same aspects, but also include the subject, its *jouissance* (enjoyment), and the unconscious.

One of Lacan's ideas is that this discourse pretends that the subject's desire can be satisfied by enjoyment connected to consumption. While desire is without any end, just an ongoing "motivating power," which cannot be satisfied by any specific goal, consumption has its satisfaction in the enjoyment of a given product. When this discourse has more or less total dominance, it constitutes a dead end for the subject, which does not seem to have any possibility to rid himself or herself of it.

This chapter will focus on the form of this discourse, the subject's dead end, and possible ways out of it.

The capitalist discourse

The main questions regarding capitalist discourse today are: (1) Is there a way out? (2) How shall we understand the apparent paradox in Lacan's description of this discourse, when he says that, on the one hand, the subject consumes himself (Lacan 1978: 32) and, on the other hand, the other seems to be the barrier preventing the subject from its enjoyment (Lacan 1986: 278), as the capitalist discourse promises the subject? How can the subject both consume himself and regard the other as the one preventing him from unlimited enjoyment?

Let us first try to answer this second question, beginning with a few remarks about the demands of this discourse. This discourse constantly pushes the subject to do more, to be more flexible, efficient, transparent, self-reflexive, etc. But a divided subject can never be transparent or self-reflexive. It cannot understand itself completely, as the capitalist discourse demands. Nor is this the case for working people, for children in schools, for students at universities, etc. The demands of being efficient etc. are demands of the cruel superego or the Other, which can be represented by the leader of an enterprise, or even by the coach or the mindfulness-therapist of the enterprise or of the school, or by the psychologist at the workplace. Hence, we see a cruel superego demanding more and more of the subject.

But the subject is not only submitted to these demands; it is also submitted to a cruel superego of enjoyment: Enjoyment is not, to repeat a well-known point, forbidden as in Freud's time, but rather commanded. You must continue to enjoy and not accept that someone else steals your enjoyment. The cruel demands of enjoyment entail tremendous jealousy and hatred toward the other, who is supposed to steal our personal enjoyment. This gives rise to racism, as we see today; but let us just focus a little more on the cruel demands of becoming more efficient and of enjoying more.

Regarding the demands of increased enjoyment, the subject is without defense. The subject succumbs, when there is too much enjoyment and when the Real becomes too present. This gives rise to anxiety. The demands of being efficient, self-reflexive, etc. also give rise to stress and depression. The dominance of the capitalist discourse seems to explain the affects that strike the subject: anxiety, stress, and depression.

However, stress is not an isolated affect caused by the capitalist discourse, but a specific form of bodily anxiety caused by this discourse. Stress is just one form of anxiety stemming from the demands of Other: The demands of efficiency, transparency, etc. Stress is caused by the enigmatic desire of the Other and its demands, prescriptions, advises, commands, etc., whether this Other be my leader, my chief, my teacher, my coach, my NLP-therapist, etc. When I do not understand the desire of the Other, I am struck by stress or pure anxiety. Anxiety is a signal of the enigmatic desire of the Other. When about one fourth of the adult Danish population feels stress and when about 49 percent of Danish students experience daily stress (Dansk Magisterforening 2017), then it manifests the dominance of the capitalist discourse and anxiety today.

But we may distinguish between two kinds of anxiety regarding the capitalist discourse: On the one hand, we have anxiety stemming from the enigmatic desire of the Other, the Other subject, and on the other hand, we have anxiety stemming from the enjoyment commanded by the capitalist discourse. Anxiety stemming from enjoyment commanded by the capitalist discourse is not caused by an enigmatic desire of the Other, but by meeting the Real of the body in this enjoyment. Hence anxiety is caused by either the linguistic, but enigmatic Other or by the body as an enjoying Other, while the body as an enjoying Other is outside language. These two kinds of anxiety are manifestations of the paradox of this discourse, which, on the one hand, promises us unlimited enjoyment, if only the other does not steal our enjoyment, and on the other hand, demands us to be more efficient, self-reflexive, etc.

The capitalist discourse not only promises the subject that it can satisfy its desire, meaning enjoying without limits, because desire no longer functions as a defense toward enjoyment, toward *jouissance*. It works also for the surplus value, as Marx underlines it. And although such a surplus value is the same as the more-to-enjoy, as Lacan stresses it (Lacan 2006a: 45), although the surplus value is the same as the *plus-à-jouir*, the capitalist discourse needs the subject to work and buy its products. The discourse cannot exist without people working, and therefore the subject is not allowed to surrender to the unlimited enjoyment or to the pure satisfaction of its drives. Even though this discourse produces addicts, subjects addicted to the enjoyment inscribed in the discourse, it still needs people to work. We are addicted, that is the triumph of this discourse; we are for example addicted to our new smart phone, computer, Nexflix, earphones, etc., but we are not addicted as ordinary drug addicts. The drug addict is excluded from the necessity to work, and though the drug addict can be seen as an emblem of this discourse, the drug addict is outside discourse as such.

Hence the smartness of this discourse, which opens to the possibility of the self-consuming subject: The smartness is that this discourse promises the subject to enjoy without limits, if only the other does not prevent the subject from doing so. The discourse tells us that the satisfaction of desire would be possible, if only the enjoyment of others did not prevent this. This may explain the hatred toward the other today.

Lacan underlines a more important aspect (1986): When one subject relates to another, whoever that other may be, the subject always presumes that the other subject is at a balance or that the other at least is happier than the subject itself. The other has an enjoyment, which the subject is excluded from. Or the other enjoys, where the subject cannot (Lacan 1986: 278). Such an understanding of the other is based on the imaginary, as the other constitutes a sort of (negative) ideal, which the subject is excluded from. This ideal represents an unpleasant reality to the subject caught in this imaginary idea.

Today we find many expressions, which sustain such imaginary ideas: For example, "They steal our money," "They are parasites," "They do not want to work," or "They rape their daughters," whereby they steal women, who could have been ours. These are expressions about "them," who are not "us." When "they" steal our money or keep their daughters to themselves, they have a possibility of enjoying that which has been robbed from us and which we are supposed to have. The others today are mostly the immigrants, the unemployed, the unbelievers, or other "races."

Lacan expresses it like this:

> It is strange that this has taken form of an idealization of the race, namely the things which are less interesting in the context. It is possible to find out where this fiction-character comes from. But what can fundamentally be said is that there is no need for the ideology to constitute racism; it is enough with the more-to-enjoy, which is recognized as such.
>
> Anyone who is interested in what may occur must say that all kinds of racism insofar as the more-to-enjoy is enough to sustain them is the agenda today; it is this which will manifest itself for us the coming year. (Lacan 1978: 30, author's translation)

Racism is founded on what one imagines about the Other's *jouissance*; it is hatred of a particular way of enjoying, of the Other's own way of experiencing *jouissance*.

We may well think that racism exists because our Islamic neighbor is too noisy when he has parties, but what is really at stake is our experience that he takes his *jouissance* in a way different from ours. The Other's proximity thus worsens racism: As soon as there is closeness, there is a confrontation of incompatible modes of *jouissance*. Racist stories are always about the way in which the Other obtains a *plus-de-jouir*: Either he does not work or he does not work enough, or he is useless or a little too useful. But whatever the case may be, he is always endowed with a part of *jouissance* that he does not deserve. True intolerance is thus the intolerance of the Other's jouissance. Of course, we cannot deny that different objective signs (e.g., color) may refer to races, but they only exist insofar as they are, in Lacan's words, races of discourse, meaning traditions of subjective positions (Miller 2008).

In his considerations of the capitalist discourse, Lacan underlines this idea about the Other's enjoyment using Marx's analysis of capitalism, saying that "we" (the subject) only have less enjoyment. "We" only have access to the less-to-enjoy, because they, the Others, have the more-to-enjoy (cf. Marx's idea about surplus value). The opposition between us and them, therefore, as mentioned, includes the imagination of a complete enjoyment, if only the other did not steal our enjoyment. The capitalist discourse promises forms of satisfaction, which are not limited. An unlimited enjoyment has of course never existed, but this does not exclude the fantasy about it.

Alternatives?

Regarding a possible answer to the second question about a possible way out of the capitalist discourse, there does not seem to be any real alternative to this dominating discourse. The communist alternative (discourse) disappeared with the fall of the Berlin Wall, and there exists no real movement with a strong discourse promoting an alternative. Hence, we must search for another way out for the subject. Two important possibilities are psychoanalysis and poetry. Regarding these possibilities, I will begin with psychoanalysis, and more precisely the subversive side of psychoanalysis.

The analyst, of course, does not say to the client that this or that discourse is repressing subjectivity, but lets the subject work with its discourses and eventually lets the subject reduce their influence. Hereby it also helps the subject to subvert dominant discourses. Psychoanalysis is thus a place where the subject can get rid of the discourse, which dominates (masters) it and its identity. Lacan named such discourse a master discourse; it is a discourse that can change character or even be reduced to almost nothing during an analytic work, and in our time, the master discourse is replaced by the capitalist discourse (Lacan 1968: 36). Such work constitutes a possible subversion of a dominant discourse, even though the analyst places himself or herself in a rather neutral position. Hence, the cure establishes a certain political act.

However, such a subversion, advanced by the subject in the cure, stresses the impossibility of joining the object of desire, while the capitalist discourse excludes this impossibility. Or this discourse precludes castration, as Lacan expresses it (Lacan 2011: 96), which does not mean that we are all psychotic, insofar as a subject cannot be reduced to a given discourse, even if such a discourse determines the form of the subject's desire and enjoyment.

But what psychoanalysis fails to do, the capitalist discourse succeeds in doing: It destroys all (other) master discourses and possible identities of the subject promising the subject its object of desire, albeit an object which is transformed to an object of enjoyment. The capitalist discourse forecloses castration, and therefore it also destroys the subject as such or at least as long as it is determined by this discourse. Psychoanalysis of today is placed between the subversion of the master discourse and a restitution of the subject vis-à-vis the demolishing capitalist discourse.

Let us briefly elaborate on the foreclosing of castration made by the capitalist discourse. It forecloses castration, insofar as it postulates the existence of an unlimited enjoyment and the possible access to such an enjoyment. The capitalist discourse proposes all kinds of objects and means to the subject so it can obtain this enjoyment. These objects and means are, for the subject, diffuse, so to say, because the discourse lets the subject believe that the division, which is the subject's very condition, can be removed. The discourse proposes not only objects to consume but also the negation of the lack and division of the subject. Hence, the subject not only consumes objects but also consumes itself.

Lacan has underlined this by stressing that the capitalist discourse not only works very well but that it works too fast (Lacan 1978: 36). Working too fast includes the consumption of the subject, and it destroys its possible master signifiers without giving the subject any alternative signifiers. The subject then goes on from its position in language to an enjoyment, which is repetitive as in the drives. Or the subject is reduced to something, which most of all is determined by repetition, as we know it from the drives.

Hence, capitalism attempts to foreclose castration and division, which the subject is submitted to, by way of objects. Such objects are often developed by science: smartphone, iPad, webcam, computer, smart-TV, mechanic sex toy, digital camera, GPS, etc. These are objects, which should annihilate the subject's division, but which precisely also in their reproducible, exchangeable, multiplication, and available forms destroy the subject. Closely connected to this destruction of the subject is, as I have said, the extinction of (all) other kinds of discourse, including those where the subject could have sustained an identity. The capitalist discourse annihilates the subject under the imperative of consumption. It makes the subject a slave of consumption in such a way that the subject reduces itself to an object, which like all other objects is intended for fast consumption—too fast. Depression is the emblem of this kind of consumption, because this consumption strangles desire. Fast consumption most of all includes division of the subject and its castration, that is all that which sustains it as a desiring subject. Fast consumption is meant to fill its lack, its castration, with objects. Hence, the subject is completely desubjectivated, surrenders completely to the place of the object. A variety of our time's psychotherapies are indirect products of the capitalist discourse, because they only promote the promise of the suspension of the subject's division. And they try to persuade the subject to believing *that you can, if you want*. Or they try to persuade the subject that it will succeed, if only it wishes to. Hereby the lack will also be removed.

But let us again return to the question regarding a possible way out of the capitalist discourse, which maintains the subject's possibility to orientate itself toward its unconscious, as psychoanalysis does. Such a question, which is central to psychoanalysis, inscribes itself into the ethics of the subject. Psychoanalysis opens up to the possibility of subverting the weight of the capitalist discourse and of reducing the influence of the master signifier.

Psychoanalysis cannot change the capitalist discourse, even though we can analyze it theoretically, and even if psychoanalysis may help in subverting the effects, which it has on the subject. Psychoanalysis is not a revolutionary force, but it has subversive effects on the position of the subjects in the capitalist discourse, because it permits the subject to change its position regarding this discourse. Besides art, psychoanalysis seems to be the only place where this discourse can be subverted, in one subject after another, one by one. This is our responsibility: To open up to possible subversions of the capitalist discourse, so the subject's answer to the Real, so the burden of that which cannot be represented in language, can be reduced.

Psychoanalysis and poetry

Lacan draws a parallel between poetry and psychoanalysis—psychoanalysis understood as the fact that a subject is in an analysis. Psychoanalysis is allied with poetry (Miller 2002–3). Psychoanalysis is an invitation to talk, not to describe, not to explain, not to justify or repeat, not really telling the truth. Psychoanalysis is an invitation simply to speak, and probably to be heard.

Lacan has designated what comes forth in an analysis as a poetic turn. To use his or her life to tell it, as the subject may do it in an analysis, this is to make a poetic effort. The daily life of each subject can be grasped and magnified by poetry in an analysis. It cannot be considered as such, realistically, but it is covered with an aura, which goes beyond any sense. The aim of interpretation is also what the subject means beyond itself.

This is what it means to have poetic effects, where Lacan pointed to a specific poetic unfolding of what happens to you contingently or in a meeting. The analysis invites you to weave, to perform beyond the brute fact. Each analytic session gives the subject space, assistance, in this poetic effort. The substance of a poetic effect is perhaps not what is described in a given talk in the analysis, but that which just happens. The poetic effect is an effort to make sense of what just happens and an effort to go beyond. When the analytic operation is just like a poetic act, who is the one who enjoys? Not the analyst. The enjoyment of the operation is not to the benefit of the listener. Enjoyment is the other side, the side of the speaker. Analytic experience highlights that the meaning may be, for the subject, turned to purposes of enjoyment, but of course an enjoyment radically different from enjoyment in the capitalist discourse. Enjoying language without going toward an unlimited enjoyment, meaningfulness, or a narrative totality is to make poetry.

Though there are significant differences between poetry as such and the poetic effects in psychoanalysis, they both represent a subversion of a given discourse. They both open up to that which the subject cannot understand and cannot bear, that is, the Real. They both do this in their own way: Poetry perhaps does this more directly than psychoanalysis, which gives the subject the possibility of not only getting rid of a dominating discourse, at least for a while, but also of going through anxiety, which this discourse or other parts of the subject's life may give rise to. Psychoanalysis gives the subject the possibility of getting rid of the cause of anxiety, and it thereby opens up to another relationship to the Real, and in that way, it also permits the subject to see its own otherness, which can diminish hatred toward the other. Poetry may also give the subject (the reader) the possibility of questioning given dominating discourses, and poetry may also give rise to anxiety, insofar as it opens up to the Real (Rasmussen 2017). Both poetry and psychoanalysis are outside the domain of management, social control, and meaning. Both poetry and psychoanalysis create holes in language and the principle of narration. In both cases, the subject assumes a new symbolic relationship to words (Cliché 2009: 54).

However, I do not believe poetry can change the subject's life, as psychoanalysis can, because the new symbolic position created by reading poetry is momentary, while the effects of psychoanalysis may be permanent. However, psychoanalysis can neither change nor undermine the dominance of the capitalist discourse as such. But psychoanalysis and poetry are both places, where one can breathe freely—without the burden of the capitalist discourse. They are some of the few "breathing spaces" in our time. There may surely be other kinds of art producing such breathing spaces, but breathing spaces do not seem to exist any longer at the university, where the cruel demands of the superego are central as we know in the evaluations, economic rapports, ECTS-points, etc. It becomes more and more evident that the university is becoming a more and more integrated part of the capitalist market, producing knowledge as this market wants it.

Jean-Pierre Siméon, a French poet, has a more optimistic point of view regarding the importance of poetry today beyond a principle of narration. Siméon claims that any poem is a concentrated piece of humanity, which opens up to the otherness of every human being (Siméon 2015: 30). Poetry is a subjective and singular detaining of reality, which transforms this reality into a complex language in relation to life (Siméon 2015: 55). Very optimistically, Siméon thus sees poetry as the only alternative to the way the world is getting worse and worse.

Although it is difficult to share this optimism, his understanding stresses the unavoidable necessity of poetry in our time: Poetry represents an ethical position in opposition to the worsening acceleration of alienation, but in the capitalist discourse, it is considered like nonsense and an obstacle to be overcome. The position of poetry in the future is therefore, according to Siméon, a first argument for a possible alternative to human destiny (78).

However, my conclusion is that poetry is only a breathing space in our common day of capitalist reality. The same goes for psychoanalysis. A real alternative to capitalist reality demands a strong counterdiscourse, and this unfortunately does not exist.

References

Bauman, Z. (2005), *Wasted Lives. Modernity and Its Outcasts*, Cambridge: Polity Press.
Cliché, A. É., "Jacques Lacan. Poésie, savoir et vérité," *Oeuvres & Critiques*, XXXIV (2): 2009. Available online: https://periodicals.narr.de/index.php/oeuvres_et_critiques/article/viewFile/1130/1109 (accessed August 6, 2018).
Dansk Magisterforening (2017), "Stress blandt de studerende." Available online: https://dm.dk/media/9005/stressblandt-de-studerende.pdf (accessed November 18, 2018).
Lacan, J. (1978), *Lacan en Italie*, La salamandra. Available online: http://www.praxislacaniana.it/wordpress/download/lacan_in_italia.pdf (accessed August 6, 2018).
Lacan, J. (1986), *L'éthique de la psychanalyse*, Paris: Seuil.
Lacan, J. (2006a), *D'un Autre à l'autre*, Paris: Seuil.
Lacan, J. (2011), *Je parle aux murs*, Paris: Seuil.
Laval, C. (2007), *L'homme économique. Essai sur les racines du néolibéralisme*, Paris: Gallimard.
Miller, J.-A. (2002–3), *Un effort de poésie*. Available online: http://www.causefreudienne.net/un-effort-de-poesie (accessed August 6, 2018).

Miller, J.-A. (2008), "Extimity," trans. Françoise Massardier-Kenney, *The Symptom*, 9. Available online: http://www.lacan.com/symptom/extimity.html (accessed August 5, 2018).

Rasmussen, R. (2017), *Kærligheden til det uden navn. Om samtidslyrik*, Hellerup: Forlaget Spring.

Siméon, J.-P. (2015), *La poésie sauvera le monde*, Paris: Le passeur éditeur.

Part Three

Application

1

The Materialist Use of Examples: Relocation, Repetition, and Reconceptualization

Brian Benjamin Hansen

"People still debate what Madame Bovary is really supposed to exemplify" (Ferrara 2008: 50). If I begin with this rather quirky statement from the Italian philosopher Alessandro Ferrara, it is because it turns our everyday understanding of the role of the example upside down. We would normally expect examples to serve the ideas or concepts they are examples of, and we would expect them to ease our understanding of the idea by concretizing or illustrating it in some way. Seen from this perspective, Madame Bovary, the famous protagonist from Gustave Flaubert's novel of the same name, could simply be an example of everything that is wrong with women's romantic fantasies, and by reading the novel, we would learn that this only leads to unhappiness and suicide. Through Bovary, we learn about some already established moral dogma; we move from the universal to the particular and back again through an already established passageway. However, this is of course not what is great about the novel at all, and Madame Bovary is exactly interesting because of the complexities of her character (not to mention Flaubert's own complication of the subject matter, when he stated: "*Madame Bovary, c'est moi!*"), creating great debate, still today, on love, marriage, sexuality, boredom, and even more topics. And this is why Ferrara is right in his approach to "the example of Bovary": What Ferrara seems to claim is that Madame Bovary is an example, and indeed a very good example, one of the best—we just do not know what it exemplifies. What I will argue in this chapter is that one should not try to solve the paradox, mend the gap between concept and example. Maybe there are examples that somehow undermine their own concept, and maybe they even first establish themselves as examples without concepts, asking us to invent new ways to conceptualize them?

When speaking about examples in the way just mentioned, we may of course vacillate on the border of what meaningfully can be called an example. Why not simply call Madame Bovary an "event" in the history of literature? Maybe this would be more in line with how a literary critic thinks about the original and remarkable literary characters and works of art he or she analyzes. The character or the artwork is not an example, because this would mean that it would be an example *of something*. As Todd McGowan has remarked, no one wants "their" artwork, their precious object of analysis, simply to exemplify a concept, and no one likes "applied psychoanalysis" or "applied Marxism" (McGowan 2014: 67). However, my wager would nonetheless be that there is another way of thinking with examples. There is a logic of examples, in which the example, even if it still is an example of something, of a concept, first and foremost exemplifies something "more." Furthermore, there is a practice of identifying good examples, as well as working with the mess that these good examples bring to our concepts. Madame Bovary is an event in the history of literature, but she is also an example in search of a new concept, and thus an intervention into thought.

The use of examples I have been outlining is what Slavoj Žižek in a brilliant description has called "the materialist use of examples" (Žižek 2012: 364). A couple of authors have, over the last decade, written very eloquently on Žižek's use of examples (McGowan 2014; Pfaller 2007; Stamp 2007), but, although Robert Pfaller has touched upon it, I think there is more work to do in expounding Žižek's materialism of the example. My claim is that this work must be done by going back to Freud. There is in both Freud and Žižek a certain priority of the example; the example intervenes brutally into already established concepts and notions, and it even serves as the impetus for the creation of new or differently structured concepts. Take Freud's famous dream of "Irma's injection" (Freud [1900] 1975: 107), which inaugurates *The Interpretation of Dreams*; it is all there, in this example; the example sets a new standard (see also Dolar 2016: 31–56), which Freud must try to live up to in the rest of the book.

The materialist example is a "*universal Singular*," Žižek claims, it is "a singular entity which persists as the universal through the multitude of its interpretations" (Žižek 2012: 364). It is as if a whole philosophical doctrine and method has been condensed in this sentence, which needs to be unpacked. For the materialist, there are "singularities"; unique cases, which do not fit into positive models and schemes, and which exactly therefore must stand at the core of theoretical work. The materialism of the example does not mean that the example is about what is concrete (i.e., tangible and easy to get), as opposed to the abstractions of the concept, but rather that there is a certain tension between example and concept at work. The materialist example is about something that disturbs a given symbolic-conceptual universe; it is some kind of a stumbling block, and it demands a certain "Freudian" practice of stumbling.

Example and intervention

A strangely overlooked fact about Freud's three great books on the unconscious, dealing with dreams, jokes, and everyday life, is that they abound with examples. All three books, from 1900, 1904, and 1905, are wondrous collections of examples; the 1904 publication, *The Psychopathology of Everyday Life*, is even almost exclusive, composed by the use of examples. There are hundreds and hundreds of examples in these books, and one should think that this would wear you out as a reader. But it does not. Even though all examples are connected to one, decisive concept, namely "the unconscious," the books are not like catalogs; they are not inventories. Also, they are not illustrations of or "content" to the abstract concept of the unconscious. The examples perform some kind of work. But what work?

What the Freudian example does is, to be short, it *intervenes*. The good Freudian example has a strange way of productively "not fitting"; it goes in another direction than you would expect, and it gives you more than you wanted. There are, I would claim, at least a handful strong materialist examples in Freud's work—"Irma's injection" (from *The Interpretation of Dreams*), "Signorelli" (from *The Psychopathology of Everyday Life*), "Fort-da" (from "Beyond the Pleasure Principle"), etc.—and these examples create a new articulation of the thing they were merely meant to exemplify. It would be wrong to say that "Irma's injection"—maybe Freud's biggest showcase, his own dream which is the first and most important dream in *The Interpretation of Dreams*—is simply and straightforwardly an example of "wish-fulfillment," the theory that Freud is working with in the book. The dream is certainly about wish-fulfillment, but the fundamental question, asked by the dream/example, is, What is a wish? It is not at all clear precisely what wish, and what kind of wish, is fulfilled by Freud in the dream. At the same time, it would be just as wrong to say that this is merely one out of many examples of what Freud means by wish-fulfillment, or even with his concept of the unconscious. No, in this example it is all there: The dream of Irma is exactly a "universal Singular," as Žižek puts it. This example is fixed, and it remains fixed, as the point for a reflection of a "non-relation"; the point where that which does not fit with the concept produces something more than was prompted for. There is an excess of possible interpretations of "Irma's injection," and what follows in the book could even be seen as a process of interpretation (by other examples) of this first materialist example. In the last chapter of the book, a new materialist example turns up—another one of the strong materialist examples—namely the example of the father who just lost his son and dreams of this boy uttering the terrifying words: "*Father, can't you see I'm burning?*" (Freud [1900] 1975a: 509 ff). As Jacques Lacan has pointed out, such "an example hardly seems to confirm Freud's thesis in the *Traumdeutung*—that the dream is the realization of a desire" (Lacan [1973] 1998: 57), and one must, I would add, thus really admire Freud for sticking to examples that almost go against the grain of his own notions and theories. "Everything is within reach," says Lacan, "emerging, in this example that Freud places here in order to indicate in some way that he does not exploit it, that he appreciates it, that he weighs it, savours it" (Lacan [1973] 1998: 35). So, once again, the example is not there to prove anything; rather, it is there to intervene, and it is for this reason it is appreciated and worthy of attention.

How is it that the example can produce more than its concept? What kind of concept would allow this? One must not think that the concept of the materialist example still somehow lies in the background of the example, providing the stage onto which the example makes a show. Following Žižek, we should distinguish between the idealist and the materialist approach to examples. The relation of concept to example takes a Platonic-idealist form, argues Žižek, whenever the idea is thought of as something that the petty examples can never live up to (Žižek 2012: 364). We have the idea of "the good," and then we have examples of good men, good horses, good chairs, etc., but they are not exactly it. However, in the Freudian enterprise—which I take to be a materialist approach—things work differently; here, you begin from and actively engage in examples that are "not it." The example *must* be something which does not fit. It *must* be "not it" in order to be "it." Generally speaking, any example is to some extent a "flaw" when compared to its concept, as it always misses or even displaces its conceptual horizon, but this failure must be turned into a criterion for the "success" of the example, and this is what Freud does. In a traditional idealist setup, what gives ontological power, even if it is in a derived form, to the example is the concept. But what gives power to the "wild" examples of Freud comes from themselves; they have no cover, no security in their concept, and they simply thrive on their own ability to "give body to what the exemplified notion itself represses or is unable to cope with" (Žižek 2012: 364). Thus, the concept of the unconscious is structurally dependent on its examples; it all begins with the examples (the dreams, the symptoms, the jokes), which do not fit.

The truth of the example

Is it possible to say something more detailed about this way of working with examples? How can one push examples to produce something more? Very schematically, I think three things go for the materialist example: It must be relocatable, it must be repeatable, and it must cause some kind of reconceptualization.

"Examples," states the philosopher Irene E. Harvey, "always exceed whatever frame one seeks to place around them, or whatever cage one tries to capture them with" (Harvey 2002: ix). This description pinpoints the first of the characteristics of the materialist example, namely that it is relocatable. The example cannot be contained; it breaks free from its frame, and it can thus be relocated into other frames. "Irma's injection" does not simply exemplify wish-fulfillment; rather, it exceeds this framework, and what Freud discovers by this example is the very peculiar character of wishes. By relocating the example, the discrepancy between concept and example is converted from a deficit to an asset. The example is a good one if it can be repeatedly relocated, and this would be the first criterion for a productive, materialist example. There is in this type of examples an indeterminacy that cannot be eliminated. The example must set in motion the process of relocation, being the center for the production of different interpretations and theoretical explanations. If the example can be immediately located ("this is an example of x"), if it can be subsumed under a concept, as Immanuel Kant would have said it, it is not interesting. But if it keeps on asking for relocation ("this is an example of x, y, z, etc."), there is something worthwhile in it. The good example pushes itself in front of its own concept and shows something new, something more than what was in the concept.

This could also be articulated by saying that the example is good if there is something original or singular in it. In this first criterion for the good example lies what could be called an "excessive hermeneutics," meaning that one can keep on asking what this example is really an example of. What is Madame Bovary an example of? What is "Irma's injection" an example of? Speaking in terms of the hermeneutical circle, the example may be a part, referring to a whole, that is, a larger horizon of understanding that it takes part in. But the materialist example is not a normal part; it breaks off from its horizon and begins to disturb and destabilize it. This part cannot be contained by a whole, but produces new lines of thought. That the example does not fit into a given theoretical framework is something which can be verified by a larger social group and thus transcend the researcher who gave or found the example to begin with. It would be the first step of the researcher simply to report on the example, passing it on to a larger community, and thereby try to universalize its singularity.

The productivity of the example can be linked to an "excessive hermeneutics," but there is also another way of understanding what is happening in the materialist example. There is more to the good example than the wild production of interpretations, namely the character of the materialist example of being "fixed." Thus, behind the productivity of the example, in terms of new interpretations, there is the example as a stumbling block. The example is a materialist example when it gives form to a theoretical impossibility, to what the theory structurally cannot come to terms with, to what is constitutively repressed in it. Every example, both in Freud and Žižek, is an attempt to short-circuit what is "not it" with what is "it." Therefore, an important way of working with the example is simply to repeat it: "A materialist," says Žižek in his short description of the materialist use of examples, "tends to return obsessively to one and the same example" (Žižek 2012: 364). He must repeat it, replay it, examine its singular core, detect the very "navel" of it. Something in the relation of the example to the concept insists in its otherness, so that this otherness itself must be understood as some kind of "passphrase"; this passphrase or formula being the place from where thought catches its energy.

"Irma's injection" is or produces such a passphrase. There is a navel of the dream, says Freud (Freud [1900] 1975a: 525), where it seems that we cannot go further, we cannot make further interpretative gestures, but this does not mean that the example is worn out, emptied; it rather means that this is the point where the very conceptual impossibility of the dream is laid bare, the point where it fixes Freud's thought and provokes it. This is what must be repeated; this is what the researcher must engage in. Is this also not what Žižek is doing with his examples of "the act"? For Žižek, a true act is something surprising; it redefines the coordinates it emerged from. In this way, the concept of the act, in the same way as the concept of the unconscious, provides the space for examples that deliver more than they should. Žižek uses the example of Keyser Söze from *The Usual Suspects* (1995), who is put into a corner, but performs the shocking act of shooting his own family to break free from his perpetrators. He also uses the example from José Saramago's book *Seeing* (2004), in which the citizens do not vote in an election for the city council, and this act of nonaction in the end causes the system itself to become paranoid and disintegrate. And he uses the example with the protesters from Occupy Wall Street, who saw that there was no ground beneath the feet of the investors on Wall Street and told them to "look down!" For Žižek, these examples are all decisive; they are perfect examples of the true act, and he does not back down from repeating them again and again in different contexts. With excessive hermeneutics, there may still be the feeling that the example must belong to some (still unknown) horizon of knowledge. We keep on producing still more interpretations, because we expect that one of these interpretations, or explanatory models, in the end will set things right, so that the example can finally be placed in a conceptual framework. The repetition of the example, however, shows that this reconciliation is a fantasy, and this displays another dimension of materialist thought. In this dimension, it is not about producing additional interpretations, reaching for the ultimate one, but about laying bare the very conditions of this production. To relocate the example, to work with different interpretations, is only the first step; it can be seen as some kind of preparation for the second step of "reducing" the example to its fundamental conflict with its concept. This could also be formulated as a move from the epistemology of the example (its production of interpretations, e.g., new knowledge) to the ontology of the example: the way it produces truth as opposed to knowledge. There is a truth of the example when it causes a breakdown of the concept, when it becomes "mere counter-example" so to speak. If there is an "ethics of the example," it is here. The question of this ethics is not, What is this an example of? It is rather: How can I show fidelity to this example? How can I keep on repeating it? How can I place myself in the (theoretical) conflict of this example?

A good example intervenes in thought; it destabilizes and fixes it in this shock. Is this not also something we know from other philosophical writers? Søren Kierkegaard would, for example, also be a user of materialist examples. Kierkegaard puts the story of Abraham and Isaac, as told in the Old Testament, into the register of a materialist example (Kierkegaard [1843] 2012). Why does Abraham set out to Moriah when commanded by God to go there to sacrifice his only and very beloved son, Isaac? What, if anything, has this to do with faith? For Kierkegaard, there is something in this story, something almost absurd, which hypnotizes thought. It causes a breakdown of concepts, and it demands another way of thinking. Another thinker, Walter Benjamin, could also be said to be a user of materialist examples (think of his example of "the arcade"), and he has almost defined a slogan for thinking through materialist examples in his *Theses on the Philosophy of History*. "Thinking involves," he writes, "not only the movement of thoughts but also their zero-hour [Stillstellung]" (Benjamin [1940] 2005: XVII). Benjamin is about to describe a materialist philosophy of history, which deploys the method of focusing on the breaks in history's homogeneous course: "Where thinking suddenly halts in a constellation overflowing with tensions, there it yields a shock to the same, through which it crystallizes as a monad" (Benjamin [1940] 2005: XVII). In this description, we find both sides of the materialist example, as discussed so far: the overflowing of tensions that gives rise to multiple interpretations and possible lines of action springing from it, and the shock at the core of it. This would in fact also be a very good description of what I have been discussing in relation to Freud's treatment of the dream of Irma's injection. This dream is for Freud precisely a constellation overflowing with tensions—it is somehow overdetermined—and this constellation gives thought a shock, causing it to curl itself around this example like a monad.

From the ethics of repeating the example, we come to the last characteristics of the materialist example, namely that it must cause a reconceptualization. Reconceptualization arises from repetition. Something happens in the act of repeating the example, in the ethics of sticking to the example. Something is created in this practice; it ensues from it as a new relation between example and concept. I would argue that this is what happens for Freud in his discovery of the unconscious. First of all, he discovers it through examples, especially one extraordinary example, "Irma's injection," that does not fit into prevalent concepts. The same goes for Žižek's concept of the act. It is not that this concept is not well-founded; it is simply that it only becomes a genuine concept in and through its examples. Only through the (singular) example of the act can the true (universal) concept of the act retroactively be posited.

This is what could be called "setting an example" (see also Bjerre 2016). For a materialist, to set an example would mean to insist on something singular as formula for a new concept (often through a radical restructuring of an existing concept, so that a new name is not always necessary for the invention of a new concept). A materialist example produces a breakdown of concepts, and from this destruction emerges a new concept; this concept was not there before, as it is structured in a completely different way: The new concept is only Itself at the mercy of its example, its Other. Thinking is thus provided not only with new material by the example but also with a new form.

The main part of the work that is done with materialist examples is done through the practice of already established material thought; examples are relocated and repeated in light of e.g. "the unconscious," Kierkegaard's "faith," Žižek's "act," etc. In this way, most examples work at an "ontic" level where the ontology of the materialist example is utilized in the service of investigations into certain academic fields, such as cultural analysis or diagnostics of the present, or interventions into fields of practice, such as aesthetics, politics, sports, economy, etc. However, the potential of the materialist example lies in its ability to create new concepts, which is contrary to a position that would claim that concepts always come first. These new concepts are of course not the same concepts as idealist concepts—they emerge on the condition that they are structured differently, as I argued—but they are still universal concepts. With the concept of the unconscious, Freud is in fact aiming for a general and fundamental concept. Through relocation a singular example is given multiple interpretations, while repetition eventually paves the way for a reconceptualization that creates a new fundamental concept.

If there is such a thing as a "power of the example," which is not only a rhetorical power, it is to be found in the materialist practice of setting an example. We are under the sway of the power of an example, not when it seduces us into certain ways of acting and thinking, but when we simply have to stick to it, because there is something more in it, because it disturbs and intervenes, ultimately giving us the task of creating new concepts.

References

Benjamin, W. [1940] 2005, *On the Concept of History*. Available online: www.marxists.org/reference/archive/benjamin/1940/history.htm (accessed August 28, 2018).

Bjerre, H. (2016), "At sætte et eksempel," in B. B. Hansen and J. H. Ingemann (eds), *At se verden i et sandkorn—om eksemplarisk metode*, 27–47, Frederiksberg: Samfundslitteratur.

Dolar, M. (2016), *Køn, filosofi og psykoanalyse*, Aarhus: Forlaget Philosophia.

Ferrara, A. (2008), *The Force of the Example: Explorations in the Paradigm of Judgment*, New York: Colombia University Press.

Freud, S. (1975 [1900]), *The Interpretation of Dreams*, SE, vol. IV, London: The Hogarth Press.

Harvey, I. (2002), *Labyrinths of Exemplarity: At the Limits of Deconstruction*, New York: State University of New York Press.

Kierkegaard, S. (2012 [1843]), *Frygt og Bæven*, Søren Kierkegaards Skrifter, electronic version 1.6. Available online: www.sks.dk/FB/txt.xml (accessed August 28, 2018).

Lacan, J. (1998 [1973]), *The Four Fundamental Concepts of Psychoanalysis*, The Seminar of Jacques Lacan, Book IX, New York/London: W. W. Norton.

McGowan, T. (2014), "The Priority of the Example: Speculative Identity in Film Studies," in M. Flisfeder and L.-P. Willis (eds), *Žižek and Media Studies*, 67–78, New York: Palgrave Macmillan.

Pfaller, R. (2007), "Interpassivity and Misdemeanors: The Analysis of Ideology and the Žižekian Toolbox," *International Journal of Žižek Studies*, 1 (1): 33–50.

Stamp, R. (2007), "'Another Exemplary Case': Žižek's Logic of Examples," in P. Bowman and R. Stamp (eds), *The Truth of Žižek*, London: Continuum.

Žižek, S. (2012), *Less than Nothing: Hegel and the Shadow of Dialectical Materialism*, London and New York: Verso.

2

On Ethics and the Unconscious in J.M. Coetzee's *Disgrace*

Kari Jegerstedt

What are we actually doing when we are transferring the psychoanalytical practice from the clinic to the analysis of society, art, and culture? What kind of knowledge does applied psychoanalysis produce? What kind of object does it produce?

The questions above, posed by the editors of *Analyzing the Cultural Unconscious*, offer a rare occasion to reflect critically on what we are doing as researchers and teachers in a time when we find ourselves submerged in what is increasingly becoming, as Mark Fisher has argued, a self-perpetuating academic knowledge-producing machine (Fisher 2009). Since the questions are linked to the aspects of *doing*, however, they cannot be given a once-and-for-all systematically and theoretically elaborated answer; any effort to approach them must be grounded in praxis. Thus, in order to begin addressing the dynamics of these questions, I offer a reading of J. M. Coetzee's novel *Disgrace* (1999) and the (or its) question of ethics. The aim is to pry out not only how psychoanalysis may inform a reading of that particular novel but also how a reading of that novel may have something to say about the kind of knowledge psychoanalysis produces when applied to society, art, and culture.

The question of ethics is at the core of psychoanalytic inquiry and practice. Lilian Munk Rösing observes, with reference to Lacan's statement in *Seminar XI*, that the status of the unconscious is ethical; Freud's ethical gesture consists in giving up the position as master, as he resigns himself to passively listening to the speech of the hysteric (Rösing 2007: 100). This is precisely the point at which psychoanalysis proper begins. How is it possible to listen, psychoanalytically and ethically, to a work of literature? And, to slightly reformulate one of the editors' questions, "How is it possible to move from the singular experience [of reading literature] to universal functions and structures in culture and society?" Although it may not be possible to answer in a general way, I pose the question here in a gesture similar to literary critic Gayatri Spivak's insistence that it is both an impossible and a necessary task to make a literary reading relevant for today's world (Spivak 2003).

Disgrace is most commonly read, we learn from Andrew van der Vlies' reader's guide to the novel, as "a rigorous philosophical working out of some compelling ideas about ethics, responsibility and identity in a postcolonial society" (Vlies 2010: ix). Its main character, David Lurie, a middle-aged English professor, is both a sufferer from and critic of recent New Public Management reorganizing of South African universities. His anachronistic romantic inclinations lead him to seduce one of his students (Melanie), after which he is charged with sexual harassment. Finding the rhetoric of his hearing committee (whose immediate extratextual reference is the South African Truth and Reconciliation Committee) purely instrumental, he refuses to express remorse and is forced to leave his position "in disgrace." He travels to his daughter Lucy's smallholding in Eastern Cape. One day three men approach Lucy's farm, shoot her dogs, rape Lucy, and attempt to kill Lurie by burning. After the attack, Lucy is "a dead person" who "[does] not know yet what will bring [her] back to life" (Coetzee 2000: 161). She refuses to report the rape to the authorities, and when she finds that she has become pregnant, she decides to keep the child. The neighboring farmer, her former gardener and "dog-man" Petrus, offers to marry her. She accepts, even though he is already married and even though he is related to one of the rapists and may even be in league with them:

"Go back to Petrus," she says [to her father]:

"Propose the following. Say I accept his protection. Say he can put out whatever story he likes about our relationship and I won't contradict him. If he wants me to be known as his third wife, so be it. As his concubine, ditto. But then the child becomes his too. The child becomes part of his family. As for the land, say I will sign the land over to him as long as the house remains mine. I will become a tenant on his land"...

"How humiliating," [her father] says finally. "Such high hopes, and to end like this."

"Yes, I agree, it is humiliating. But perhaps that is a good point to start from again. Perhaps that is what I must learn to accept. To start at ground level. With nothing. Not with nothing but. With nothing. No cards, no weapons, no property, no rights, no dignity."

"Like a dog."

"Yes, like a dog." (Coetzee 2000: 203)

At the end of the novel, Lurie returns to Lucy's farm and finds that she has indeed grown back to life. He starts helping out at the nearby animal clinic, disposing of dogs that have been put to death. Gradually forming closer ties to the animals, he develops a special relationship with one of the dogs, which he gives up for lethal injection at the end.

Much has been written about Lurie's possible ethical transformation in his dealing with the abandoned dogs—dogs that he has to *learn* to love. His initial, and in fact enduring, sentiment toward the kind of charity work the animal clinic is involved in is rather harsh and aggressive. "[A]nimal-welfare people are a bit like Christians of a certain kind," he tells Lucy: "Everyone is so cheerful and well-intentioned that after a while you itch to go off and do some raping and pillaging. Or to kick a cat" (Coetzee 2000: 73). When he promises to help out, it is only on the condition that he will not make the work affect him personally: "All right, I'll do it. But only as long as I don't have to become a better person. I am not prepared to be reformed. I want to go on being myself. I'll do it on that basis" (Coetzee 2000: 77). Whether or not Lurie actually does change, or reach a higher level of knowledge, through this work is a point of contention in Coetzee-scholarship. The most common reading, however, links Lurie's dedication to dogs—or more specifically to *dead* dogs, which he makes sure are disposed of one by one instead of beaten by shovels "into a more convenient shape for processing" (Coetzee 2000: 146)—to a Levinasian-inflected notion of a responsible "response to the other." As Derek Attridge puts it in his influential book *J.M. Coetzee and the Ethics of Reading*, Lurie thus resists "the generalization implicit in the category 'animal', preferring the impossible task of acknowledging the singularity of each individual creature," hence also "manifesting a dedication to a singularity that exceeds systems and computations" (Attridge 2004: 188).

A Lacanian reading of the novel, however, makes possible a different take on the question of ethics—and, equally importantly, a different take on *who* is, in fact, the ethical *subject* in the novel, namely Lucy. However, such a reading is only possible through a shift of perspective that must involve the question of sexual difference. The link between ethics and sexual difference is not accidental. As several critics have argued, for Lacan the question of ethics and the question of sexual difference are thoroughly and fundamentally intertwined. Indeed, Lacan introduces his *Seminar XX: On Feminine Sexuality, The Limits of Love and Knowledge (Encore)* by pointing out that he is "still (*encore*) here" because there is still something to be said about ethics, something that did not make it into *The Ethics of Psychoanalysis*, a seminar he decided not to publish (Lacan 1999: 9).

Thus Joan Copjec writes in *Imagine There's No Woman*: "In considering feminine sexuality," Lacan "returns to the problematic of ethics by returning to and now foregrounding the question of *being* (as such)" (Copjec 2002: 6), that is, being as not-all. "[I]f it is woman who is privileged in Lacan's analysis," Copjec argues, "it is because she (the not-all) remains closer to the truth of being, while man (defined through the exception) obfuscates this truth through a nostalgic, secondary operation that allows him to maintain a belief in the plenitude of being to come" (Copjec 2002: 7). The point is not that woman is ethical, but that the ethical act as such is feminine. Yet, to pose the question of ethics in terms of sexual difference, Copjec argues, entails developing a new thinking of ethics—hitherto "theorized in terms of the superegoic logic of exception or limit"—as "an ethics of inclusion or of the unlimited, that is, an ethics proper to the woman" (Copjec 1994: 236). It is my contention that *Disgrace* opens sexual difference to the question of ethics through the choices and nonchoices of Lucy. Read this way, *Disgrace* is not simply "a rigorous philosophical working out of some compelling ideas about ethics, responsibility and identity in a postcolonial society," as van der Vlies suggests but, more precisely, a fictional-philosophical investigation into the question of sexual difference, and into the relationship between sexual difference and change.

Yet, if we are to follow this line of inquiry, the question is: What kind of object is thus produced? Firstly, it must be remembered that it is no accident that we are talking here about a work of art, a work of literature. And literary work, the *singularity* of literature—that which makes literature literature—is, as Derek Attrigde argues, the "staging of the fundamental processes whereby language works upon us and upon the world" (Attridge 2004: 130). Thus literature may have a special affinity to the Lacanian sexed subject, which is nothing but a function in and of language. As Copjec reminds us in *Read My Desire* (1994), for Lacan "our sexed being… is not a biological phenomenon, it does not pass through the body, but 'results from the logical demands of speech'" (Copjec 1994: 213). Most importantly, since those logical demands arise from a fundamental impasse in language, sex is but "the stumbling block of sense" (Copjec 1994: 204) marking "the subject as unknowable" (Copjec 1994: 207). A careful reading, then, of literature as "a staging of the fundamental processes whereby language works upon us and upon the world" will, we can hypothesize, eventually hit upon these impasses, and thus the place that sex, according to Copjec, "comes to be" (Copjec 1994: 161, 167). Such a sexual reading—the reading of sex not as sense, but as that which marks the subject as unknowable—is closely linked to what Attridge (from a Derridean perspective) argues is the ethics of reading, a response to its singularity:

> The literary work demands a reading that does *justice* to the formal elaboration of these processes [whereby language works upon us and the world], a reading in the sense of a performance, a putting-into-action or putting-into-play that involves both active engagement and a letting-go, a hospitable embrace of the other. (Attridge 2004: 130)

What distinguishes a *psychoanalytic* reading, however, is its attunement to the unconscious, to unconscious desire; or—to refer once more to Copjec—since desire may only register itself negatively in speech, to read psychoanalytically, to become literate in desire, is "to learn how to read what is inarticulable in cultural statements" (Copjec 1994: 14). Psychoanalysis, as an ethical encounter, starts precisely at the moment when you begin to listen to the unconscious. Applied to literature, we can rephrase Attridge's definition, highlighting the *unconscious* "processes whereby language works upon us and the world," a reading that stages "a hospitable embrace" of the unconscious. Yet what kind of status does an object so produced have; what is its *ontological* status, so to speak? And whose unconscious are we talking about? Is it the unconscious of the character, of the text, of the author, the more general cultural unconscious, or is it, in fact, the unconscious of the reader? Maybe all of them? In short: Whose desire is speaking?

The unconscious that insists

It would seem that a proper ethical engagement with a piece of literature would have to begin with a very careful reading of the text itself. The question is, when does such a reading start? What is its temporality? The first time I read *Disgrace*, I thought it was quite good, but I wasn't *taken in* by it, so I put it down, read different stuff, moved on.

It was not until later that the novel kept coming back to me, or, in fact, Lucy kept coming back to me, "haunting" me as it were. And she did not do so because I had decided to take a second look at the novel; she did so as a kind of response to a certain irritation in me, an irritation that was awakened by a completely different issue. As a matter of fact, I had in the meantime started my academic affiliation as a gender studies researcher and found myself constantly going to national gender studies conferences, visited by researchers and bureaucrats alike, where the question of how gender research could contribute to make a better and more just society was repeatedly being debated. What irritated me, or rather made me increasingly uncomfortable, was not necessarily the topic of the debate in itself, but the kind of instrumentality I, like Coetzee's Lurie, felt myself being submerged in. This instrumentality was not only political but also theoretical, since it had to do with how gender was being thought. For instance, Judith Butler's initially groundbreaking theory of gender as performatively constituted had, when put into the wheels of the academic-bureaucratic knowledge-machine, led to the notion that gender is something that is forever negotiated and renegotiated, making it possible—in turn—to investigate exactly *how* gender is negotiated—or "performed"—on every little scene in the whole of society. Similarly, the concept of intersectionality, initially posed as a sophisticated analytical tool to aid in the theoretical complexities of thinking differences between women as multiple constructions along various axes of gender, race, sexuality, and class, made it possible not only to claim that these categories exist as empirical givens but to investigate—and denominate—exactly how these now reified categories intersect, again on every scene in all of society, whether public or private or in-between. In fact, this research—or "institutionalized critique"—had come to constitute an elaborate knowledge production, which is, at the very same time, an extensive mapping not only of hegemonic discourses but of "what is," of every public and private space available to the scrutinizing eye. It felt as if the naming of gender constructions had become a formidable industry in its own right, the result being a reification, rather than radicalization, of differences—a reification of bodies and of sexes.

As several critics have pointed out, this dispersion of multiple identities, or subjectivities, corresponds quite neatly to the dispersion of consumer society, to labor migration in the wake of colonialism, to a rapidly expanding tourist industry, and to the new ontologies associated with technological advancement and genetic engineering.[1] In advanced global capitalism, feminist philosopher Rosi Braidotti points out, we are all "human bodies caught in the spinning machine of multiple difference," in a society where the "consumption of 'difference' [has become] a dominant practice" (Braidotti 2005). Within this world system, the institutionalization of feminist research of "de-constructible differences" runs the risk of becoming a supplement to a state machinery that *cannot but* adapt to the needs of capital—even as it tries to minimize, or atone for, its destructive effects. The state, or even global governance institutions, demands research into gendered differences through mechanisms such as gender-mainstreaming in order both to ensure the smooth functioning of the work force *and* to guarantee the individual a minimum of rights, objectives which are, of course, essentially "good." Yet at the same time, within this scenario the more radically critical—and *revolutionary*—potential in feminism is subsumed under the needs of policy making and thus effectively neutralized by instrumental reason: "the servicing of goods."

It is quite easy to point out this problem; the difficult question is to figure out what the possibilities *are* of thinking gender critically within the present regime. Are there alternative ways of thinking resistance and change in our age of multiple identities, from a feminist point of view? It was when pondering this question that I started to hear, in a *nachträglich* mode, Lucy insisting that her act—that is, starting again "[w]ith nothing," "[l]ike a dog" (Coetzee 2000: 203)—had an ethical import that addressed this very same problematic. Thus I went back to the novel to investigate if this might in fact be true. From that point on, my "listening" to the novel was considerably altered, or sharpened, and yes, I could hear Lucy "speak" in another tongue.

Still, the question remains as to whose desire is speaking in the reading of Lucy's act as an ethical act. In fact, posing her as the ethical agent runs counter to most criticism of the novel: The figure of Lucy is consistently seen as the most problematic aspect of the novel and has even earned its own "Lucy syndrome," referring to the idea that "white South Africans must be prepared to accept abasement and abnegation to atone for wrongs of the Apartheid era" (van Vlies 2010: 76). If that were indeed the sentiment that Lucy's actions conveyed, it would of course be preposterous to claim that her act could be read as a psychoanalytical ethical act (ethics does not play a zero-sum game). However, I found some support, mainly from Gayatri Spivak, for reading Lucy's actions differently. Spivak's argument is a purely *literary* argument. "The literary text gives rhetorical signals to the reader, which lead to activating the readerly imagination," she writes in the essay "Ethics and Politics in Tagore, Coetzee, and Certain Scenes of Teaching" (2002). "Literature advocates in this special way," she argues, and continues:

> What rhetorical signal does *Disgrace* give to the canny reader? It comes through the use of focalization… *Disgrace* is relentless in keeping the focalization confined to David Lurie. Indeed, this is the vehicle of the sympathetic portrayal of David Lurie. When Lucy is resolutely denied focalization, the reader is provoked, for he or she does not want to share in Lurie-the-chief-focalizer's inability to "read" Lucy as patient and agent. No reader is content with acting out the failure of reading. This is the rhetorical signal to the active reader, to counter-focalize. (Spivak 2002: 22)

In Spivak's reading, Lucy's decision to start over again with nothing, like a dog, makes her "equal in disgrace" with all (Spivak 2002: 19), thus conveying something of the *cost* of the necessary process of communal construction, *not* to get even (as the "Lucy syndrome" suggests) but to start *anew*. However, her decision can never be construed as a political message: Literature is not a blueprint for action; it can only point to the new while *remaining* literature. As such, the knowledge produced by a literary reading belongs to a different order of truth. "[W]hat literary reading teaches us," Spivak argues, "is to learn from the singular and the unverifiable" (Spivak 2003: 34)—the unconscious perhaps?

Spivak's point is that the ongoing process of learning to read literature can foster an "un-coercive rearrangement of desire" (Spivak 2007: 108). I share Spivak's take on *Disgrace*, but as a gender theorist, I undertake my reading from a slightly different angle. My underlying wagers are here, firstly, that the Lacanian schemas of sexuation, especially as they are laid out by Joan Copjec in the now classic "Sex and the Euthanasia of Reason" (included in *Read My Desire*), offer a far more radical avenue into theorizing how sexuality and gender work on the global scene, and also how change may come about, than do most mainstream gender studies theories based on concepts of gender-performativity and intersectionality. Secondly, that the Lacanian formulas only do so insofar as we *also* take heed of the various feminist critiques—postcolonial, black, queer, and so forth—of feminist thinking, which have, and rightly so, exposed and contested *both* the white, heterosexist, middle-class bias prevalent in dominant, mainstream feminism *and* the implication of Western feminism in imperialist discourses.

Psychoanalytic feminism is in no way exempt from these critiques, quite the contrary. Not only does it posit a concept of "sexual difference" (instead of "sexual difference*s*") at its core, it also runs the risk of reinscribing an imperialist framework by posing the question of sexual difference in a universalizing way, claiming for instance that the Oedipal drama, to the extent that it shows itself, always appears as universal. *Disgrace* addresses both of these premises, or stakes: As a fictional-philosophical investigation into the question of sexual difference and into the relationship between sexual difference and change, Lacan is indispensable for a reading of the novel. At the same time, the novel is very much concerned with the limits of European modes of thought and writing—of which Lacanian psychoanalysis is part—in a once colonized, still colonized, space. *Disgrace* persistently warns us not to "deal in abstractions" (Coetzee 2000: 112) and universality, only "this particular time, this particular place" (Coetzee 2000: 112, 141), thus insisting on the singularity not only of the ethical question as it pertains to the present South African condition but also of its own status as a literary artifact.

Sexed acts of resistance

How, then, can we move from a singular experience of reading to functions and structures in culture and society? In order to be opened up to the question of ethics, Lurie and Lucy's different actions and decisions must first of all be construed as "acts." These acts are acts of resistance; they consist in saying *no*. *Disgrace* dramatizes two different ways of saying "no": a "masculine" and a "feminine" way. These "no's" can be described by a detour through Alain Badiou's concept of *subtraction*. Addressing the possibilities for a revolution, Badiou defines subtraction as "the *affirmative* parts of negation" and opposes it to *destruction*, which is "the *negative* parts of negation" (Badiou 2007). Destruction is that which simply destroys the old; subtraction, on the other hand, points to the new that arises apart from the old—that is, to that which cannot be thought within the old but is new to the *precise extent* that it is *indifferent* to the laws of the old. Within the horizon of the revolution, the relationship between the two parts of negation—subtraction and destruction, the affirmative and the negative—is always a dialectical one. However, as Badiou argues in an interview with Filippo de Lucchese and Jason Smith, the problem is that at the present time violence can only be destructive, and thus revolution is discounted. In its stead, we must enact a preliminary—or "originary"—subtraction: a "withdrawing of oneself from under the dominant laws of the political reality of a situation—including institutionalized politics—in order to create an autonomous space in which revolutionary possibilities can be fostered, or thought, anew" (Lucchese 2008: 653). Yet this "originary subtraction" cannot in itself create the "new": It must be thought as a purely formal gesture. The main aim of this gesture is to bring about a point of autonomy—a "new space of independence... from the dominant laws of the situation, [which is] neither derived from nor a consequence of destruction as such" (Lucchese 2008: 653).

Initially, this sounds like a promising strategy for feminist gender studies that are caught up in state politics of instrumental reason. Yet, as Žižek points out in his critical gloss on Badiou's concept of subtraction, merely to "withdraw oneself from" the participation in institutionalized politics is hardly a subversive gesture as such, nor will it occasion serious ruptures in the dominant society (Žižek 2009: 408). Subtraction, Žižek suggests, must therefore ideally coincide with *reduction*, a "destructive intervention into the multiplicity of a given field in order to reduce this multiplicity to its basic antagonism—a 'minimal difference' which has the potential to illuminate the basic opposition which constitutes the field as such" (Žižek 2009: 410). It is this "minimal difference," I suggest, which is dramatized in *Disgrace*. At the most basic level of the signifier, it can be detected as a difference in phonemes. The naming Lurie/Lucy (rie/cy) inscribes a minimal difference that inflects the whole sound of the name, making them more different than how they first appear. A more contextual reading would suggest that the novel dramatizes this "minimal difference" within a scenario that is very similar to that with which Badiou is concerned: a scenario in which violence can seemingly only be destructive. Moving from a "letteral"[2] to a contextual reading, *Disgrace* can be analyzed as an intersectional intervention into the basic assumptions of the nation-building process of the so-called New South Africa, also known as "the Rainbow Nation." Counting on economic growth and foreign investment to make up for the lack of a more radical politics of redistribution, the earlier revolutionary agenda of the ANC has been displaced by an effort to create a cosmopolitan, multicultural, multiracial nation-state along (neo)liberal lines. Within this scenario, a long history of racial and sexual exploitation has to be "smoothed out," as it were, in order for the new nation-state to function. At the same time, "women's rights" and gender and sexual differences have to be recognized and accounted for as a founding gesture of the very multiplicity of "the Rainbow Nation" as such. The neat juxtaposition of the different voices in the sexual harassment committee to which Lurie is submitted makes this logic perfectly clear: Racial and sexual exploitation have to be exposed, but only to be lamented and apologized for, in order that society may get back to business as usual. On the one hand, Lurie is reminded of the graveness of the situation, considering the longer history of racial injustice of which his act of seduction, and possible rape, takes part. On the other hand, he is told by another member of the committee that "we are not your enemies. We have our weak moments, all of us, we are only human... We would [only] like to find a way for you to continue *with your career*" (Coetzee 2000: 52, my emphasis). What this logic effectively displaces is the continuation of the racial dividing lines created under apartheid—and also, much earlier, as part of the colonial conquest—along the axis of class. It is precisely this complex juxtaposition of race, class, and gender that is problematized in Coetzee's novel, and it does so by introducing the theme of sexual violence, leading up to an act of withdrawal.

In this way, the novel restores both sexuality and the racialized body to the intricacies of resistance—aspects that seem to be lost in Badiou's and Žižek's musings on revolutionary politics. When David Lurie refuses to express—or rather, prove—remorse for his actions, even as he pleads guilty as charged, he effectively withdraws his body, his sexual desires, from under the dominant laws of the situation. The hearing committee that charges him in Coeztee's novel is, of course, a direct comment on The Truth and Reconciliation Committee's hearing, which similarly demanded "full disclosure" as an alternative to punishment, or justice, in a gesture which may be seen to comply with what Lurie describes as "a public thirst for abasement," a mere "spectacle" (Coetzee 2000: 56). As such, Lurie's actions can be read as a critique of the kind of hearings in which repentance and reconciliation are confined within the institutions of instrumental reason, serving nothing but the status quo, the urgent need for society to get "back to business as usual." At the same time, however, his withdrawal of his body and sexual desires from the demands of the committee resonates uneasily with former president P. W. Botha's refusal to testify in front of the TRC, calling it a "circus."

When Lucy is later robbed and brutally raped by, what we are led to assume are, three black men, she enacts a similar withdrawal, reporting the robbery but not the rape. Thus, as Meg Samuelson has pointed out, she is "driving a wedge between her body and property... refus[ing] the construction of white women's bodies as 'property to be defended' through the ritualized 'black peril' panics," which "casts black men as natural-born rapists, white men as protectors and white women as bounty" (Samuelson 2007: 148), a discourse that has circulated since the very beginning of imperialist endeavors, yet escalating in post-apartheid South Africa. Like her father, then, Lucy can be seen to withdraw her body *and* her sexuality from under the abject scripts that sustain the public discourses of righting wrongs available on the (then) current South African scene. Thus we have two subtractions, one "male" and one "female," both involving the body as well as sexual violence, but from opposite perspectives, so to speak, and related to different intertexts: the TRC, on the one hand, and the "black peril" discourse, on the other.

However, even if these two acts of withdrawal, or "formal" subtraction, are both similar and "opposite," they are not symmetrical. It is precisely at this point that Coetzee's novel encroaches on the issue of sexual difference and on the relationship of sexual difference to *change*. Yet it is important to stress that the novel only does so to the extent that it is read as and allowed to remain a piece of literature and thus also, in itself, a purely formal gesture. As Molly Anne Rothenberg has argued, even if an artwork always makes use of a historically given material, it is through the "formal reconfiguration of those materials [that it] exposes the possibility that *something could be otherwise*" (Rothenberg 2010: 180). It can only do so, however, if we do not confuse literature with politics: It is the illusory character of the artwork that allows for an engagement that is suspended from "the ontic qualities of the world," thus "creating a formal space for the new to emerge" (Rothenberg 2010: 180).

At this point, the Lacanian distinction between "symbolic acts" and "acts proper" can help us to further investigate how this formal gesture works in *Disgrace*. Further support can be found by comparing it to another representation of a literary subtraction, that of Melville's Bartleby's "I would prefer not to." The debate over Bartleby's "I would prefer not to" typically turns on the relation between destruction and construction. A case in point is the different readings of Bartleby given by Žižek and Badiou, linking his refusal to the question of subtraction. According to Žižek, it is precisely because "Bartleby does not negate the predicate," but "affirms a non-predicate"—that is, because he doesn't say "he *doesn't want to do it*; [but] says that he *prefers (wants) not to do* it"—that he is able to move "to a politics which opens up a new space outside [both] the hegemonic position *and* its negation" (Žižek 2006: 381–2). The reason for Bartleby's effectiveness is, in other words, that his act of refusal refuses the symbolic as such. However, that also means that his act of refusal cannot serve as the basis for constructing something "new." Quite the contrary: It must forever remain the foundational void of the "new." For Žižek, herein resides precisely the strength of Bartleby's paradoxical "no." For Badiou, on the other hand, the lack of "construction" in Bartleby's refusal is precisely the problem. That is so because the "new" must always break forth from the very situation it is embedded in. Bartleby's refusal negates, but it doesn't go further than that, since it refuses any further engagement with the signifiers of its situation, thus not being able to break the way open for the "new" to emerge (Badiou 2006).

The juxtaposition of a "male" and "female" "no" in *Disgrace* turns *both* on Žižek's differentiation between saying "no, I don't want to" and "I want not to," *and* on Badiou's call for an "engagement with the signifiers of the situation." In contrast to Lurie's withdrawal from the disciplinary committee, which takes form as an absolute refusal, "I won't do it" (Coetzee 2000: 58), "I wouldn't oblige" (Coetzee 2000: 66), "I am not prepared to be reformed" (Coetzee 2000: 77), Lucy's withdrawal is both more conditional *and* more affirmative, working along the lines of "I would prefer not to": "As far as I am concerned," she tells her father, "what happened to me is a purely private matter. In another time, in another place it might be held to be a public matter. But in this place, at this time, it is not. It is my business, mine alone" (Coetzee 2000: 112).

At the same time, neither Lurie's nor Lucy's refusals are purely grammatical; they are both situational (unlike Bartleby's, which constitutes, as Žižek puts it, "the formal gesture of refusal as such" (Žižek 2009: 384)). In fact, the text repeatedly insists that they must be understood on the background of "*this* [particular] place, at *this* [particular] time" (Coetzee 2000: 112, 141, emphasis added). What the novel effectively asks us to do, then, is precisely to read the very signifiers of this situation—to engage with them, as it were. But the novel also does more than that: It thematizes reading, or the lack thereof, as forming an integral part of the two differently gendered refusals, thus pitting them against each other, albeit in an asymmetrical way. The male "no" proceeds through an obstinate refusal to read—and what it in effect fails to read, is precisely the way the signifiers "sex" and "race" function in the situation—whereas the "female no," on the other hand, proceeds through a profound revelation of the very personal impact of the signifiers of the situation, thus taking upon itself the whole weight, the heaviness, of the situation as such.

However, insofar as the whole story is focalized through Lurie, we cannot get to Lucy's story, her female "no," directly. As Spivak argues, we must rid ourselves of Lurie's view. And Lurie's problem is also one of reading: He consistently stages his encounter with the hearing committee as a heroic "standing up for a principle"—the "freedom to remain silent" (Coetzee 2000: 188). If we decide to read this "standing up for a principle" from Lurie's own perspective as a fight against instrumental reason—as Derek Attridge suggests we can—then *Disgrace* tells the story of "a man's self-destructive opposition to a new collective insistence upon accountability and moral rectitude" (Attridge 2004: 105). Transferred to the sexual scene, however, Lurie's "romantic" version of resistance, construing himself as the "servant of Eros" (Coetzee 2000: 52, 89), serves merely the need for self-justification. When quoting one of Shakespeare's sonnets—"a woman's beauty does not belong to her alone. It is part of the bounty she brings into the world. She has a duty to share it... She does not own herself" (Coetzee 2000: 16)—his rendering of these lines in South Africa in precisely this time and context quite literally reads, "she [Melanie, a woman of color] does not own herself," thus invoking a longer history of slavery. Yet, Lurie himself cannot grasp the signifiers of the situation, reading only "sex" where he should also read "race"—thus glossing over the complicity of his own act in a prevailing racial history.

Lurie makes a similar, though inverted, misreading when encountering his daughter's rape. When Lucy recounts the effect of shock that the rape imparted on her, she stresses the fact the rapists made her feel hated: "It was so personal [she says], It was done with such personal hatred. That was what stunned me more than anything. The rest was... expected. But why did they hate me so? I had never set eyes on them" (Coetzee 2000: 156). Lurie's response is to conjure up an explanation that is, in fact, purely historicist: "It was history speaking through them... A history of wrong... It may have seemed personal, but it wasn't. It came down from the ancestors" (Coetzee 2000: 156). Again Lurie confuses the terms "sex" and "race," but the other way around: While Lucy tries to make sense of the rape in sexual terms—wondering "[m]aybe, for men, hating the woman makes sex more exciting" (Coetzee 2000: 158)—Lurie keeps insisting that had the rapists been *white* (like himself), she "wouldn't talk about them in this way" (Coetzee 2000: 159).

Unable—or unwilling—to read the broader implications of the signifiers "race" and "sex" in relation to his own actions, the principle Lurie can be seen to stand up for is then, ironically, *not* the "right to remain silent," but the *right to remain the same*. If we read Lurie's refusal (his withdrawing of his body and sexual desire from the instrumental rationality of the hearing committee) along the lines of Lacan's distinction between "symbolic acts" and "proper acts," where proper acts produce a radical change of the agent's identity, Lurie's "no" is a purely symbolic act. His constant posing of the wrong signifiers is an act through which he "states" and "performs" what he is, asserting his own subjective position. His "no," carried on by a series of misreadings, is—to borrow from Joan Copjec's reading of *Antigone*—a "fixation," an insistence on "stubbornly conform[ing himself] to [his] own personal history" (Copjec 2002: 44). Lurie is, in fact, conforming himself to the superego's demand to enjoy.

Lucy's "no," on the other hand, is of a completely different order: When acting as she does, she takes the whole meaning of the vexed, complicated intersection of race and sex in the past and present situation in South Africa to bear upon her own body. Indeed, her decision to become "like a dog"—to "start at ground level. With nothing"—suggests even more than that, echoing the last sentence of Kafka's *The Trial*, where K. is disposed of, precisely, "Wie ein Hund!... es war, als sollte die Scham ihn überleben" (Kafka 2002: 272). As *Disgrace*'s preoccupation with dead dogs—and with the disposal of dead dogs in particular—suggests, the signifier "dog" is intrinsically linked to the theme of disposability. What is revealed to Lucy during her rape is precisely the ultimate terror of pure disposability: "I meant nothing to them, nothing. I could feel it" (Coetzee 2000: 158). After the rape she is also, like K., a "dead" person, or—in Lacanian terms—between two deaths: between symbolic death and actual death.

The theme of disposability can be seen in relation to wider, global political issues. As Rosi Braidotti notes, the mechanism of disposability is already inscribed in the spinning machine of global capitalism, producing bodily differences (woman/native/others) "to become disposable commodities to be vampirised" simply as body parts (Braidotti 2005). If Lucy's withdrawal of her own body from under the dominant discourses of righting wrongs amounts to anything, then, it is not to offer real, political solutions, but to intervene in a multiple field of difference to reveal a "minimal difference" that illuminates how sexual difference interacts with the haunting, traumatic real of disposability. Yet, unlike the story of Kafka's K.—and unlike Bartleby's too—Lucy's story is first and foremost a story of survival. When she decides to become "*like* a dog," to start anew with "nothing," she also becomes *other* than a dog, other than a victim: She becomes a survivor. The distinction is crucial. As Badiou writes in his book *Ethics*: "The status of the victim [is the status] of suffering beast, of emaciated, dying body, [it] equates man with his animal substructure, it reduces him to the level of a living organism pure and simple" (Badiou 2002: 11). A survivor, on the other hand, is "an animal whose resistance… lies not in his fragile body but in his stubborn determination to remain other than a victim, other than a being-for-death, and thus: *something other than a mortal being*" (Badiou 2002: 11–12). Lucy's "no"—her withdrawal of her body as a victim from under police authorities—thus constitutes an "act proper"; it is an act of genuine self-transformation and hence also an ethical act. As her father notes when he sees her growing back into life, tending to her flowers, pregnant with her mixed-raced child: "[H]ere she is, solid in her existence… With luck she will last a long time" (Coetzee 2000: 217).

How, then, are *we* to deal with her decision; how are we, in fact, to *read* it? Is it at all possible to argue that her act of refusal can inform feminist thought, even feminist practice, today? Pondering the enormous historical weight carried by Lucy's refusal to report her black-on-white rape, Mary Eagleton suggests that "if one accepts the ethics of… Lucy's choice to remain silent, then the ethical act for the reader must be… to work for a world where such self-sacrificing heroism is no longer necessary" (Eagleton 2001: 200).

Although Eagleton's political solution to Lucy's ethical dilemma might seem like a "happy ending" to this story, her appropriation of Lucy's situation to bear *directly on* the reader's situation—*not* as a subject within the circulation of violence, but as subject in the *position of righting wrongs*—runs the risk of diminishing the impact of Lucy's act. It does so by subtly reinscribing the dynamics of what Badiou calls an *ideological ethics*, that is: An ethics which posits "a general human subject… universally identifiable" but in effect *split into two*, so that "this subject is both, on the one hand, a passive, pathetic, or reflexive subject—he who suffers—and, on the other, the active determining subject of judgement—he who, in identifying suffering, knows that it must be stopped by all available means" (Badiou 2002: 9). This is in fact the very ideology that Lucy's withdrawal of her body cuts across. *Neither* purely passive *nor* purely active, she asserts her subjectivity, *not* in an act of self-sacrifice but of self-transformation, thus also allowing for something "new" to take place. As Coetzee's novel finally suggests, Lucy's act is an act to be read—to be identified and named, *truthfully*, or, as it were, in "grace."

Notes

1 See for example the discussion between Judith Butler, Ernesto Laclau, and Slavoj Žižek in *Contingency, Hegemony, Universality* (2000).
2 "The truly literal meaning of 'literal' is, in fact, not 'actual,' 'real,' or 'lifelike,' but 'letteral'—having to do with letters and with the reading of letters grouped into words (as in the sense of 'literate')" (Quilligan 1976: 67).

References

Attridge, D. (2004), *J.M. Coetzee & the Ethics of Reading: Literature in the Event*, Chicago: University of Chicago Press.

Badiou, A. (2002), *Ethics: An Essay on the Understanding of Evil*, trans. Peter Hallward, London: Verso.

Badiou, A. (2006), *Logiques des mondes: L'être et l'événement 2*, Paris: Éditions du Seuil.

Badiou, A. (2007), "Destruction, Negation, Subtraction—On Pier Paolo Pasolini." Graduate Seminar, Art Center College of Design in Pasadena, February 6, 2007. Available online: http://www.lacan.com/badpas.htm (accessed January 19, 2019).

Braidotti, R. (2005), "A Critical Cartography of Feminist Post-Postmodernism," *Australian Feminist Studies*, 20 (47): 169–80. Available online: https://www.researchgate.net/publication/46662743_A_Critical_Cartography_of_Feminist_Post-Postmodernism (accessed January 19, 2019).

Butler, J. et al. (2000), *Contingency, Hegemony, Universality: Contemporary Dialogues on the Left*, London: Verso.

Coetzee, J. M. (2000), *Disgrace*, London: Vintage Books.

Copjec, J. (1994), *Read My Desire. Lacan against the Historicists*, Cambridge and London: MIT Press.

Copjec, J. (2002), *Imagine There's No Woman: Ethics and Sublimation*, Cambridge: MIT press.

Eagleton, Mary (2001), "Ethical Reading: The Problem of Alice Walker's 'Advancing Luna'—and Ida B. Well's and J.M. Coeztee's Disgrace," *Feminist Theory*, 2 (2): 189–203.

Fisher, M. (2009), *Capitalist Realism. Is There No Alternative?*, Hants: O Books, John Hunt Publishing.

Kafka, F. (2002), *Der Process*, Frankfurt am Main: S. Fischer Verlag.

Lacan, J. (1999), *On Feminine Sexuality, The Limits of Love and Knowledge (Encore)*, New York: Norton.
Lucchese, F. and J. Smith (2008), "'We Need a Popular Discipline': Contemporary Politics and the Crisis of the Negative," interview with Alain Badiou, *Critical Inquiry*, 34 (4): 645–59.
Quilligan, M. (1979), *The Language of Allegory. Defining the Genre*, Ithaca and London: Cornell University Press.
Rothenberg, M. A. (2010), *The Excessive Subject: A New Theory of Social Change*, Cambridge and Malden: Polity Press.
Rösing, L. M. (2007), *Autoritetens genkomst*, København: Tiderne Skifter.
Samuelson, Meg (2007), *Remembering the Nation, Dismembering Women? Stories of the South African Transition*, Durham: University of KwaZulu-Natal Press.
Spivak, G. C. (2002), "Ethics and Politics in Tagore, Coetzee, and Certain Scenes of Teaching," *Diacritics*, 32 (3): 17–31.
Spivak, G. C. (2003), *Death of a Discipline*, New York: Columbia University Press.
Spivak, G. C. (2007), "Thinking about the Humanities. A Talk," transcript from a Columbia University lecture. Available online: stjenglish.com/wp-content/uploads/pdfs/6-1/08Spivak.pdf (accessed February 7, 2019).
Vlies, A. van der (2010), *J.M. Coetzes Disgrace*, London and New York: Continuum.
Žižek, S. (2006), *The Parallax View*, Cambridge: MIT press.
Žižek, S. (2009), *In Defense of Lost Causes*, London: Verso.

3

When I Am beside Myself; or, Why Beckett Is Good for Nothing

Linus Nicolaj Carlsen

Presence of absence

The narrators of Samuel Beckett's works and indeed most of his characters are haunted by a nothingness in the sense that they are no longer *of* this world yet continue to exist *in* it and to speak as if possessed, as if compelled to speak in an impossible space of neither life nor death. The French philosopher Maurice Blanchot writes of Beckett that he "evokes something of this malaise of a man fallen out of the world, eternally hovering between being and nothingness, henceforth as incapable of dying as of being born, haunted by his creature, meaningless ghosts he no longer believes in" (Blanchot 1986: 147). The Beckettian narrator is caught up in the same language that he harbors a profound distrust toward, and all the stories that he tries to tell ultimately fail. But in this failure a certain kind of absence peeps out from the work—an emptying of the literary subject that makes of it neither a some-thing nor a no-thing.

While Beckett would most likely have scoffed at the notion of "understanding" his works via philosophy, he might not have been completely averse to the philosophy of Blanchot—seeing how the latter attempts a blurring of the line between philosophy and literature to the extent that the categorization specific to (one type of) philosophy goes out the window in favor of a thinking that does no more than ask—a thinking that happens in and through literature. The so-called "ordinary language" is concerned with categorizing and naming, it is the way in which we make things (and ourselves) appear to us as meaningful; the literature advocated by Beckett and Blanchot, by contrast, tries to erase, to "make-forget." Language becomes literature when it becomes a question to itself.

What is enacted in Beckett is a sort of positivized negativity that signifies a "going-beyond" the notion of Self. Slavoj Žižek has convincingly argued for the necessity of distinguishing between "person" and "subject,"[1] but if we want to get close to what happens in Beckett, especially in his so-called "middle period," we need more specifically to consider the relation between language and subject as being fundamentally about *nothing*. My argument is that there is a certain type of nothingness inherent to the human experience, and that this presence of absence comes eminently to the fore in Beckett as an "agency without agens."[2]

In the following, I will try to elucidate how Beckett's works can be said to embody this nothingness that links it to both Jacques Lacan and Martin Heidegger, and more specifically that this comes out most forcefully in his 1953 novel *The Unnameable*, the final instalment of the trilogy, preceded by *Molloy* and *Malone Dies*, and arguably his most inaccessible book. Caution is certainly advised when it comes to linking the thoughts of these writers, but I think that there is a place where all three can be seen to be on the same page: in the distrust of the Cartesian subject as it relates to language.[3] Beckett's unique vision draws attention to the way in which existence goes beyond the subject: a "wounded space" (Blanchot), devoid of Self but shimmering with existence—enacted by a literature that is a continuous failure. This is why the three central words in the following are *murmur*, *gnawing*, and *failure*. All of these keywords point us in the direction of Beckett's method as a slow and stumbling movement, whereby "nothing is happening."

The murmurs of *The Unnameable*

When, in the beginning of the novel, the narrator wonders, "How proceed? By aporia pure and simple?" (Beckett 2006a: 285), it gives a clue to the constant questioning and undermining that characterize the work. This self-questioning that gives *The Unnameable* its stumbling motion is literature as enacted thinking, hell-bent on getting to something authentic—which it is always unable to, seeing how the words are obscuring what it tries to grasp. Ironically, the book is a dizzying jumble of words that points out all the shortcomings of words. But it seems as if this spewing of words is a prerequisite for approaching this very delicate presence that the Beckettian narrator hears in the margins of the stories. A murmur that is indicative of *the presence of absence*: "I... never stopped telling stories, to myself, hardly hearing them, hearing something else, listening for something else" (Beckett 2006a: 405).

Though Beckett will come to perfect a minimalism in his later works, such as *Imagination Dead Imagine* and *Worstward Ho*, there is an unresolved tension in his trilogy from 1951 to 1953 that has something to do with the lingering need to tell stories and a growing distrust of language. But while *The Unnameable* is the most radical of the trilogy's deconstruction of narrative, even here stories abound, albeit almost as quickly torn apart again. Where the works from the later minimalist period seem somehow more tightly knit, having a clearer sense of expression, *The Unnameable* seems stuck in an unbearable and unsolvable conflict with itself that results in a seemingly endless outpouring of words:

> But when it falters and when it stops, but it falters every instant, it stops every instant, yes, but when it stops for a good few moments, a good few moments, what are a good few moments, what then, murmurs, then it must be murmurs, and listening, someone listening, no need of an ear, no need of a mouth, the voice listens, as when it speaks, listens to its silence, that makes a murmur, that makes a voice. (Beckett 2006a: 402)

The writing in *The Unnameable* is the written equivalent to *murmur*, a low, indistinct, continuous flow. One aspect of murmuring is that it is an enunciation without enunciated; or, to put it differently, it is an enunciation where the very absence of verifiable communicative content makes of the enunciation something uncanny.[4] It makes it inhabited by a spectral doppelgänger; an underside to language that, as Blanchot mentions, "no one speaks" because they are busy saying some-thing. This other language is "nothing but a voice murmuring a trace… like air leaves among the leaves" (Beckett 1967: 133). If it is spoken by no one, it is because it is not there for us to speak or to write, but can only be felt in its effects as a faltering or be guessed at as a meaning behind the mumble.

This is how we should understand the nature of the speaking voice in Beckett: something that tries to enunciate the very impossibility of enunciation—an empty site in which a message without content resonates; what Lacan in "The Subversion of the Subject and the Dialectic of Desire in the Freudian Unconscious" calls "(a)n enunciation that denounces itself, a statement that renounces itself" (Lacan 1977: 300). The murmur is simply a way for language to speak without signifying, thus derailing any claim to truth-content, which, however, does not lessen the weight of the enunciation but in fact makes it all the more overwhelming.[5] There are two sides to this issue: not only is the murmur enunciated as a theme, always surrounding the narrator with barely perceived voices; it is also the enunciation, the writing itself, that takes on this indistinct, continuous nature—the text becomes a murmur: "the words fail, the voice fails, so be it, I know that well, it will be the silence, full of murmurs, distant cries" (Beckett 2006a: 406). The trickle of words breaks off and trails somewhere else, only to soon after halt and turn yet again, leaving the reader with a bunch of open-ended fragments.

No-thing?

But what are we to make of this absence that is not the absence of a thing, but somehow absence in itself? One of the challenges of putting *nothing* into words is its complicity in *something*; that is, the very word "no-thing" indicates that there is an object somewhere to be found—it speaks in the same language as presence. So does the word *absence* (ab-esse; from-thing). As such, language always already closes itself off to any authentic representation of nothingness by insisting on the simple negation of presence, and thus fails to enunciate the way in which language is haunted by its own undoing. But language as *literature* is capable—in spite of itself—of enacting what Heidegger calls an openness toward Being, which in his vocabulary is indeed a kind of nothing; that is, because this openness lets us experience *that* there is existence ("es gibt") rather than showing us what *kind* of existence or beings, it is first and foremost a disappearance of our categories of comprehension.

The philosopher Miguel de Beistegui writes in his book on Heidegger that "life tends to understand and interpret itself on the basis of its own fallen state, that is, on the basis of its own practical, concernful absorption in the world… This tendency is reassuring and *tranquilizing*" (de Beistegui 2005: 18). This absorption obscures the disappearance or erasure that leaves beings in the wake of its withdrawal, a *raum-gebend* ("space-giving") that allows beings to appear to us. Angst is one of Heidegger's modes of openness because—as opposed to fear—it is not related to any positive being; angst is objectless.[6] This uncanny experience coincides completely with who we actually are—in anxiety we are face-to-face with ourselves as emptied. What this means is that the subject "is" at heart nothing but openness. But exactly because the nakedness of the self is terrifying, we imagine ourselves as a person.

In *Letter on Humanism*, Heidegger argues that "language is the House of Being. In its home man dwells" (Heidegger 2000: 83). The only way to be counted as human at all is to emerge as such through language, but our emergence is as an absence born of the inconsistencies of language.[7] The house that Heidegger imagines is run through with cracks. This means that it is the signifier that institutes lack. Its very fullness is at the same time the harbinger of nothing. Lack and overabundance coincide. The word gives body to a special kind of absence by being "a trace of nothingness," as Lacan notes in "Function and Field of Speech and Language": "Through the word—already a presence made of absence—absence itself gives itself a name" (Lacan 1977: 65).

When language turns into literature, it is *not* somehow mastered by an artist who uses it "better"; rather, the artist makes language (and thus his or her own art) *fail*. He or she makes language into a question directed at itself, effectively (as in Beckett) consisting of nothing but its own undermining. When language makes itself impossible, it has made itself possible, and as such into art. There is a side effect to this: Since the idea of an "I" is a function of language, the failing of language at the same time enacts "the tense failing of an identity—the failing that exposes the subjectivity which is without any subject" (Blanchot 1995a: 78). This is the continuous collapse that takes place in *The Unnameable*: "This voice that speaks, knowing that it lies, indifferent to what it says, too old perhaps and too abased ever to succeed in saying the words that would be its last, knowing itself useless and its uselessness in vain, not listening to itself but to the silence that it breaks" (Beckett 2006a: 308).

Raiders of the lost subject

It has been argued that Beckett's characters—especially in the plays—aren't really characters, but more like placeholders for a voice. But instead of seeing it as a flaw in his writing, we should rather see it as emblematic of the way in which his writing constantly executes the gap between voice and person: "(H)is voice continued to testify, as though woven into mine, preventing me from saying who I was, what I was, so as to have done with saying, done with listening" (Beckett 2006a: 303). Beckett's characters are always besides themselves even as they try to make sense of their situation.

The Unnameable traces a thinning out of the proper name, analogous to the way in which the trilogy as such traces an effacement of Self. Here, as mentioned earlier, we still have the attempt to tell stories about persons, but gradually these characters become more and more void—they transform, grow less: from Basil over Mahood to Worm until the attempt at narrative is finally abandoned, narrowed to the point of an impossible imperative: "you must go on, I can't go on, you must go on, I'll go on, you must say words, as long as there are any, until they find me, until they say me" (Beckett 2006a: 407). Lacan subverts Heidegger's notion of *Es ruft* in order to turn it into *Ça parle*—it speaks, something speaks through me, even in my silence there will be speech. Lacan refers to this phenomenon as "a discourse in which the subject... is spoken rather than speaking" (Lacan 1977: 69).

This certain type of nothingness that cannot be relocated back to a lost object is connected to the crumbling subject with which Beckett wrestles: "[P]erhaps that's what I am, the thing that divides the world in two, on the one side the outside, on the other the inside, that can be as thin as foil, I'm neither one side not the other, I'm in the middle, I'm the partition" (Beckett 2006a: 376). This middle ground, this nothing other than that which introduces a cut, is subjectivity—an in-between characterized by a subject constantly being dismantled by doubt: "It is not a question of knowing whether I speak of myself in a way that conforms to what I am, but rather of knowing whether I am the same as that of which I speak" (Lacan 1977: 165). Another way of saying this is that Beckett's narrator inhabits the "space" between enunciation and enunciated, the partition. Subjectivity is here nothing but the movement toward inhabiting the signifier (in this case the "I"), but since this movement is at all times stunted by a distrust of language, Beckett's narrative is more akin to a trembling on the spot; that is, there is movement, but not the kind that brings us forward—"it falters every instant."

What we are dealing with is *"subjectivity without any subject"* (Blanchot 1995a: 30), what Blanchot also refers to as *"le Neutre."* This kind of existence is not what we can catch a hold of by even the most blatantly confessional autobiography, but the properly uncanny experience of "just existing"; uncanny because suddenly "I" am not there, only "there is."[8] In Beckett, this is the terrifying experience of an element in language that is somehow in excess of the subject that speaks it—to be seized by something "extimate" that marks the impossibility of silence: "When the talking stops, there is still talking; when the language pauses, it perseveres" (Blanchot 1986: 141).

But this seemingly endless flow of words not only annuls the narrator and the narrative but also to some extent annuls the reader. Reading *The Unnameable* is in some ways boring—but it is boredom in the Heideggerian sense.[9] When we read, we hope to be transported away from our dreary everyday, and the usual way is through narrative, character, and empathy. And at the same time, we make this reading into part of what Sartre would call our "original project"; that is, we are always already once removed from the reading, being aware in a reflexive mode "that-we-read" and fitting this into our notion of what kind of person we are.

Beckett refuses to give us this—instead, his works are deliberately hard to read because they refuse to let literature be reassuring ("reassuring" of course not taken to mean "everything's gonna be alright" but "ah, there is coherence and meaning"). Sometimes when reading the novel, the words somehow lose their meaning, the book its direction, and you realize that you have at the same time lost your sense of purpose in reading. And that, I think, stems from a certain expectation we have to literature; even Joyce, Beckett's one-time idol, still tells *stories*. Beckett, on the other hand, just *gnaws* at all the presuppositions of language.

The gnawing of failure

In 1937, Beckett wrote a letter in which he hinted at his poetics: "To bore one hole after another in language, until what lurks behind it—be it something or nothing—begins to seep through" (quoted in Gontarski 1986: 5). The central point in this letter is *not* the "nothing" behind language, but "to bore." Beckett's nothingness does not lurk behind the words in an imagined beyond, but happens as a side effect while language actually attempts to say something; that is, it is not a question of succeeding in pointing out nothingness, but of failing to point out presence. Direct representation somehow betrays the nothingness inherent in language, whereas the literary enunciation teases out the cracks in language by trying to write something and miserably failing.

The literary illustration of this can be found in a sentence from the prose work *Worstward Ho* from 1983: "All gnawing to be naught. Never to be naught" (Beckett 2006b: 484). First off, the homophonic resemblance between "gnaw" and "naught" infects the sentence with a sort of minimal difference that makes it tremble; the sentence itself, independently of its content, illustrates a failure to come to rest. Both at the level of form and content, it is the striving toward an authentic articulation of this nothingness that determines man, but it can never fully articulate it. However, this is exactly the point. In *Less Than Nothing*, Slavoj Žižek writes: "the split between substance and subjectivity, Being and reflection, is insurmountable, and the only reconciliation possible is a *narrative* one, that of the subject telling the story of his endless oscillation between the two poles. While the content remains un-reconciled, *reconciliation occurs in the narrative form itself*" (Žižek 2013: 14). To slightly alter the vocabulary of Žižek's comment: the reconciliation mentioned is precisely the *lack* of such—it is what keeps the narrative and the sentences unsettled and unsettling. Beckett's fiction is no longer in any conventional sense storytelling, but rather the un-telling of stories, the articulation of impossibility. This is why "failure" takes on an ontological character through Beckett's work.

The absence disappears in a form of representation that necessarily fails it as soon as it tries to grab it; therefore, the only valid approach to absence is a literature that enacts an effacement—or rather, that attempts to capture its very "drawing-back." Absence can thus only be represented as the failure of something else—the failure to tell stories, to describe the self, and so on. The literary moment is in this sense that which falls between the words, the echo of the said. What Beckett puts into play is this gap between the Being and naming, giving voice to the nothing through failure—and this might very well be the reason why Blanchot wrote that *The Unnameable* fails as a work of art.

Thus, Beckett's art is concerned with the *lack* of the signifier, the signifier as bearer of nothing. What at first glance appears to be a fault in language is actually its most sublime moment, and this is what literature as a form of thinking is capable of: It uncovers *nothing*. Heidegger writes that "[i]f man is to find his way once again into the nearness of Being he must first learn to exist in the nameless" (Heidegger 2000: 86), and this movement towards the nameless was, as we saw earlier, also the movement of *The Unnameable*—an attempt to write the empty site bereft of subject, but where subjectivity as a presence freed of agent murmurs and gnaws in the margin.

This gnawing of language is the nothingness as "infinite disquiet, formless and nameless vigilance" (Blanchot 1995b: 326). If it is formless and nameless it is because these are the methods by which language creates meaning, coherence, logic, and harmony. The real fall into nothingness is not the one that speaks it, but the fall that annuls itself while saying something else: the failing literature.

Nothing moves

To sum up, we might remember why Blanchot considers Orpheus as the artist par excellence regarding the failing art. The movement up through the underworld, where Orpheus is forbidden to look at Eurydice, is an illustration of being in the presence of absence in as much as Eurydice is not yet reconstituted to the world of the living. Orpheus' mistake is to want to grasp her in her radical otherness *directly*, that is, as an image, which is exactly what blows the whole deal. This presence of absence, for which Eurydice becomes a figure, can only be approached sideways while actually doing something else, attempting to tell stories: "it seemed to me I only barely heard it, because of the noise I was engaged in making elsewhere, in obedience to the unintelligible terms of an incomprehensible damnation" (Beckett 2006a: 302).

While Beckett's narrator is busy telling stories, he becomes aware of something humming along—a murmur at the edge of his ability to express. This murmur is that of Eurydice as self-effacing art, the one that gives room for this voice from the underworld, not to let it speak, but to let it murmur. "For it is difficult to speak, even any old rubbish, and at the same time focus one's attention on another point, where one's true interest lies, as fitfully defined by a feeble murmur seeming to apologize for not being dead" (Ibid). As soon as the subject comes into existence—as the one who writes "I"—it is haunted by a lack. And what a murmuring and gnawing literature such as Beckett's does is to "write out" this lack so that it can be felt as a palpable presence.

This is the problem in literature that Beckett makes visible: How to speak one's Self if the moment of enunciation puts us right back into the same-old mess? If the moment of appearance is at the same time a *dis*appearance, and what is left is only the contours of outside stuff—what the narrator calls his "pensum"—who is "I"? But at the same time, and this is where the Beckettian conundrum is spot on, there would not even be the trace of authentic Being, which is all we can ever experience (its withdrawal), if we did not *engage and fail*. This is why Buddhism and meditation are not viable options concerning this particular ontological dilemma, because they are essentially ways to escape the deadlock of an inherent nothingness that is not an *entity* but a *movement*.

The Beckettian gnawing and murmuring may only result in failure, but because of this, it is able to write out an experience of nothingness that does not "represent" it: "there is no silence if not written" (Blanchot 1995a: 8). We should take Beckett's oeuvre as asking us this: How does the Self exist as a subjectivity beyond itself? How does the nothing speak? How do we name it? In its drilling of holes, Beckett's literature is akin to the psychoanalytic contribution to cultural criticism as it highlights the noncomplete nature of human experience, resulting in a "non-knowledge."

Notes

1 For example in *Less Than Nothing* (2013).
2 This formulation is borrowed from Benjamin Noys. See Noys (2010).
3 The interest in language is certainly characteristic of the later Heidegger, where he tries to rid himself of any vestiges of subject-oriented thinking.

4   Although the word itself does not pop up frequently in the plays, the very staging of them certainly displays a murmuring quality, especially *Play* and *Not I*.
5   This aspect is not unlike Lacan's play on *jouissance* as *jouis-sens*.
6   Heidegger here relies heavily on Søren Kierkegaard's discussion of angst.
7   This is what Lacan, borrowing from Ernest Jones, calls *aphanisis*. See Lacan (1998).
8   This is Emmanuel Levinas' notion of the "*il y a*." See Levinas (1947).
9   The critic Alfred Alvarez wrote: "*The Unnameable* comes perilously close to being the Unreadable." Quoted in Bair (1993: 402).

References

Bair, D. (1993), *Samuel Beckett. A Biography*, New York: Touchstone.
Beckett, S. (1967), *No's Knife. Collected Shorter Prose 1947–1966*, London: Calder and Boyars.
Beckett, S. (2006a), *Samuel Beckett. The Grove Centenary Edition II. Novels*, New York: Grove Press.
Beckett, S. (2006b), *Samuel Beckett. The Grove Centenary Edition IV. Poems, Short Fiction, Criticism*, New York: Grove Press.
Blanchot, M. (1986), "Where Now? Who Now?" in *On Beckett: Essays and Criticism*, ed. S. E. Gontarski, New York: Grove Press.
Blanchot, M. (1995a), *The Writing of the Disaster*, Lincoln, London: University of Nebraska Press.
Blanchot, M. (1995b), *The Work of Fire*, Stanford: Stanford University Press.
de Beistegui, M. (2005), *The New Heidegger*, London: Continuum Press
Gontarski, S. E. ed. (1986) *On Beckett : Essays and Criticism*, New York City: Grove Press.
Heidegger, M., *Letter on Humanism*, in *Global Religious Vision*, transl. Bruce Fink, July 2000, vol. 1/1.
Lacan, J. (1998 [1973]), *The Four Fundamental Concepts of Psychoanalysis*, The Seminar of Jacques Lacan, Book IX, New York/London: W. W. Norton.
Lacan, J. (1977), *Écrits. A Selection*, New York: W. W. Norton.
Levinas, E. (1947), *De l'existence à l'existant*, Paris: Librairie Philosophique Vrin.
Noys, B. (2010), *The Persistence of the Negative: A Critique of Contemporary Continental Theory*, Edinburgh: Edinburgh University Press.
Žižek, S. (2013), *Less than Nothing. Hegel and the Shadow of Dialectical Materialism*, London, New York: Verso.

4

Analysis Sounds Boring

Anders Ruby

Modern electronic music seems to be ridden with the problem of subjectivity. There is an unsatisfying or even unsettling absence of "humanity," "feeling," or similar platitudes in the cold, inorganic functioning of music machines. The concert performance of electronic music is usually accompanied by excessive performative elements that are entirely nonfunctional in terms of musicality, as to cater to the "lack of humanity." Or to be more precise, to cater to the lack of transference: a specific position to which one can pin understanding and ultimately enjoyment. My claim is then that instead of merely stuffing this gap in the machine's lack of humanity with more humanity, there is an opportunity in this discontent—an analytic opportunity even. Electronic music gives voice to a body that is not to be found in its place. And as such, it stands in contrast to "played music"—music played by human beings that is—in that machine music does not give us the opportunity to identify with the performer quite so easily. No matter how obscure or unpleasant a "played" musical performance might be, we always have the opportunity (or way out) to simply identify with (our own imaginary projection of) the enjoyment of the other: "I might not understand this, but the artist seems to be somehow enjoying it." Machine music obscures this transference. For is it not precisely in the performative elements of a specific technê, a rehearsed artistic technique such as that of an experienced cellist, that we open a door to transference and close one to analysis? A technê that arguably disappears along with the sought-after "humanity" in the performance. And is this not precisely the setup and schism that we know from analysis? Impressive technique and a captivating performance are rather things the analyst should shy away from, as to not simply identify with this position of Other that the analysand offers to transfer to the analyst. So could stupid, repetitive modern electronic music thus perhaps be closer to the analyst's position within the artistic domain than Beethoven, Wagner, or Bach?

The concert setting

There is something strange about concerts. Even if we just attempt a simple definition—a setting for the experience of a musical performance—something remains excluded. For such a description would also fit the watching of a musical performance on a television, for example, which we would not outright accept as having been to a concert. There is an element of "being there," meaning being engaged. So the concert is a setting where one is engaged in the experience of a musical performance. How, then, is one engaged? Once again, a strangeness arises in the description—even on the basic level. One is engaged as an audience, which, in most cases, means to be standing or sitting in front of the stage in a large group, reduced to only a single signifier; that of desire. The crowd can clap, shout, wave their hands, or show similar cheering gestures, but not engage in actual conversation with whoever is on stage. Even if this type of dialogue is often feigned in the concert setting: "Do you want to hear more?," "Are you having a good night?," "Do you see what's going on in the world right now?" More often than not, the crowd *does* want to hear more, they *are* having a good night, and they *do* see what is going on in the world right now, even if no one knows what is being referred to. The crowd at a concert is an audience in the most literal meaning of being an assemblage of those who listen, which is also why one of the worst things that can happen at a concert is the sudden reversal of roles, as some jaunty musician insists on involving the audience as an active participant in the performance. The audience is not there to be engaged as agency, but rather to play the role of desire itself. For the performer, the audience is the generalized Other, while for the audience, the performer is the particularized version of the Other. A "star"—an effective performer—is someone who is able to sustain desire, to keep desire flowing in this particular setup. In fact, I think this is precisely what stardom means today: It is neither something that can be measured or judged on the level of technique nor something that can be judged on the merit of some aesthetic quality, but rather the true mark of "a star" is to keep desire flowing—someone who is fully willing and able to identify with this position above the crowd, precisely *as if* it were based on some sublime quality, the factor *x* or another bromide.

In fact, is this relationship (which is of course) between performer and audience not the most clear-cut version of transference that we know from popular culture? Does "the star," above the crowd, subject of the spotlight, whose voice is amplified ten times over, not precisely embody the imaginary position of a subject-supposed-to-know? And does the performer not also in most cases identify with the position to a degree where a truly imaginary relationship can emerge, in which crowd and performer can slide into a kind of circle of recognition—or circle of desire?

As Lacan writes in seminar XI:

> As soon as the subject who is supposed to know exists somewhere there is transference. What does an organization of psychoanalysts mean when it confers certificates of ability, if not that it indicates to whom one may apply to represent this subject who is supposed to know? (Lacan 1977: 232)

What is a concert stage, if not precisely such a certificate? With all its superfluous ornamentations of lights, visuals, and fireworks surrounding the name in the middle. And what is the performer, if not such a subject-happy-to-accept-transference? Indeed, this is a feature that somehow seems equally important to that of the performance itself. In fact, it is not rare to see concert reviews stating that "nothing was wrong with the music, but the band just didn't seem to enjoy it." This circular relationship is precisely what the analyst's own analysis—also know as the training analysis—is supposed to prevent: that the relationship gets stuck in perversion. Stuck in a place where the analyst unconsciously begins to enjoy either giving or withholding answers to the analysand—whereas the analysand enjoys the fact that the Other knows—has the knowledge that he or she seeks. Needless to say, the interdependent nature of such a relationship does not nurture the psychoanalytic process; nor does it allow for the subject to actually begin thinking.

Now, this might sound a bit harsh; concert settings are perverse environments with nothing but regressive fantasy structures, and to go to a concert, one would have to be a pervert, let alone the endeavor of performing at one. My point is a bit subtler. Even if, as a kind of wild analysis, the above statement might not be entirely wrong.

Performance and perversion

Musical works of art *do* have a very hard time escaping perversion, especially in the concert setting, as the piece does not begin to emerge without a certain level of technê, creating an inescapable bond between the work and the performing ego.

It is striking that Lacan speaks of a two-edged ax when speaking of transference and the desire of the analyst (Lacan 1977: 235), since it is transference that is needed to initiate analysis; yet if it is applied with too much force, analysis gets stuck in this transference. This is indeed also the case here in our current setting: Technique is what allows the pianist to play the piece, to bring it into existence, but it is also inevitably what stands between the audience and the work. On a phenomenological level, we meet the musical work of art as always-already interpreted through another human being. But the problem here is not simply Kantian—that we can never really reach the noumena as some sort of pure artistic core, but rather that if we engage in the work at all, we do so as a kind of falling in love. The purity of the tones, the precision in the intonation, the agility and speed of the fingers—all so utterly fascinating!

But, even if the technê of a performer is not extraordinarily impressive, or if the work is the most free-form, avant-garde noise-jazz you have ever heard, it is not that transference disappears altogether. The Other can function as the gravity of transference even if it does not achieve the status of a full subject-supposed-to-know. The crack through which transference can slip in can easily be a crack in "perfection," so that the traction of the Other rather becomes something like a subject-supposed-to-enjoy, or maybe even a subject-supposed-to-suffer (for more on this point, see Žižek 1998). At the very least, the ego of the performer opens some biographic details that allows for the ever-so-popular idea of the "unlocking" of the message, so that we can understand what the piece was *really* about. Its very merit becomes the fact that it is a personal story or that someone's suffering becomes clear. Even if the audience does not "understand" what is going on, the very certificate of the stage, the setup of transference, allows for enjoying the enjoyment of the Other.

What we get in electronic music is a kind of resistance within this circle. The Other is missing in its place. Of course, machines can serve as Others (as Lacan explores in *Seminar II*), but what we expect in the concert setting is an Other in the flesh—of flesh. Precisely at the place where we expect a placeholder for our projections toward the performing stage, something lacks to which we can attribute the pains and pleasures that the performance gives us. A specific Other, in relation to whom we can have these feelings. Electronic music is boring in the sense that it is not interpreted by a real human being, bringing it vividly to life right in front of our eyes. But this is a very specific kind of boredom. Something is lacking on the level of transference, because it is excessively present on the level of technê. This is a paradox, since I did claim that precisely technê was what allowed for transference to get going in the first place. But here, a certain boundary has been crossed. That the computer is able to play faster, cleaner, and more precise than any human subject is simply uninteresting. It has eliminated the very question of technê. The on-stage machine amounts to a ghostly presence, playing regardless of our ability to understand it. But that is not the end of it. It is not just that the machine is "out there," playing, as something completely external to my body and reality. The real problem arises as the music has the possibility of moving the audience, the subject, in spite of this lack of an "interesting other"—but doing so with no clear place to bind transference. Something is lost in machine music, something we expect to be at the core of our experience, a concrete other, and yet, the experience remains.

The point is not that what we hear in electronic music is the pure message, or a pure work of art, undistorted by the self-interested ego. Rather, we hear everything that is usually surrounding such a message, such a content; however, we do not hear this in the pure form either. It is not that we finally hear the piece without the performance, the work without the technique, or the pure, artistic idea, or something like that. Clearly, there is technê involved in electronic music as well. Good technique and bad technique. Clever, surprising, and delicate programming, and blunt, uninventive, or crude programming, for instance. Just as an obvious objection would be that there *are* usually people on stage in the context of machine music, either performing on electronic instruments or otherwise operating the machinery. Yet, the way that we experience such a performance, where it is obviously the machine that does *the work*, the machine that plays the music, right here, right now, despite what thoughts, ideas, and divine inspirations that might precede this very moment, still forces us to see a rather fundamental split in the relation between subject and Other. If one is "taken" by a musical piece, this experience, this enjoyment would under "normal circumstances," that is, those of a human body performing the piece, rest upon a certain dwelling on the performer. One is "grabbed," "taken," "taken away," "gone," or one of the countless other metaphors for being mesmerized or swept off one's feet. There is quite obviously an element of falling in love. Transference *is* an offer of love, and such an offer can either be accepted or be rejected. Both can lead to an even stronger, or deeper fall. In the case of a human performer, after the applauding offer of love from the audience, the Other of the stage must respond with either a bow (an acceptance), a "thank-you" (an acceptance with a return gesture), or some other version of establishing a firm circle of transference. The machine does not allow for any of those functions. Neither acceptance nor rejection. It is simply indifferent. But this indifference, all the way down to the indifference to my bodily presence, allows for a different kind of experience. An experience of love without an Other, but one that remarkably is able to define itself as such while still being at the opposite end of narcissism. I shall return to this point after a little further development.

A lack of lacks

If no one is able to accept my offer of love, of transference, and thus to frame my own enjoyment, a certain lack arises in the Other. This is quite obvious in the case of machine music. Such a lack, Lacan tells us, forces the subject to respond with its own preexisting lack, and so we have the formula for separation: the infamous overlapping or coincidence of two lacks. Within this, the object a, the very object cause of desire, that which brings it about, is brought into play again and a window is left open. A window through which we can get out of perversion. Out of the affirming relationship with the musical performance in which the symbolic order is simply confirmed, and into an open constellation of signifiers in which desire and fantasy are actually brought into play. But this engagement with object a is no small endeavor—rather it is the very threshold that must be crossed for one to "subjectivize" desire, to actually move something in analysis.

But how can electronic music, which precisely has no kinks, no slips, and no nicks, bring about a more "subjectivized" experience than one full of feeling, unsuspected turns and small, interesting, human mistakes? Precisely because something happens in this lack of interesting, subjective interpretation. In the lack of a knowing and enjoying position in contrast to the subject. When this position disappears, I claim one of two things can happen. Either we get a version of a ventriloquist performance, in which the trick embarrassingly falls apart. The performer attempts to uphold the position that the audience calls for by the audience through excessive gesticulation and pushing of meaningless buttons. One might have seen examples of this in popular culture, as when famous DJs open large stadium events for instance. An outcome in which nothing changes in terms of imaginary roles and subjectivization. We sustain the illusion that such a position exists, but unfortunately the performer simply was not able to live up to it. To deliver, so to speak. This is no different from an analytically failed "fall of the Other," in which the analyst might demonstrate (intentionally or not) that he or she is in fact not knowing—not filled with the information and truth that the analysand seeks. Yet, this insight does not lead to a fall of the Other as such, but rather the fall of this concrete other in front of me. The position of Other remains unchanged and it is simply a matter of finding the right other, then. A new analyst. A new idol, a new life coach, or someone willing to take on the imaginary role that will reenable my enjoyment. This seems to be the level at which machine music, and especially electronic music performances, is stranded today. It does not seem to be able to remain interesting to its partner, the audience. It is too boring to look at. Some even consider it fake in some sense. It is not sufficiently willing to take control and swipe us off our feet. So just like in any other relationship, it must renew itself. Find new and excessive ways of staying within the imaginary realm that will bind the other's interest—ours. Laser-shows, dancers, holograms, fireworks, pyrotechnics.

But there is also another possibility. Potential, even. One in which it is not simply the concrete other in front of me that falls, but rather the structural element that ensures or even enables my enjoyment. The Other. The breaking point in any analysis is a moment where the subject comes to the realization that the Other is not desiring, and thus not demanding, in the specific way that was imagined by the subject. But since the desire remains present even in its foreign form, the subject must himself or herself assume responsibility for the enjoyment. In the concert setup, this would amount to the realization that in spite of the lack in the Other; in spite of the mis-belonging or detached nature of the sounds that I am hearing in machine music, desire is still present. I am captivated by the object a, but I cannot fully ascribe it to, nor enjoy it through, the Other.

The foreignness of the sounds, their origin, their source, becomes explicit when performed by the machine, yet everything about the situation remains known, familiar. It is precisely not the experience of some sort of radical foreignness; in fact, the reverse is closer to the truth. What is experienced is the known-ness, the familiarity of the whole setting, *yet* with the small but fundamental shift that there is a certain lack of bibliographic adherence. I am unable to clearly understand what it is that the Other wants from me, and thus I am unable to give it. I am, in a sense, left with my own desire, and to engage in a musical experience of this sort is, almost by necessity, to assume my own desire. For the voice that hangs emptily in the room, whether it be the analyst's office or the concert hall, belongs to no specific other, and to approach it as object a is at the same time to assume responsibility for it myself.

The analytical discourse is precisely that which speaks from the position of the small *a*, not the capital *A*, which is to say, that it is desire, rather than an Other, that does the talking in analysis.

Counter-love

So by this logic, would it not be better to just sit quietly at home and listen to a record? With no elevated other, no point of transference or place of identification? Again, the parallel to the analytical situation seems obvious, and so we can ask, Would analysis be better without the analyst in the room? Despite being an effective way of getting rid of transference—no, of course not. We cannot simply write off transference as something that must be avoided at all costs. In fact, it is the supposition of knowledge that initiates analysis in the first place. In this way, transference has a dialectical nature in that it, on the one hand, remains an obstacle for analysis to overcome, but, on the other hand, functions as a fuel that drives it forward. Analysis works precisely because there *is* an other in the room. However, it does not work *through* this other, but rather *in relation to* this other. One of the difficulties of analysis is figuring out whom the analysand is addressing—symbolically. At the moment where a cardinal symbolic role starts shaking, analytical potential arises, and it is in such a moment that the analyst must confront his or her own narcissism and cast off the temptation of making the analysand's enjoyment dependent on the analyst's presence and recognition. Cast off the temptation of getting a "fan."

In the musical setting, this would amount to rejecting a certain position offered in transference. To reject, on the one hand, the position of someone who either has some divine insight or elitist technê, thus remaining the access point of the audience's enjoyment and, on the other hand, the fundamental offer of love available here. Not only the love that the audience is offering *but, even more fundamentally, the love of oneself.* I realize that in today's therapeutic climate, this sounds rather controversial, so let me elaborate.

The relationship needed for transference to work properly disrupts as the computer—the ghostly music machine—enters the setting and makes "countertransference" (if we accept this Freudian/early Lacanian term; otherwise, we can just call it transference) impossible, since the computer does not have unconscious feelings toward the listener. Or at least, that question goes way beyond the scope of my inquiry. This leaves an impossibility in the stable circle of recognition or the establishment of a relationship with a kind of master/slave dialectics. In other words, the computer, the music machine, on behalf of being intellectually stupid, yet athletically superior, in some sense, functions as an intermediary that can relieve the subject of a very specific kind of enjoyment: narcissism.

One should not engage in art to be loved. Just as one should not engage in psychoanalysis to receive love. One engages in psychoanalysis to be able to love *outside* of that setting. Analysis *itself* is boring, or at least, it should not be made exciting.

The drop of the Other

So how, then, can desire still be flowing in this setting? With the machine on stage, disrupting our means of engagement—obscuring transference. The machine might very well mean a lack of countertransference, but the setup *itself* allows for desire to be flowing even in spite of this lack. Desire flows as if the "clinic" itself—the surrounding technique and materiality—acts on behalf of this lack of obvious anchor point. The concert setting, the clinic, bears a certain promise. It promises knowledge, technique, desire. Machine music is a very specific way of not delivering on that promise. It lures you into the clinic and leaves you there. But before the disappointment that there is no one there to love you back, or even to accept your offer of love, several steps have already been taken, setting desire in motion. One has shown up, others have shown up, there is a certain technique in place, and there is a certain spatiotemporality in that one knows that the concert is about to happen, desire is about to happen—here and now. In this respect, what I claim to be structurally different about machine music is neither on the level of sound nor on the level of composition, but quite simply on the level of transference, something that comes about through the way we perceive the composition, through the way that it sounds in a certain setting. Analysis does not work because analysts give extraordinarily good advice. It works because they are good at this positioning, in which the setup itself starts speaking. And what is a modern electronic music concert if not a setting in which the concert itself speaks?

On the one hand, we could bring up the vast amount of experimental artists working in this realm. Artists working with generative music, acousmatic listening sessions, live coding, and countless other ways in which the classical concert format with all its imaginary identifications is being challenged. However, a somewhat more subtle, yet perhaps more interesting, shift can be detected on the popular music scene—in fact, at the very heart of this scene. If one listens to the current wave of popular music, quite often one will come across a musical phenomenon that has become known as "a drop." And in all its stupidity, there is something quite wonderful about this phenomenon, which has a long history in EDM (Electronic Dance Music). I shall return to this in a moment.

For decades, pop music has been structured around the chorus. Songwriters are orbiting this meaty centerpiece on the table and developing everything else from it. The chorus justifies everything else in the song, and it is the natural climax of the pop song structure. A poor song with a good chorus is still a good song. It has been the selling point of pop music for as long as pop music has been around. Where other parts of the song might have different leading roles, the chorus is ruled by the star, who must in this part shine brighter than ever.

In EDM, things work a little differently. Most electronic dance music is instrumental and the songs are not made in radio-friendly bite-sizes, but are hard-pumping marathons made for sweaty underground clubs and enormous masses of people. Here, the climax is not the chorus. It speaks more directly to the body. The climax is "The Drop," meaning the part where, after a very long and slowly graduating buildup, the heaviest of the rhythmical instruments "drop in." The drop functions quite a lot like the drive, moving pulsatingly beyond the logical climax and into infinity. Very clearly shown by the way that the drop is dramatized and delivered in an obviously orgasmic manner: The rhythm intensifies by adding more and more subdivisions, the volume intensifies, and the pitch goes up and up and up until the whole thing is concluded in a small break before being resolved in "The Drop." Such a buildup can last several minutes, and if one witnesses this event at a concert where the orgasmic hinting in the music is too subtle, then one can always rely on giant foam cannons spraying the audience into the sustained trance that comes right after the drop.

However, the interesting thing about the fact that this drive, the drop, has found its way into popular music is that opposed to the traditional climax in the chorus, the drop is an instrumental part: As we know from Freud, drives are silent. So where we would have previously found the full manifestation of the imaginary whole character of the Other, we get instead what we could perhaps call "the drop of the Other," to paraphrase Lacan's infamous "fall of the Other." The Other as relieved of its duties by the music machine—the signifying machine.

Consider how one of the arguably biggest pop-hits of late, "Lean On," by Major Lazer, featuring DJ Snake and MØ, one of the most streamed Spotify-songs in history, stands as a clear example of the incorporation of the drop (of the Other) in pop music (Pentz et al. 2015). If one attends one of MØ's concerts, nothing initially seems off, as we are welcomed in the usual setting, with the certificate, or the musical clinic in place. Transference works. The main character, MØ herself, a beautiful young woman with all the characteristics of a modern pop star, leads us in via the verses, bridges, buildups, breaks, and so on. But then, as we approach the chorus, something shifts as the break turns into a drop. A drop of the Other in which the whole scene is left open. You can almost feel the television producers' panic, as the cameras restlessly search for a place to focus, as the Other, who was supposed to accept the love of the camera's gaze, transference, and so on, just starts dancing with no choreography, as a member of the audience would have danced, before she usually walks down from the stage altogether to actually join the audience in a kind of rejoicing. But what are they in fact "leaning on"? What are they celebrating—what are they enjoying? On stage stands a lonely music machine, and the line between agent and other is blurred.

It is hard to avoid the comparison to the communist speakers, who at the end of the speech would themselves join the audience to applaud what had been said. As in recognition of the fact the speaker himself or herself was subordinated to the signifier—to what had been said. MØ seems to like the music, and maybe she is enabled to do so without the narcissistic pitfall, precisely on behalf of the machine. On behalf of the way that computer music opens the possibility of an enjoying position, not in relation to an Other that can make the world whole, but in relation to the signifier itself, which can make the world open.

References

Lacan, J. (1977), *The Four Fundamental Concepts of Psychoanalysis (Seminar XI)*, trans. Alan Sheridan, New York: Norton.

Pentz, T. W., Leacock, C., Walsh, Meckseper, P., Leighton, P., Grigahcine, W. S. É., and Andersen, K. M. A. Ø. (2015), "Lean On." Peace Is the Mission, artist name: Major Lazer feat. DJ Snake & MØ. 2015, Mad Decent; Because; Warner.

Žižek, S. (1998), "The Interpassive Subject," The European Graduate School. Available online: www.egs.edu/faculty/slavoj-zizek/articles/the-interpassive-subject (accessed January 29, 2019); http://www.lacan.com/zizek-pompidou.htm (accessed January 29, 2019).

Part Four

Materiality and the Signifier

1

Lol V. Stein to the Letter

Ida Nissen Bjerre

In 1964, Lacan wrote an "Homage to Marguerite Duras." He had just been reading her latest novel, *Le ravissement de Lol V. Stein*, and he was ravished—"it turns out that Marguerite Duras knows, without me, what I teach," he proclaimed (Lacan 1987: 9). Not only did Duras write about the themes that occupied Lacan, there was also something in her special way of writing about these themes that resonated in Lacan: "In paying homage to her, all that I shall show is that the practice of the letter converges with the workings of the unconscious" (Lacan 1987).

The working of the unconscious in the practice of the letter was part of Duras' experience when she wrote *Le ravissement* and was "seized," perhaps even ravished, by her own writing: "I was writing when I suddenly heard myself screaming, because I was seized with fear," she reports, adding: "I don't know why. It was a fear… a fear of losing my mind" (quoted in Porte 1977: 101–02). Years later, in her book *Écrire*, she wrote that writing means being confronted with "all the unknown in oneself, in one's head, in one's body" (Duras 1993: 64). This does not mean that Duras' madness is the key to understanding her works. In his essay on Duras, Lacan goes against psychologizing readings pretending to explain "an author's avowed technique" by some neurosis of the author's. "Boorishness," "stupidity" (Lacan: 1987: 8)!

Instead of searching for the meaning outside the text—in the author's childhood, the historical context, or elsewhere—the reader should follow the example of the analyst and adhere to the speech or the text in its very materiality, that is, its sounds and letters. When we become too obsessed with understanding the hidden meaning "behind" the signifier—that is, behind the analysand's, or narrator's, speech—we often fail to listen to the *way* in which the speaker conveys what she says—we fail to listen to the sound of her words, to the tone of her voice, to slips and slurs and hesitations. Lacan often spoke ironically about certain analysts' use of their so-called "third ear," with which they claimed to sense a meaning beyond the meaning that could already be heard in the analyst's speech (Reik: 1998). According to Lacan an analyst has no need for such an ear; on the contrary, "it sometimes seems that two [ears] are already too many."

> I repeatedly tell my students: "Don't try to understand!" and leave this nauseating category to Karl Jaspers and his consorts. May one of your ears become as deaf as the other one must be acute. And that is the one that you should lend to listen for sounds and phonemes, words, locutions, and sentences, not forgetting pauses, scansions, cuts, periods, and parallelisms, for it is in these that the word-for-word transcription can be prepared, without which analytic intuition has no basis or object. (Lacan 2006b: 394)

Whereas people like Jaspers and Reik tried to hear their own theories in the analysand's speech, Freud listened patiently and with his "freely floating attention" that would attach itself to such peripheral and "unserious" things as slips, puns, dreams, jokes. In Lacan's wording Freud would take "the description of an everyday event as a fable," "a prosopopoeia as a direct interjection," "a simple slip of the tongue as a highly complex statement, and even the rest of a silence as the whole lyrical development it stands in for" (Lacan 2006a: 209).

In his homage to Marguerite Duras, Lacan not only testifies to the workings of the unconscious in Duras' writing but also makes it work in his *own* writing. His *Écrits* are notoriously known for their many neologisms, homologies, ambiguities, surreal imagery—all the stuff that the unconscious is made of, or "structured like."

In what follows, I will try to zoom or rather tune in on this "literary" dimension of Lacan's text. To paraphrase the title of a book by Bruce Fink, I will read Lacan to the letter (Fink: 2004). Where Fink is also dealing with the letter in its "mathèmematical" dimension, I will primarily stick to the letter in its material dimension. Focusing on a few paragraphs from Lacan's "Hommage to Duras," I shall try to unfold Lacan's "literal," associative reading of *Le ravissement de Lol V. Stein* and show how much is going on at the level of the signifier itself. But let us first have a brief look at the novel.

Was will Lol V. Stein?

The novel revolves around a primal scene: At a ball the eponym character Lol V. Stein sees her fiancé falling instantly in love with another woman, dressed in black, the mysterious wife of a visiting ambassador. They dance all night while

Lol watches them from a dark coin in the ballroom. Only at dawn does she reveal herself, trying to stop them from sneaking away, but with no success: "With lowered eyes, they moved past her... Lol's eyes followed them across the garden. When she could no longer see them, she slumped to the floor, unconscious" (Duras 1986: 12).

After this dramatic event, Lol is brought back to her room in her parents' house and stays for weeks in her bed, almost speechless: "The only times she did speak was to say how impossible it was for her to express how boring and long it was, how interminable it was, to be Lol V. Stein" (Duras 1976: 164). People around her presume that she suffers from her broken heart: "Her extreme youth would soon bring her out of it. Her condition was easily explainable" (Duras 1986: 15). But is that really so? If we are to believe the witnesses from the ball she did not feel repelled, rather the contrary: "Lol could not have been more fascinated"; "she seemed to love them" (Duras 1986: 8). In the narrator's poetic wording, Lol simply seems to have forgotten "the age-old algebra governing the sorrows of love" (Duras 1986: 80–81).[1]

The ball scene is established as a primal scene ten years later when Lol—after having lived a sterile life in a shallow marriage—starts to restage its choreography of desire with new actors, one of those being a man whom she randomly spots in town:

> Did he look like her fiancé from [T.] Beach? No, not in the slightest. Did he have certain mannerisms that reminded her of her dead lover? Yes, no doubt he did, especially the way he looked at woman. He too, like the other one, must have been an incorrigible ladies' man, must have borne the burdens of his body only with them, this body which, with every glance, demanded more. (Duras 1986: 43)

Lol discovers that the man has a secret affair with her friend from childhood, Tatiana Karl, and she starts to spy on the couple when they meet in secret. In a recurring scene we are told how Lol lies in a rye field behind a hotel at the outskirts of town, looking up at the window of the room where the adulterous couple meets.

> Living, dying, she breathes deeply, tonight the air is like honey, cloying sweet. She does not even question the source of the wonderful weakness which has brought her to lie in this field....
>
> The rye rustle beneath her loins. Young, early-summer rye. Her eyes riveted on the lighted window. (Duras 1986: 52–3)

...

[Now,] Tatiana Karl, naked in her black hair, crosses the stage of light, slowly. It is perhaps in Lol's rectangle of vision that she pauses. She turns back to the room where the man presumably is. (Duras 1986: 54)

It turns out that the man in the window is the narrator, Jacques Hold. A third into the novel he reveals himself as not only the first-person narrator but also a character in the story. We thus understand only retrospectively that the images of the ravished Lol—in the rye, in town, during the ball—are on his account. Jacques Hold imagines what Lol imagines (sometimes even imagining what she imagines that he imagines) and speaks of himself in the third person ("*He must have been an incorrigible ladies' man…*" etc.). Even after having revealed himself as the narrator, he recurrently speaks of himself in third person, which leaves us with the feeling of a decentered narrator; the "I" of this story is not the master in his own narration. Besides being the one who speaks, he is spoken. "He does not, in any case, simply display the [narrative] machinery, but is in fact one of its mainsprings," Lacan writes, "and he does not know just how taken up in it he is" (Lacan 1987: 8).

Jacques Hold himself describes his narrative method in archeological terms: His ambition is "to level the terrain, to dig down into it, to open the tombs wherein Lol is feigning death" (Duras 1986: 26). The archeological metaphor of depth and surface invites us to regard the narrator's project as a hermeneutic project. By bringing the night of the ball into the light, Hold hopes to understand what Lol desired during the ball, what she wanted, and not least what she wants (with him) for now: "what is there about me I am so completely unaware of and which she summons me to know?" (Duras 1986: 95–6). "What did you desire?" (Duras 1976: 150), he asks on several occasions. "What did you want?" (Duras 1976: 103). "But what is it you want?" (Duras 1976: 112). These questions could all be heard as variations of Cazotte's famous *Che vuoi?*, "What do you want?," which to Lacan is the essence of the neurotic subject's question to (and from) the big Other. More specifically the questions echo Freud's famous question to Marie Bonaparte: *Was will das Weib?* What does woman want?

Soon Hold realizes, though, that the knowledge he is looking for cannot be stated in positive terms: "to know nothing about Lol [V.] Stein was already to know her. One could, it seemed to me, know even less about her, less and less about Lol [V.] Stein" (Duras 1976: 81). This may look like the resignation of Freud when he refrains from answering his famous question *Was will das Weib?* and proclaims woman's libido to be a dark continent (Freud 1948: 241), but contrary to Freud, and in line with Lacan, this "non-knowing" is still regarded by Hold as a kind of knowledge, if not a knowledge that lends itself to positivization, then still a knowledge that can be described indirectly or circumscribed.

Such an approach to Lol V. Stein comes close to Lacan's approach to *Lol V. Stein* (the novel), or to fiction in general. In his essay *Lituraterre* (from 1971), Lacan states that what literature reveals is not so much a failure of knowledge (*échec du savoir*) as a knowledge to be found in failure (*savoir en échec*) (Lacan 2001: 13). To repeat what Lacan repeated again and again: "Don't try to understand!" "May one of your ears become as deaf as the other one must be acute. And that is the one that you should lend to listen for sounds and phonemes, locutions, and sentences... " With this earful mind, let us now turn to Lacan's "Hommage to Duras, on *Le ravissement de Lol V. Stein*."

In the game of love

Lol V. Stein: wings of paper, V, scissors, Stein, the stone, in the game of morra you lose yourself.

One replies: O, open mouth, why do I take three leaps on the water, out of the game of love—where do I plunge? (Lacan 1987: 122)

[Lol V. Stein: ailes de papier, V ciseaux, Stein, la pierre, au jeu de la mourre tu te perds.

On répond: O, bouche ouverte, que veux-je à faire trois bonds sur l'eau, hors-jeu de l'amour, où plongé-je ?] (Lacan 1985: 7)

In this paragraph, Lacan clearly seems to be associating "Lol V. Stein" with the game of rock-paper-scissors, reading the name almost like Freud would read a dream: as a small picture puzzle. Initially he picks out the two L's in the "*Lol*," suggesting that the two letters could be seen as two wafer-thin, or "paper-thin," wings, flapping around an *o*—like outstretched hands rounding up the rock in the game of rock-paper-scissors. In other words, the *l*'s on the page are associated with the *l*'s of the palm, the palm miming both the L's written on the paper and the "paper-L's" of the hand, "*ailes de papier*" (homophonic with L's de papier[2]).[3] In a similar way, he reads the initial letter *V* (in Lol V. Stein) as a typographical illustration of the hand's V sign miming the scissors. The surname "Stein" he reads in German meaning "Stone" associated with the clenched fist, the "rock."

At the end of the sentence a similar hand-signing game is evoked, namely the game *morra*: "in the game of morra, you lose yourself [*au jeu de la mourre tu te perds*]." What gets lost in my translation is, of course, the homophony between the "la mourre" and "l'amour": Not only in the game of morra (*la mourre*) but also in the game of love (*l'amour*), you run a great risk of losing—losing your way or losing your money, or maybe even losing yourself ("tu te perds" holds all these connotations). Lacan might also hear the fatal destiny of the *morra*-player augured in the homography of *morra* and "mourra" (a future form of "mourir," i.e., "to die"). In the game of *morra* the object is to guess whether the sum of the fingers shown will be odd or even: If you guess wrong, or the opponent guesses right, you lose, and the game is over.

In the game of rock-paper-scissors the risks are equally high: Ultimately, one of the players will be crushed by the rock, cut to pieces by the scissors, or enveloped by the paper. Again, a similar principle could be said to apply in love—at least with Marguerite Duras. In almost all her "love stories" one of the characters will ultimately get his heart broken, go to pieces, or end up in the palm of the other's hand.

In *Le ravissement de Lol V. Stein*, during the ball, the only thing that Lol picks up from the couple's conversation are the words "... that she might die [... *peut-être qu'elle va mourir*]," suggesting that their adultery might kill her. The remark turns out to be prophetic, yet not so much for Lol V. Stein as for Michael Richardson. After the ball, he sells all his properties and follows the Ambassador's wife to Calcutta only to learn that she doesn't have any intentions of leaving her husband. That he might actually end up dying by his own hand is suggested by Duras in other contexts.

Love can also be something of a "guessing game," so we are reminded by the translation of "jeu de la mourre" as "love's guessing game" in the quote above. Being in love, one can become almost obsessed with the thought of guessing the other's thoughts: What is she thinking of? What does she think that *I* think? What would be a clever move in this situation? What can I expect? What does *she* expect from me? What does she want?—questions that can all be heard as paraphrases of Jacques Hold's *Che vuoi*-questions.

The subject in love is a neurotic subject: someone who doesn't really know how to play the game of love. He is sidelined—"out of the game," "hors-jeu de l'amour" as Lacan put it in the quote above. Word for word "hors-jeu" means "outside-game." In football lingo, though, it means "off side." The metaphor draws an image of the subject in love as an overzealous lover, always one jump ahead of the other, *acting out* in the Lacanian sense of the term. (The dialectic counterpart to this type of "love player" would of course be the obsessional type circling around the thing, in every possible way delaying the game. "Mora" spelt with one *r* actually means "delay.")

The subject in love has a terrible timing: he's either too early or too late; he is *hors-jeu*, which can also be heard as (a pun on) *hors-je*, literally, "outside-I," a neologism that comes close to the French expression *hors de soi*, that is, "beside oneself," or maybe even "out of one's mind," in other words: *ravi*, ravished.

The Other *jouissance*

In his twentieth seminar, Lacan connects love with female *jouissance*. One often associates this *jouissance* with some kind of mystical/hysterical *ravissement* that words fail to express. Like the one we see on the front cover of *Seminar XX* in the figure of Saint Teresa sculpted in marble by Bernini. Lacan does not doubt that Saint Teresa's religious ecstasy is of a sexual kind: "you need but go to Rome and see the statue of Bernini to immediately understand that she's coming [*qu'elle jouit*]. There's no doubt about it" (Lacan: 76). Luce Irigaray comments:

> In Rome? So far away? To look? At a statue? Of a saint? Sculpted by a man? What pleasure are we talking about? Whose pleasure? (Irigaray 1985: 91)

To Irigaray, Lacan does not speak of woman's pleasure, but of man's: "Where the pleasure of [*Teresa*] is concerned, her own writings are perhaps more telling" (Irigaray 1985).

While I think Irigaray's feminist objections to Lacan's images of feminine *jouissance* are appropriate, I think one should, however, be careful to equate these *images/examples* of feminine *jouissance* with his *definitions* of female *jouissance*. If we take Lacan literally, feminine *jouissance* is defined by being something that cannot be defined or can only be defined by formal intuitionistic definitions that would not be accepted in classical logic: It is an *other* jouissance than the phallic one, it is a *supplement* to the phallic one, but Lacan cannot say what it actually is, neither can women.[4]

Thus Saint Teresa as an image of the other, feminine *jouissance* is something like a contradiction in terms: Her ecstatic face is to be found everywhere in our (patriarchal) symbolic order, for instance in (Jacques Hold's images of) Lol V. Stein's *ravissement*. Perhaps Lacan's pointing to Bernini's Teresa is more ironic than Irigaray presumes. Perhaps Lacan is actually making fun of the masculine fantasy of woman's *jouissance*. At all times "[men] have been begging [women], begging them on their hands and knees—to try to tell us [about their *jouissance*], not a word! We've never been able to get anything out of them" (Lacan 1998: 75).

Lola V~~alerie~~ Stein

One may wonder why Duras' novel is not at all mentioned in *Encore*, as there are so many parallels between Jacques Hold's image of (the *ravissement* of) Lol V. Stein and Jacques Lacan's image of (the *jouissance* of) woman. Lying in the rye field with flickering eyelids and some kind of connection to God, Lol seems to be a parody of a masculine fantasy of feminine ravishment; a repetition of good old Bernini's ecstatic Teresa. With her "extremely vague identity" (Duras 1986: 32), her empty eyes (Duras 1986: 155; 173), and lack of voice (Duras 1986: 30), Lol contains all the partial objects, *les petits objets a*, that Lacan adds to Freud's more prosaic list of desirable objects: nothingness, gaze, voice.

Thus she is described by her husband:

> He liked her. She aroused in him his special penchant for young girls, girls not completely grown into adults, for pensive, impertinent, inarticulate young girls [*sans voix*]. (Duras 1986: 19–20)
>
> ...
>
> He loved this woman, this Lola Valerie Stein, this calm presence by his side, this sleeping beauty who never offered a word of complaint, this upright sleeping beauty, this constant self-effacement which kept him moving back and forth between the forgetfulness and the rediscovery of her blondness, of this silken body which no awakening would ever change, of this constant silent price of something different which he called her gentleness, the gentleness of his wife. (Duras 1986: 23–24)

Lol is a blank screen on which men can project their fantasies. On the other hand, one can argue that there is something subversive about Lol's "extremely vague identity." Her refusal to be predicated makes of her a perfect example of woman as Lacan defines her, or rather refrains from defining her. Lacan insists that "nothing can be said about woman" (Lacan 1998: 75), and Duras insists that nothing meaningful can be said about Lol V. Stein: "She doesn't make sense" (Quoted in Porte 1977: 101). Tatiana's statement about Lol as "strangely incomplete" (Duras 1986: 71) is echoed by Lacan's statement about woman as not-all, *pas-tout*. Woman is not completely enrolled in the conventional (phallic) economics of desire, and Lol is not-all either (or, indeed, *as well*). Anyway, that is what Tatiana says: "She says that in school—and she wasn't the only person to think so—there was already something lacking in Lol, something which kept her from being, in Tatiana's words, 'there [*là*]'" (Duras 1986: 2–3).

> [P]art of her seemed always to be evading you, and the present moment. Going where? Into some adolescent dream world? No, Tatiana answers, no, it seemed as though she were going nowhere, yes, that's it, nowhere. Was it her heart that wasn't there? Tatiana apparently inclines toward the opinion that it was perhaps, indeed, Lol [V.] Stein's heart which wasn't—as she says—there [*là*]. (Duras 1986: 3)

That Lol is not completely… there, not completely… *là* is taken to the "letter" after the ball when Lola insists to be called just Lol, so that the "la" of her name is cut off. Also she cuts down her middle name Valérie to "V" and insists on her family name *Stein*: "Lol V. Stein, this was how she referred to herself" (Duras 1976: 13). From a Lacanian perspective, it is tempting to read the new name as an expression of the symbolic castration to which Lol is subjected by the separation from her fiancé. The "V" could be seen as a symbol of the separating function of castration, if we regard it, in the manner of concretism, as a pair of scissors, which is what Lacan does when associating Lol V. Stein with stone-*scissors*-paper. Lol's insistence on her family name, Stein, is also an affirmation of the symbolic castration if we read it as an insistence on the father's name, *le nom* (non) *du père*.

When Lol, after the ball, cuts off the last syllables of her first names and insists on her patronymic, it can thus be read as an expression of her acceptance of symbolic castration, including sexuation. In this operation, though, the feminine markers disappear from her names: Lola loses its feminine suffix *a*, and "Valérie" is cut down to the neutral "V." One may read the abbreviations and their reduction of sexual difference as literal resistance to the sexuation of symbolic castration. Or one may read them as expressions that there is something feminine about Lol V. Stein that cannot be contained by the symbolic order and its masculine logic of desire, cf. Lacan: "Woman is not-whole—there is always something in her that escapes discourse" (Lacan 1998: 33).

According to Lacan, "Woman does not exist"—*La* femme does not exist: "*La* cannot be said *(se dire)*. Nothing can be said of woman" (Lacan 1998: 33). The omission of the feminine *a* in "Lol*a*" can be read in line with the barred feminine article in "La femme." The last syllable in Lol's name is no longer "la," Lo*la*. Neither "Lol" nor "La femme" is completely… *là*. But even if Woman is not *là*, she has a relation with S($\cancel{A}$), which is the matheme for the lack of the big Other (Lacan 1998: 81), that is, the point where the symbolic (patriarchal) order is exceeded, by "the Real."

It should have been a hole-word

In a somewhat cryptic paragraph, Lacan writes that the double ravishment of Lol V. Stein, her own ravishment as well as the rapture she arouses in the narrator, is "knotted together in a cipher that is revealed in a name skillfully crafted in the contour of writing: Lol V. Stein" (7). Compared with Tatiana's observation that part of Lol always seemed to be evading you and the present moment, being nowhere, exactly nowhere, then one could read this "part of Lol" literally: as the middle part of "Lol," that is, the letter o, which—read as a 0, a zero—reveals the contours of a cipher, perhaps the cipher that Lacan is hinting at. Remember that *chiffre* is the term used for "digit" in French. Often, Lacan would use just this digit, the number zero, as a metaphor for *a*, his notion for this "something" (or "nothing") in the other that is more than the other.

Like the 0 in a series of numbers, the *a* in lacanian terminology refers to an absence, or a negativity, but a constitutive one, namely the one around which desire pulsates. We only desire what we don't have. So, object *a* is both something real and something imaginary: a real lack and an imaginary, fantasmatic covering up of this lack. In the register of the Real, object *a* can be compared with the hole, or the gap, in the Other (*l'Autre*, hence the matheme Ⱥ). In the novel this gap is felt as a dis-synchronization between Lol's body and her voice. When Lacan says "O, open mouth," we should perhaps regard "open mouth" as an apposition defining "O." "One replies: *O, open mouth*" Perhaps the reply "O" is not an outspoken "O!," but a graphic illustration of an open mouth, a mute scream like the one that cuts into our eyes when we are in front of Edward Munch's *The Scream*, Caravaggio's *Medusa*, or Francis Bacon's *Pope Innocent X*.[5] The real voice, or the voice of the Real, is a mute scream stuck in the throat (Žižek 1997: 52; Dolar: 156–59). To this silent scream, this voice zero, corresponds Lol's gaze described as sad and zero—*triste et nul* (Duras 1976: 173)—that gaze, which is elsewhere in the novel called a "non-gaze." While there is definitely something quite creepy about Lol's appearance—her ghostlike traits, her dead eyes, and her lack of voice—this is also what makes her so desirable. As Mladen Dolar has once put it apropos the famous automaton Olimpia (from Hoffmann's tale *The Sandman*): "A blank screen, empty eyes, and an 'Oh!': it is enough to drive anybody crazy with love" (Dolar 1991: 9).

Lol's silent voice and non-gaze, her "constant self-effacement," add to her attractiveness: "they vied for her affection at school—although she slipped through their fingers like water [*eau*]—because the little they managed to retain was well worth the effort" (Duras 1986: 2). This water, this "eau," to which Lol is compared, gives us yet another "o" besides the one in the middle of her name, as "eau" and "o" are pronounced the same way in French. O is the number 0, the open mouth of the silent scream, and "eau," water.

Jacques Lacan, not unlike Jacques Hold, tries to get "hold" on Lol V. Stein by fixing her name on paper: Literally she is an "o"—an absence, a hole, a zero—surrounded by two L's, two *ailes de papier*, wings of paper. To capture Lol in writing, though, turns out to be as impossible as catching water with your hands. Something is lost: "Lol is not to be understood, she is not to be saved from ravishment," Lacan emphasizes (1985: 11).

Lol V. Stein is like a slippery skipping stone, a "skipping *Stein*," that slips out of one's hand and makes "three leaps on the water," "trois bond sur l'eau [o]"—just like the letter *o* skips across the line of Lacan's text:

> On répond: O, bouche ouverte, que veux-je à faire trois bonds sur l'eau, hors-jeu de l'amour, où plongé-je? (1985)
> [One replies: O, open mouth, why do I take three leaps on the water, out of the game of love—where do I plunge?] (Lacan 1987: 122)

Lol V. Stein gets us in to deep water, Lacan suggests. To chase her is to chase a fata morgana: "[when] speeding up our steps [*à presser nos pas*] behind Lol's steps [*sur les pas de Lol*], which resonate through the novel—we hear them behind us without having run into anyone" (Lacan 1985: 7). This is reminiscent of the situation in Zenon's famous paradox. The swift-footed Achilles can never catch up with the tortoise, which has been given a head start. While Achilles runs to catch up, the tortoise gains another lead, which he will then have to cover, and so on. Theoretically he gets infinitely close to the tortoise without ever overtaking it. In Lacan's version Achilles has no problems in overtaking (*dépasser*) the tortoise. What he cannot do is to join her (*la rejoindre*).[6] I intentionally translate "la" by "her" and not "it," because according to Lacan, the tortoise might as well be called Briseïs, the name of the woman Achilles took as his sex slave during the looting of Troy, without ever "reaching" her.

> When Achilles has taken his step, gotten it on with Briseis, the latter, like the tortoise, has advanced a bit, because she is "not whole," not wholly his. Some remains. And Achilles must take a second step, and so on and so forth. (Lacan 1998: 8)

To sum up: There is something about the feminine subject (whether Briseïs or Lol or Saint Teresa) that you cannot completely grasp: "there is always something in her [*chez elle*] that escapes discourse" (Lacan 1998: 33). There is (quite literally) something in "Lol" that escapes Jacques Hold's narrative: a central absence, marked by the letter *o*, and an ineffable femininity, the cut-off feminine suffix *a* that would destabilize the symmetry of the palindrome "Lol," reminding us that something escapes speech, "something" that to Lacan has to do with the *jouissance* or *ravissement* of woman.

Notes

1. Translated into Lacan's mathemes, one might say that Lol simply seems to have forgotten the formula for the functioning of desire: $ <> a.
2. Seen from the side, the thumb and the forefinger could be said to form a capital L;
   Seen from above, or from underneath, the hand makes a lower case l, a line in the air.
3. In French "ailes" [ɛl] is pronounced like L [ɛl], also in plural.
4. Since the scope of this article doesn't allow me to develop further on the issue, I can only refer to the vast number of theoretical interpretations of the logic behind the female sexuation formulas starting with Joan Copjec's classic essay "Sex and the Euthanasia of Reason" from 1994. For a more specific discussion of the prevailing critique of Lacan's concept of and other "female" jouissance, see Alenka Zupančič 2000.
5. Michel Foucault compares Duras' characters to the figures that Bacon painted: distorted, morcellated bodies, often with a kind of vacuum (like an open mouth) in their middle (Foucault 1994: 765).
6. "A number has a limit and it is to that extent that it is infinite. It is quite clear that Achilles can only pass the tortoise—he cannot catch up with it. He only catches up with it at infinity (*infinitude*)" (Lacan: 1998: 13; eng. 13).

References

Copjec, J. (1994), "Sex and the Euthanasia of Reason," in trans. J. Copjec, *Read My Desire: Lacan against Historicists*, 201–36, Cambridge, Massachusetts: MIT press.

Dolar, M. (1991), "I Shall Be with You on Your Wedding-Night: Lacan and the Uncanny," *October*, 58: 5–23.

Duras, M. (1976 [1964]), *Le ravissement de Lol V. Stein*, Paris: Éditions Gallimard.

Duras, M. (1986), *The Ravishing of Lol Stein*, trans. Richard Seaver, kindle edition, New York: Pantheon Books.

Duras, M. (1993), *Écrire*. Paris: Éditions Gallimard.
Fink, B. (2004), *Lacan to the Letter: Reading Écrits Closely*, Minneapolis: University of Minnesota Press.
Foucault, M. (1994), *Dits et écrits II*, Paris: Éditions Gallimard.
Freud, S. (1948 [1926]), "Zur Frage der Laienanalyse. Unterredungen mit einem Unparteiischen," in *GW Band 14*, Wien: Imago.
Irigaray, L. (1985 [1977]), *This Sex Which Is Not One*, trans. Catherine Porter, Ithaca: Cornell University Press.
Lacan, J. (1985 [1965]), "Hommage fait à Marguerite Duras, du ravissement de Lol V. Stein," *Ornicar? revue du Champ freudien*, 34: 7–13.
Lacan, J. (2001 [1971]), "Lituraterre," in *Autre écrits*, 11–20, Paris: Éditions du Seuil.
Lacan, J. (1987), "Homage to Marguerite Duras. On *Le ravissement de Lol V. Stein*," in *Duras by Duras*, trans. Peter Connor, 122–9, San Francisco: City Light Books.
Lacan, J. (1998), *On Feminine Sexuality. The Limits of Love and Knowledge. Book XX: Encore 1972–1973*, trans. Bruce Fink, New York: W. W. Norton.
Lacan, J. (2006a), "The Function and Field of Speech and Language in Psychoanalysis," in *Écrits*, trans. Bruce Fink, 197–268, New York and London: W. W. Norton.
Lacan, J. (2006b), "The Situation of Psychoanalysis and the Training of Psychoanalysts in 1956," in *Écrits*, trans. Bruce Fink, 384–407, New York and London: W. W. Norton.
Porte, M. (1977), *Les lieux de Marguerite Duras*. Paris: Les Éditions de Minuit.
Reik, T. (1998 [1948]), *Listening with the Third Ear—The Inner Experience of a Psychoanalyst*, New York: Farrar, Strauss and Giroux.
Žižek, S. (1997), *The Plague of Fantasies*, London and New York: Verso.
Zupančič, A. (2000), "The Case of the Perforated Sheet," in *Sexuation: SIC 3*, 282–96, Durham and London: Duke University Press.

2

Lacan and the Archeology of the Subject

Carin Franzén

Contemporary subjectivity has been claimed to be in crisis, for good or for bad, and in current post-humanist theory, a suggestion to solving this crisis has been to "bracket the question of the human," to use Jane Bennett's phrase in her book *Vibrant Matter* (2010: ix). Furthermore, Bennett argues that it is time to let go of the question "where subjectivity begins and ends" because it is "too often bound up with fantasies of a human uniqueness in the eyes of God, of escape from materiality, or of mastery of nature" (2010: ix). A starting point for this kind of "new materialism" in human and social sciences was Bruno Latour's seminal work *We Have Never Been Modern* and his denouncement of the "semiotic turns" (1993: 63). The problem with the primacy given to the signifier according to Latour is that it leaves "the rest of the world with nothing but simple mute forces" (1993: 138).

At any rate, there is an ongoing discussion regarding the status of the modern subject, which reflects social and cultural changes and turns history into an interesting arena for theoretical appropriations, to which both Michel Foucault and Jacques Lacan have offered valuable perspectives. In this chapter, I will try to revisit Lacan and Foucault in order to better assess the specific materiality of the subject in Lacanian psychoanalysis that differs from both naturalistic materialism and post-human new materialism. Furthermore, by allusion to Foucault I will use the term "archeology" to highlight the condition of the subject as subjected—both to the signifier and to the other—that a present liberal and neoliberal humanism tends to hide by a naturalization of modern subjectivity in terms of self-realization and individual autonomy. This neoliberal subjectivation has consequences not only for the contemporary subject. As sociologists Luc Boltanski and Eve Chiapello have shown in *The New Spirit of Capitalism* (2007: xliii), there is also a "waning of critique" vis-à-vis an engulfing business culture that seems to absorb every resistance by new and subtle methods of exploitation, such as project-based forms of organization demanding flexibility and adaptability at any cost.

Historical conditions

A first approach to an understanding of the historical dimension in Lacan's thinking is given by Foucault as he, in his "archaeology of the human sciences" during the high days of structuralism, describes psychoanalysis along with Claude Lévi-Strauss' ethnology as dissolving what is taken to be granted as human in the humanities by uncovering the subject's unconscious condition (Foucault 1989: 413). This break with a certain humanist tradition anchored in Descartes' *cogito ergo sum* could be said to have started with Freud's archeological excavation of the idea of human sovereignty, which he talked about in terms of offended narcissism (Freud 1955: 139). Lacan continues along this path when he in *Seminar XI* says of Freud's method, that if it is Cartesian, it is so by the displacement of the certainty of the *cogito* to the field of the unconscious: "It is because Freud declares the certainty of the unconscious that the progress by which he changed the world for us was made" (Lacan 1977: 36). This break also has consequences for the history of subjectivity. In fact, it reveals that we have never been modern or at least that Freud by his disclosure of the unconscious opened a new door in the wall of modernity, which changed our approach to history (the subject's history as well as the history of the subject).

Freud's references to history, especially ancient myths and literature, were often used to lay bare universal structures determining human subjectivity, such as the Oedipus complex. To be sure, the concept of the symbolic in Lacan's work can be said to have the same universal function, but it also attaches the subject to a specific materiality that he describes as "the play of signifier" (Lacan 2006: 392) that produces different cultural techniques throughout history. While Foucault sees these techniques in Western subjectivity as part of Christianity and its obligation to confess and to put oneself into discourse (Foucault 2014), Lacan's turn to history highlights a constitutive impediment at the core of this obligation that is due to the "heteronomy of the symbolic" and its effect on the subject of the unconscious. "The fact that the symbolic is located outside of man is the very notion of the unconscious" (Lacan 2006: 392).

Lacan's many references to historical texts—ancient philosophers, medieval theologians and poets, early modern moralists (the list goes on)—are thus parallel to but also deviate from Foucault's project of writing a history of Western subjectivity. The major difference is that while Foucault is interested in "techniques by which the individual is led, either by himself, or with the help or under the direction of another, to transform himself and modify his relation to himself" (Foucault 2014: 345), Lacan focuses on different ways of dealing with a structural limit that conditions the subject throughout history.

When a medievalist such as Sarah Kay points out that Lacan "sees modern subjectivity as deriving from the erotic configurations of medieval courtly love poetry" (Kay 2001: 26), it is because this specific code of behavior and regulation of the sexual relation in feudal society during the eleventh and twelfth centuries dealt with a certain impossibility of the sexual relationship (to which I will return). Kay's point is nevertheless important because it makes us see that there are different ways in which the Western subject enacts its own subjectivation. Not only by an obligation to truth such as confession, which Foucault emphasizes, but also by the specific techniques that lead to poetry and art.

Before I come back to this point, I want to underline the fact that Lacan uses historical references, for instance medieval literature, not in order to explain the specificity of medieval subjectivity, but to better analyze the formation of modern subjectivity. In this respect, Lacan's perspective is similar to Foucault's use of history, namely "to cut diagonally through contemporary reality" (Foucault 2014: xiv). From an archeological point of view, it is always an actual question that directs the re-reading of history, which in turn can sharpen the understanding of the present. The overall question for both Lacan and Foucault could therefore be: What is a subject?, or as Lacan puts it, Do we "know what the term *subject* means" (1977: 37)? And the answers that are taking shape in their works undermine in different ways "fantasies of a human uniqueness in the eyes of God, of escape from materiality, or of mastery of nature" to use Bennet's words (2010: ix).

A point of departure for Foucault is that Western subjectivity is grounded in "the relationship of self to self, the exercise of self on self, and the truth that the individual may discover deep within himself" (Foucault 2014: 128). Subjectivity in this sense is inseparable from the organization of power in Western society and Foucault goes back to early Christianity to trace its genealogy. He also reminds us that Descartes' affirmation *cogito ergo sum* was based on the specific Christian self-technology that reveals itself in the famous episode of the evil genius in the philosopher's second meditation to which Foucault refers as follows: "[T]he idea that there is something in me that can always deceive me and that has such power that I can never be completely sure that it will not deceive me is the absolutely constant theme of Christian spirituality" (2014: 303). Yet, Foucault also claims that Descartes tips "the truth-subjectivity relationship in a different direction," when he, in Foucault's words, concluded: "there is in any case something that is indubitable and in which I am not deceived, which is that for me to be deceived, I must exist" (2014).

What psychoanalysis with Lacan does in turn is to anchor this certainty of Descartes' *I am* in the unconscious. This definition also makes Lacan focus on what escapes the search for the secrets of the heart and the confessional techniques developed in the Christian tradition for that purpose. In other words, Lacan uses historical references to highlight how the subject of the unconscious always already works through other discursive manifestations of subjectivity in the West. Thus, when he returns to Descartes and his philosophical affirmation of the *cogito*, he insists that "the subject of the unconscious manifests itself, that it thinks before it attains certainty" (Lacan 1977: 37). By this statement, Lacan, in the wake of Freud, undermines the Cartesian idea that human reason is what can "make ourselves as it were the masters and possessors of nature" (Descartes 2008: 51). Let us look a little more closely at some aspects of this archeology of the subject and its consequences for the way in which Lacan reads other historical texts.

Subjective aporias and ignorance

"Ai, las! tan cuidava saber/d'amor, e tan petit en sai!" ("Alas! I thought to know so much of love, and I know so little of it"), sings the Occitan troubadour Bernard de Ventadour (1999: 262), apparently sensitive to a specific knowledge of the subject of the unconscious. At any rate, the poet expresses a certainty of not knowing not unlike Socrates' famous insistence on his fundamental uncertainty in everything except love. In *Seminar VIII*, where Lacan's key text is Plato's *Symposium*, he identifies the analyst's position not only as the subject supposed to know but as that of the incarnation of the "Other's desire" (Lacan 2015: 105). The troubadour's desire leads him to the conclusion that he does not know, a position that could be used to describe the dimension of knowledge in the psychoanalytic experience of transference between analyst and analysand. But what kind of knowledge are we dealing with here? What is it to know that what you knew is "tan petit" ("so little")?

As a matter of fact, it is not skepticism that is "holding the subjective position that *one can know nothing*"—an impossible position after the emergence of the modern subject, according to Lacan (1977: 223). As a subjective position, skepticism nevertheless points to a certain formation of the subject of which psychoanalysis can give a new interpretation. As Lacan says in *Seminar XI* (1977: 222–3), the Cartesian approach to knowledge distinguishes itself from the skepticism that can be felt in Montaigne's essays and subsequently in the writings of the classical moralists during the seventeenth century. Although this position has become impossible in modernity, it can nevertheless serve as a guide to better assess the subject in crisis as a divided, alienated subject that has built its certainty on the repression of its real condition.

Lacan actually alludes to the legacy of skepticism on various occasions, and in *Écrits*, La Rochefoucauld is the one among early modern writers to whom he most often refers (Doubrovsky 1980: 204). One reason for this could be the moralist's articulation of *amour propre* (self-love), a topic widely discussed during the seventeenth century. One of the more striking features in La Rochefoucauld's maxims (first publication 1665) is the acceptance of the rather autonomous character of the passions that Descartes thought we could master by using reason correctly (Descartes 2015: 280). Much more pessimistic, La Rochefoucauld dethrones the sovereign subject in a way that anticipates Freud: "A man often believes himself leader when he is led" (La Rochefoucauld 18731, maxim 43). Or as stated in one of his most famous and, significantly, suppressed maxims about the nature of *amour-propre*:

> We can neither plumb the depths nor pierce the shades of its recesses. Therein it is hidden from the most far-seeing eyes… In the night which covers it are born the ridiculous persuasions it has of itself. (La Rochefoucauld 1871, Suppressed maxim 1)

But the non-reflective character of this passion does not preclude its cleverness, its self-preservation, which is to say that it thinks before the Cartesian *cogito* attains certainty.

> In fact, in great concerns and important matters when the violence of its desires summons all its attention, it sees, feels, hears, imagines, suspects, penetrates, divines all… in fact, caring only to exist, and providing that it may be, it will be its own enemy. (La Rochefoucauld 1871, Suppressed maxim 1)

In this maxim it is not only egocentric or egoistic interests that are revealed as motives behind a virtuous behavior or action but this fundamental passion is in itself without any other foundation than self-preservation. It escapes reason—"the most far-seeing eyes"—and one can argue that it is in the very "night which covers it" that one can see another aspect of the modern subject take form. A subject that is not master in his own house, or as Lacan puts it in *Seminar XI*, that "is 'at home' in [the] field of the unconscious" (1977: 36).

Thus, if love could be said to be an important guideline for Lacan's theory of the subject, it is because it makes manifest a certain dimension of truth through its deceiving character, and this is also crucial for the analytical experience, defined by Jean-Pierre Klotz as follows:

> Lacan emphasizes the dimension of love that lies or misleads, suggesting that this misleading belongs, as such, to the dimension of truth. Lacan develops the idea that it is impossible to encounter the dimension of truth without being misled. Love is the point of encounter, i.e., transference is the point of encounter which introduces the dimension of truth into analytic practice itself. (Klotz 1995: 92)

In addition, by his insistence on different *aporias* in the history of subjectivity, Lacan indicates a difference from other truth regimes in Western civilization— such as the one Foucault connects to Christianity as well as the one based on the Cartesian subject of certainty—a difference that I would like to highlight further by returning to the topic of courtly love and its historical vicissitudes.

Love and the dimension of truth

When Lacan points to ignorance as essential to truth in analytic experience, he sustains this claim not only by referring to Socrates. He also takes up the appropriation of courtly love during the Renaissance by Marguerite de Navarre, both in *Seminar VII* and *VIII*, but above all in a short text paying homage to Marguerite Duras. And it is clear that all these references are about certain configurations of love and desire tied to a dimension of truth.

In the text where Lacan refers to the two Marguerites, the twentieth-century writer and the Renaissance queen, he says that both, in their writing, bear witness to a certain "locus of truth" (Lacan 1987: 128). This locus determines subjectivity in a way that precedes and surpasses the form of power related to the self-technique of putting one's own truth into discourse, which Foucault sees as essential to the formation of Western subjectivity. What is this locus?

Lacan claims that these women writers' configuration of love and desire— "this strange way of loving" (Lacan 1987: 128)—articulates something that has to do with the very structure of the subject of the unconscious and its desire, and that both writers seem to have learned from the courtly love code. In *Seminar XX*, Lacan describes this cultural and literary code among the feudal aristocracy as a "highly refined way of making up for the absence of the sexual relationship, by feigning that we are the ones who erect an obstacle thereto," making it clear that the "we" to which he refers is male: "Courtly love is, for man—in relation to whom the lady is entirely, and in the most servile sense of the word, a subject— the only way to elegantly pull off the absence of the sexual relationship" (Lacan 1998: 69). In this approach, the courtly love code is regarded as a specific solution to what is taken to be a structural lack in the constitution of the subject, which the other is supposed to fulfill.

So, how is the courtly love code treated by the two Marguerites and why do they reveal a locus of truth while the male troubadours that invented the code just "pull it off" in an elegant manner? In his homage to Duras, Lacan refers to historian Lucien Febvre's assessment of courtly love as a cultural impediment to the realization of desire by what he calls a "negative ideal," that is by not satisfying it sexually. Thus, the courtly love code is a way of handling dissatisfaction, and Febvre sees in this an "ethical revolution" in Western civilization (1944: 228). Accordingly, Lacan defines the ethical function of courtly love in terms of specific techniques giving persistence to "the purposes of the pleasure principle" (Lacan 1992: 152), which postpones the imaginary wish for completion. At the same time and from a historical point of view, courtly love remains a way of loving that deviates from the demand of chastity and confession in early Christianity. If Christian vigilance oriented toward "sinful" thoughts has similarities to the instance Freud called superego, the technology of courtly love is more like an art of love that transforms desire into words and songs, but it could also be seen as an art of not giving up "on that part of yourself that you do not know," which is Alain Badiou's (2001: 47) explanation of Lacan's famous maxim from *Seminar VII*: "From an analytic point of view, the only thing one can be guilty of is having given ground relative to one's desire" (1992: 319).

At any rate, Lacan does not so much discuss the historical context of this code but its way of handling "the dimension of truth" that is the fundamental lack at the core of the subject. There is no demonic deceiver, no Satan in the subject's heart, but an imaginary relation to the other hiding that which constitutes subjectivity in the first place, the heteronomy of the signifiers, which points to the limit or lack determining the subject's desire. If the masculine position covers up this lack by creating an object—the idealized unattainable woman— for his desire, women may use this fantasy as an imaginary support for a subject position in a social order where they are usually designed as objects, but also more lucidly reveal the impossibility inherent in every dream of love as union. Thus, "this strange way of loving" points to a true way.

Subjective materiality and ethics

The fundamental heteronomy of the subject and the lack that constitutes it can be handled in different ways. Today, there is a new potential for this psychoanalytic insight to counteract the formation of the modern subject as rational, autonomous, and "possessor of the nature" to use Descartes's words. As already pointed out by Freud, there are three events that introduce a truth dimension into the "narcissistic illusion" connected to this kind of human "self-love" (Freud 1955: 139—140). First Copernicus' establishment of heliocentrism, then Darwin's break with the idea of an ontological difference between man and animal, and finally Freud's own discovery that *the ego is not master in its own house* (Freud 1955: 143). With Lacan it also becomes clear that this truth is connected to a specific materiality that he specifies as "Freudian materialism" to be distinguished from "naturalist materialism" because of its "Symbolic form" (Lacan 2006: 390).

In Lacanian psychoanalysis, the "semiotic turn" is what suspends the very formation of a subject of certainty that it is supposed to sustain. Language is the cause of the subject of the unconscious, or as he states: "The fact that the symbolic is located outside of man is the very notion of the unconscious" (Lacan 2006: 392). Thus, the Lacanian version of Aristotle's definition of man as the animal that possesses *logos* is turned inside out.

> What we must say, following Aristotle's lead, is that it is not the soul that speaks but man who speaks with his soul, on the condition that we add that he receives the language he speaks and that, in order to bear it, he sinks more into it than his soul: he sinks into it his very instincts whose ground resonates in the depths only to throw back the signifier's echo. (Lacan 2006: 392-3)

This subjection to the signifier is what makes "human uniqueness," but it is not a foundational stone for a subject who thinks that he masters himself and the rest of the world. For this specific subjective formation to come through, a repression of the very condition of the subject is necessary. Furthermore, Lacan's archeology of the subject reveals several historical instances where this condition has other articulations than the one found in Descartes or in a general belief in human sovereignty. For example, in the courtly love code that reveals an *art of the impossible*.

Coda

The aim of this very schematic reflection on an archeology of the subject was not to look for precursors to the Lacanian theory of the subject but to make its subversive side more tangible. Lacan not only describes Freud's discovery of the unconscious as a *revolutionary* event but also presents a series of examples of historical modalities of subjectivation that can highlight the particularity of this event and disclose the impossibility at the core of the subject. This impossibility clears a path for desire to not obey, for example, to not obey the obligation to speak the truth of oneself or neoliberal demands of self-realization. Thus, Lacan is not so much interpreting history as he is revealing how some of its major philosophical, religious, scientific, or poetical discourses can cut through contemporary reality, introducing a dimension of truth permitting us to consider our present time and its subject formation in a critical light.

References

Badiou, A. (2001), *Ethics. An Essay on the Understanding of Evil*, trans. P. Hallward, London: Verso.

Bennett, J. (2010), *Vibrant Matter. A Political Ecology of Things*, Durham, NC: Duke University Press.

Boltanski, L. and E. Chiapello (2007), *The New Spirit of Capitalism*, trans. Gregory Elliott, New York: Verso.

Descartes, R. (2008), *A Discourse on the Method of Correctly Conducting One's Reason and Seeking Truth in the Sciences*, trans. Ian Maclean, Oxford: Oxford University Press.

Descartes, R. (2015), *The Passions of the Soul and Other Late Philosophical Writings*, trans. M. Moriarty, Oxford: Oxford University Press.

Doubrovsky, S. (1980), "Vingt propositions sur l'amour-propre: de Lacan a La Rochefoucauld," in *Parcours critique*, 203–34, Paris: Galilée.

Febvre, L. (1944), *Autour de l'Heptaméron: Amour sacré, amour profane*, Paris: Gallimard.

Foucault, M. (1989), *The Order of Things: An Archaeology of the Human Sciences*, London: Routledge.

Foucault, M. (2014), *On the Government of the Living: Lectures at the Collège de France, 1979–1980*, ed. M. Senellart, trans. Graham Burchell, Hampshire: Palgrave Macmillan.

Freud, S. (1955), "A Difficulty in the Path of Psycho-Analysis," in *Standard Edition XII*, ed. James Strachey, London: The Hogarth Press.

Kay, S. (2001), *Courtly Contradictions: The Emergence of the Literary Object in the Twelfth Century*, Stanford: Stanford University Press.

Klotz, J. P. (1995), "The Passionate Dimension of Transference," in Reading Seminar XI: Lacan's Four Fundamental Concepts of Psychoanalysis, Albany: State University of New York Press.

La Rochefoucauld, F. de (1871) *Reflections; or, Sentences and Moral Maxims*, trans. J. W. Willis Bund and J. Hain Friswell, Simpson Low, Son, and Marston, 188, Fleet Street. Available online: https://www.gutenberg.org/files/9105/9105-h/9105-h.htm (accessed August 26, 2018).

Lacan, J. (1977), *The Seminar XI: The Four Fundamental Concepts of Psycho-Analysis*, trans. A. Sheridan, London: Penguin.

Lacan, J. (1987), "Homage to Marguerite Duras, on 'Le ravissement de Lol V. Stein,'" in *Marguerite Duras*, trans. Peter Connor, 122–9, San Francisco: City Light Books.

Lacan, J. (1992), *The Seminar VII: The Ethics of Psychoanalysis*, trans. Dennis Porter, London: Routledge.

Lacan, J. (1998), *The Seminar XX: Encore*, trans. B. Fink, New York: W. W. Norton.

Lacan, J. (2006), *Écrits*, trans. B. Fink, New York: W. W. Norton.

Lacan, J. (2015), *The Seminar VIII: Transference*, trans. B. Fink, Cambridge: Polity.

Latour, B. (1993) *We Have Never Been Modern*, trans. Catherine Porter, Cambridge, MA.: Harvard University Press.

Ventadour, B. de (1999), *Chansons d'amour: A Bilingual Edition of the Love Songs of Bernart de Ventadorn in Occitan and English*, trans. Ronnie Apter, Lewiston: E. Mellen Press.

3

The Signifiers of *Cherry Ripe*: On the Repetition of an Art Historical Motif

Jakob Rosendal

For more than two centuries, the art historical motif known as "girl in a mobcap" has been endlessly reproduced. The two perhaps best-known instances are Joshua Reynolds' *Penelope Boothby* from 1788, which is central to the onset of the motif in the 1780s, and John Everett Millais' *Cherry Ripe* from 1879, which was commissioned to be yet another recurrence of Reynolds' Boothby-portrait (Figures 15.1–15.2).[1] The great popularity of the motif, strengthened by different periods of Romantic or Victorian nostalgia and the development of mass reproduction, has resulted in it being reproduced again and again in thousands and hundred thousands of copies (Warner 2009; Bradley 1991)—and not just as poster reproductions but on a great variety of commodities such as postcards, playing cards, puzzles, tin cans for soap and biscuits, decorative plates and figurines.

Why such an abundance of reproductions when it comes to this image of a little girl? Something more than plain popularity, commercial success, print-technological progress, and periodic nostalgia seems to be involved in the motif's century-long recurrence, something that has to do with *repetition* (rather than reproduction) and *the signifier* (rather than the motif as a sign of a specific type of girl). The argument of this text hinges on seeing the repetition of images as constituting a cultural chain of signifiers within which a symptomatic breakdown or gap emerges. A gap that is indicative of a certain unconscious traumatic point, or what we could call the real of the girl. Focusing on *Cherry Ripe*, this text will first deal with the gaps that can be detected by focusing on its reception history before turning to Millais' painting in order to argue for a Millaisian sensibility for the real of the girl.

Symptomatic reception: Displacing *Cherry Ripe*

Something is amiss about the reception of *Cherry Ripe*. However, the following is not an attempt to present a thorough critical analysis of that reception history, but will simply sketch out the ways in which the reception symptomatically seems to stumble over the repetitive imagery that constitutes the visual cultural phenomenon that is *Cherry Ripe*.[2]

In most of the literature that deals with *Cherry Ripe*, it is reproductions of Millais' painting that are considered (so that what we see as readers of this literature are reproductions of reproductions). Strangely, it is never the first reproduction, the poster supplement from the 1880 Christmas Number of *The Graphic* (Figure 15.3), which is reproduced in this literature, but rather what appears to be the poster reproduction from another Christmas publication, the *Pears' Annual* from 1897 (Figure 15.4). To the best of my knowledge, this is the first time any work on Millais has ever brought an image of the poster reproduction from *The Graphic*'s 1880 Christmas number (Figure 15.3). A couple of texts acknowledge that they are reproducing the print from the 1897 *Pears' Annual* (Pointon 1993; Warner 2009), while most write, although that is not the case, as if they were dealing with the initial reproduction from *The Graphic* (Bradley 1991; Higonnet 1998; Mavor 1996; Reis 1992). Furthermore, these reproductions are all cropped in different ways. In most cases the white frame and text—a commercial paratext with information about the original, the seller, and the price—around the image have been left out (Bradley 1991; Higonnet 1998; Mavor 1996; Warner 2009), but in one case a large portion of the image itself has been deleted (Reis 1992).

We thus have here the first potentially symptomatic gaps in the reception of *Cherry Ripe* in the form of several displacements (the often unacknowledged shifts of focus from one reproduction to another) and a removal of part of the image or at least its commercial, textual frame. The result of these displacements is that the understanding of *Cherry Ripe* as one specific reproduction has come to dominate and thus cover over any other possible readings that other versions of *Cherry Ripe* might entail: The repetitive phenomenon of *Cherry Ripe* is understood through a single instance (the 1897 print) rather than the range of *Cherry Ripe*s. The reception of *Cherry Ripe* is thus based on cropped versions of a reproduction printed seventeen years after it first appeared in print in *The Graphic*—a reproduction that displays remarkable and important differences from the painting of 1879 by Millais and its first reproduction."

Considering the reception history of *Cherry Ripe*, what is even more striking—especially in the light of the long-standing popularity of the "girl in a mobcap"-motif and the art historical attention devoted to this motif and the work of Millais—is the fact that, surprisingly, there exists next to no art historical reception of Millais' original painting and certainly no detailed analysis of it. In the painting's reception history, as far as I have been able to map it, only a few texts actually bring a photographic reproduction of it and then only to mention it in passing (Funnell 1999; Gallati 2004; Greenberg 2015; Millais 1979; Polhemus 1994). Unfortunately, these texts all bypass the opportunity to engage with the painting and merely reiterate prior readings.

Millais'—that is Geoffroy Millais' (the great-grandson of John Everett Millais)—and Funnell's reproductions of the painting are accompanied by texts that just seek to assert a narrative of Millais' success and popularity by alluding to *The Graphic*'s 500,000 or 600,000 copies and its Empire-wide dissemination (Funnell 1999: 22–4; Millais 1979: 68). Polhemus, Gallati, and Greenberg all, to different degrees, affirm Reis' earlier sexual reading of *Cherry Ripe*, which runs counter to the predominant reading of *Cherry Ripe* as an image of asexual innocence, but then quickly moves on to other images. In Greenberg's case she valuably goes on to argue against a critique of post-Freudian anachronism leveled at the sexual reading and for the possibility of reading sexuality in images of children from the Victorian era (Greenberg 2015: 130–1). Polhemus and Gallati strangely end up returning *Cherry Ripe* to the status of a simplistic innocence, after which they pursue their respective analyses of Millais' earlier painting *The Woodsman's Daughter* (1851) and of John Singer Sergeant's child-paintings, as they deem those works more interesting (less sentimental and more profound) (Polhemus 1994: 433–50; Gallati 2004: 23–5).

The reception history of *Cherry Ripe* thus presents us with another, more important potentially symptomatic gap constituted by the complete avoidance or forgetting of Millais's original painting. A gap that occurs either by not addressing and not reproducing it or, when it is reproduced, by presenting the painting simply alongside a biographical narrative or by agreeing with previous readings of *Cherry Ripe* and moving on to other images, that is, by considering it to be less significant than other images and implicitly somehow already sufficiently analyzed. In all cases, what occurs is a missed encounter with the painting, which appears to be based on a kind of reluctance to look.

Finally, there also appears to be something symptomatic about the reception of *Cherry Ripe* at the level of content. As indicated above, the readings of

Polhemus and Gallati display a hesitancy with regard to any sexual reading and ultimately cast *Cherry Ripe* as an image of asexual innocence. In other words, the authors appear *ambivalent* about the image, but end up preferring an asexual interpretation. When it comes to the reception history of *Cherry Ripe* more broadly, this ambivalence appears as an outright *contradiction* between a sexual reading and a more predominant asexual reading.

This predominant reading casts *Cherry Ripe* as an image of "the quintessential English little girl" representing "timeless purity" (Bradley 1991: 192) and as a prolonging of the "romantic child" as a "socially, sexually, and psychically innocent" child (Higonnet 1998: 24). In both cases no image of *Cherry Ripe* is analyzed *as image*, but *Cherry Ripe* is precisely rather simply placed in the role of asexual innocence. Both in Bradley and Higonnet as well as in most other cases this asexual reading is supported by some version of the judgment that *Cherry Ripe* is "emphatically Reynoldsian" (Warner 2009: 230), thus making of it a direct heir to the work of Joshua Reynolds as the most prominent painter of romantic childhood. This judgment finds support in the fact that Millais' painting was commissioned as a new version of Joshua Reynolds' *Penelope Boothby* (1788). However, any comparison between the two paintings should quickly dispel such a reading of a straightforward heritage. What we encounter here is thus yet another displacement—this time from Millais' *Cherry Ripe* to Reynolds' *Penelope Boothby*—that also causes the reception history to loose sight of Millais's painting.

A critique of Bradley's asexual reading initiates the opposed sexual reading, which sees *Cherry Ripe* as an image of "erotic display and sexual aggressiveness" and even one with a "pronounced pedophilic appeal" (Reis 1992: 201). In this exchange with Bradley, Reis is the first to really engage analytically with a *Cherry Ripe* image as image, but she claims to be analyzing the print from *The Graphic* while reproducing a cropped version of the 1897 poster from *Pears' Annual*, and unfortunately she does not consider the painting of *Cherry Ripe*. Here, the problem is not only how the displacement has caused her to lose sight of *Cherry Ripe* but also how she misses an opportunity for a more nuanced analysis of the sexual content as she too quickly jumps from a sexual reading to one of pedophilia. It could be argued that she effectively ends up conjuring the figure of the pedophile as a fetish, which allows her to disavow the sexuality of the pictured girl.

All of these potential symptoms—the displacements and cropping, and the ambivalent and contradictory readings—seem to reveal that there is something unsettled about the reception of *Cherry Ripe*. This emerges most importantly as certain noticeable gaps: the absence of the 1880 poster print from *The Graphic* and the absence of Millais' painting or the nonengagement with it the few times it has been photographically reproduced in the literature on *Cherry Ripe*. In Lacan's words from *Seminar XI* on Freud's discovery, "[w]hat occurs, what is *produced*" in such gaps "is presented as the *discovery*" of the unconscious (Lacan 1998: 25). What now remains to be done is the work of recovering the painting *Cherry Ripe* as a potential discovery of the unconscious of Anglo-American visual culture.

The real of the girl: Recovering *Cherry Ripe*

Even though much has been said about the cultural phenomenon that is *Cherry Ripe*, its reception history has effectively somehow still missed Millais' painting. We have in a certain sense yet to look at this painting—and even more so to start analyzing and interpreting it. As of today, Millais' painting is, however, practically inaccessible: Sotheby's last auctioned it off in July 2004, and the private owner has "asked not to be contacted" (from personal communication with Sotheby's). In trying to deal with an image as indicative of a cultural unconscious, this is a somewhat ironic situation considering the fundamental inaccessibility of the unconscious, the way it is "always ready to steal away," as Lacan puts it (1998: 25). Even though we are stuck at the level of reproductions, the available photographic reproductions are certainly good enough to begin looking and begin the work of recovery.[3]

Let us start with the expression of the girl: Her head is slightly tilted forward and her eyes turned upward; this makes her fringe almost cover her eyebrows, thus giving her more of a closed and stern facial expression. One that is not altered by her mouth, which remains in a neutral, relaxed state. At the same time her gaze is directed at the viewer, as it runs in a forceful straight line from and perpendicular to the surface of the painting. Even though the severity of the girl's gaze and the strength of its perceptual line give the girl an air of assertiveness, there is simultaneously a timidity to the lowered head and an uncertainty to her eyes. She thus directs her uncertainty in an assertive manner toward the viewer, thereby raising a "*Che vuoi?*" question, a "What do you want?" at the other in front of the painting (Lacan 2007: 689–91).

This forceful yet tentative and questioning confrontation with the spectator is emphasized by two other formal means. First, the elongated shape of the canvas allows the surroundings of the girl to inscribe her in a large dark oval with a blurry outline. This shape is then repeated in her body, the arms together with the hair, and again in her hands. The result is a series of embedded ovals, slightly displaced in relation to each other, that grant the image a kind of telescopic effect. This makes the eyes of the viewer jump in and out of the image by moving from oval to oval, either zooming in on the girl or being pushed outward away from the girl. The two bright spots of color that make up the thumbs of the girl underscore this telescopic push-pull effect. Isolated against the dark black fabric of her fingerless mittens, the brightness of these spots both attract the eye and shoot out another forceful perceptual line, perpendicular to the surface and thus akin to that of the gaze of the girl. Thus, both the ovals and the color spots of the thumbs work to emphasize a tensional confrontation with the viewer; they both exert a pull into and push out of the picture, thereby emphasizing the tension resulting from the questioning of the other in front of the image.

At the same time the bodily presence and the sexuality of the girl is clearly an important aspect of the painting and its way of relating to the viewer. The hands of the girl are pressed rather deeply in between her legs, as we can see from the dark shadow in the fabric of the dress to the right of her hands. They are also placed right in front of the crotch area and folded in a decidedly vaginal shape with a black line stretching vertically across it. Furthermore, the visible fingers are kept in much darker reddish tones than the rest of the visible skin of the girl, indicating an increased blood circulation and making this part of her body appear fleshier. As such and due to the placement and shape of the hands, their redness becomes interpretable as a physiological sign of sexual arousal.

The way the hands are pressed in between the legs of the girl also stretches the fabric of the dress tightly around the left leg, emphasizing the body hidden underneath the layers of white fabric. This is highlighted both by the dark shadows that appear on the left side of the left leg and by its contrast with the right leg, which is completely hidden underneath the undulating white fabric. Finally, the feet of the girl: Just the fact that they are shown also adds to her corporal presence. In their suspension above the ground, and with both feet turned slightly inward and the point of the left shoe raised faintly above the right one, they also appear to be dangling, and thus come to evoke a subtle bodily movement. Now, this tensional state of her feet, their moving stillness, seems to repeat the girl's relation to the viewer: She appears frozen under the viewer's gaze, yet her own gaze still pushes back. Furthermore, the feet with slippers in themselves and in their evocation of movement and mid-air suspension draw the image in the direction of the highly conventional sexual symbolism of slippers and swings. For instance, and just to mention art history's most famous examples, the slippers in Edouard Manet's *Olympia* (1863) and the slippers and swing in Jean-Honoré Fragonard's *The Swing* (1767).

The painting *Cherry Ripe* could thus be said to present us with a representation of a girl caught between her own body as erogenous and sexualized cultural references, which relies on the knowledge of a sexual symbolism on the part of the viewer. This further increases the tension of the relation between the painting and its spectatorial other by way of the sexualization of this relation. As viewers of this painting, we are both confronted with our knowledge of cultured sexuality and the lack of knowledge thereof on the part of the girl, which occurs at the same time as her sexual body is made present. The "*Che vuoi?*" question of the image, as expressed with the assertive uncertainty of the gaze of the girl, thus comes to concern the place of sexuality in the interrelation of child and viewer. What we have here is therefore a rare image that acknowledges the sexually desiring interrelation of child and adult, and importantly not in a perverse pedophile manner, but in a way that allows for the question of desire to emerge.[4] This emergence arises, interestingly, in between the flesh of the girl and the cultured symbolism of the viewer, but also, reversely, in between signifiers of girlhood and embodied spectatorship (an experience of embodiment that hinges on the penetrating force of the girl's stare). In this way, the image acknowledges the placement of child and adult—or the viewer—on either side of the signifier.

That positioning is even more pronounced if we turn to the symbolic fruit of the title. The title of the painting, *Cherry Ripe*, suggests a metaphorical usage of cherries. At the time of the painting, according to the *Oxford English Dictionary*, the word "cherry" was used in slang to signify lips, hymen, and virginity. The title also refers to a poem of 1617 by Thomas Campion, making the painting a repetition of yet another piece of art. This poem is highly metaphorical and uses the cherry as a metaphor for the lips of a young beautiful woman, who has yet to be "kissed" (Campion 1912 [1617]: 203–4). I mention these linguistic and poetical connections not to explore them further here, but for the way they already show how one could expect the cherries to signify the femininity and virginity of the girl, to ascribe to her a certain sexual identity, one that may usher in a future fruitful maternity.

However, such an expectation is severely disappointed by the painting. In it we do *not* find a strong metaphorical connection between the cherries and the girl. The cherries are relatively inconspicuous: They are small, kept to the side, and in dark colors. And they are not directly related to the girl, only the leaf on which they are placed touches or overlaps with the right side of the girl's dress, and just barely. This is in sharp contrast with the contemporary visual culture's stereotypical usage of cherries and fruit-metaphors in general. A striking example comes with the *Illustrated London News* of March 24, 1866, in which we find another *Cherry Ripe* by L. T. Peele (Figure 15.5). This girl holds a single cherry in one hand and a basket filled with cherries that is pressing against her stomach in the other, while several cherries are placed in her lap. Here, the closeness of girl and cherries secures a strong metaphorical relation. At the same time her gentle expression and smile grants the image the function of a fantasy in which the question of desire is screened out. Even within the context of the 1880 Christmas number of *The Graphic*, in a small advertisement for Rowlands's cosmetic articles, we find a similar, although less elaborate, fantasy image of a girl in direct, happy, pleasurable contact with a couple of cherries (Figure 15.6).

Lacking such a strong relationship between girl and cherries in Millais' painting, the cherries are not allowed to fulfill their ordinary metaphorical functioning. This has two important consequences: The cherries are not presented as a fulfilling object of desire, whereby they contribute to the painting's emphasis on the question or the lack of desire; and the cherries are not turned into a sign of the symbolic sexual identity of the girl. Instead, the cherries appear as a more undecided element hovering indeterminately between the girl and the viewer. As the connection of the cherries inside the painting and outward vis-à-vis the viewer falters, they turn into a signifier or, with Tom Eyers' fitting formulation, they are shown as a "signifier-in-isolation" that is detached from the relations of ordinary meaning-making (Eyers 2012: 36–60). As a result, the normal functioning of cherries as a quilting point of femininity and as a central element in cultural fantasies of the girl is impeded.

With Millais' painting then, do we not have a pictorial exposition of the Lacanian definition of the signifier as that which represents the subject for another signifier (Lacan 1998: 218 and 236)? The cherries represent the girl for the viewer: The cherries, turned into a signifier, are indicative of or represent the girl as subject as they fail to grant her a certain symbolic meaning of femininity, as they fail to represent her symbolically speaking; the cherries thus represent the girl for the viewer, not as specific other, but as someone who finds him or herself in the place of the big Other as the battery of signifiers. The girl as subject emerges in Millais' work both as an opening up of the lack of desire through her questioning gaze and through her avoidance of the cherries as satisfying object and, importantly, as an opposition to and a disconnection from the usual symbolism of cherries, that is as a gap within the typical functioning of signifiers.

This in turn brings out the extent to which the pictured child and adult viewer are placed on either side of the signifier so to speak: Where the ordinary viewer will seek out meaning through the interrelation of signifiers, the girl breaks up the meaning-making relations, effectively creating a gap in the chain of signifiers. Interestingly, this gap has a material presence in the painting itself in the form of the black oval shape in which the child is contained. As this black hole surrounds the girl, she almost appears to be suspended in a void, without a definite relation to the natural surroundings around her, at the same time as this nature itself becomes immersed in darkness and as such is not really creating a legible environment for the girl, that in turn could have made the girl herself symbolically legible as natural or as of nature. A few red flowers bend toward her, but rather than creating a signifying connection, they seem to highlight the blackness of the background that separates flowers and child and therefore also the distance between them.

Recognizable flowers and leaves are scattered throughout the surroundings, but as we approach the girl, the background turns increasingly darker. It is as if the painted natural elements returned to a state of pure materiality, in which they are no longer visible or legible as specific representational elements, but only as paint. We are here in the domain of what art historian Georges Didi-Huberman calls *the pan* ("*le pan*") and later *the symptom* of images, that is the areas where the materiality of paint reveals a symptomatic non-meaning within representational and symbolic meaning (e.g., Didi-Huberman 1985: 45–7). The girl in Millais' painting is thus placed between the potential, but failing meaning-making of signifiers and a gap of non-meaning, between cherries and flowers and the encompassing hole of darkening paint.

In this way, Millais' painting reveals a striking kinship with the unconscious as that which, in Lacan's words, "shows us a gap" in the chain of signifiers that "connects with a real," which belongs to "the order of the *non-realized*" (Lacan 1998: 22). What I would like to call *the Millaisian real of the girl* then concerns the gap of the painting of *Cherry Ripe*, its hole of dark paint, as it carves out a zone of the nonrealized. A lack of realization that finds painterly expression through the girl's defiant gaze, bodily sexuality, and semantic opposition. Tellingly, this figure of the nonrealized finds her place on the threshold: between objects of desire and the lack of desire, sweet fruits and a questioning gaze; between adult cultured sexuality and the real bodily sexuality of the child; between the representational and the nonrepresentational, motif and paint; between meaning and non-meaning, sign and signifier.

Looking back, it is this that the reception history appears to be covering up or screening out by way of both earlier "girl in a mobcap"-images and later *Cherry Ripe* reproductions, but which nonetheless appear to show up in certain gaps, which connect with the real of the girl and lead us to recover Millais' *Cherry Ripe*.

Figure 15.1 LI190.1 Joshua Reynolds, *Portrait of Penelope Boothby*, 1788. 75 × 62 cm. Oil on canvas. Lent from a private collection. Image © Ashmolean Museum, University of Oxford.

Figure 15.2 John Everett Millais, *Cherry Ripe*, 1879. 134.6 × 88.9 cm. Oil on canvas. Private collection. © Bridgeman Images.

Figure 15.3 John Everett Millais, *Cherry Ripe*, 1880. A supplement from the 1880 Christmas Number of the journal *The Graphic*. 70 × 45 cm. © The British Library.

Figure 15.4 *Cherry Ripe*, 1897. Poster from the Christmas publication *Pears' Annual*. 84 × 54 cm. © Jakob Rosendal.

Figure 15.5 L. T. Peele, *Cherry Ripe*, 1866. From *The Illustrated London News*, March 24, 1866. © Jakob Rosendal.

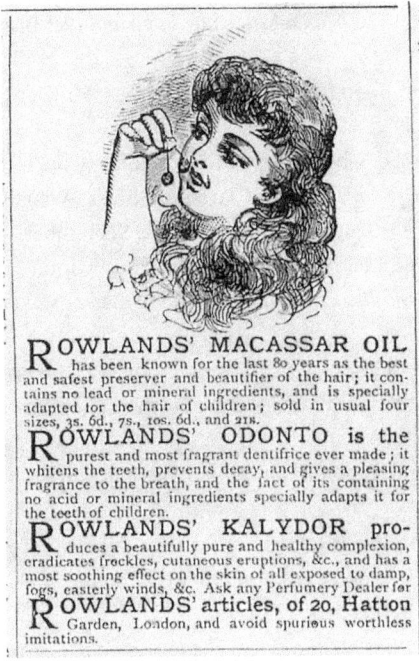

Figure 15.6 Rowlands' advertisement, 1880. Printed in the 1880 Christmas Number of the journal *The Graphic*. © The British Library.

Notes

1 Thanks to VELUX FONDEN (The Velux Foundation) for project funding (project number 00021290) enabling the completion of this article.
2 I plan to take up this broader critical work on the reception history of *Cherry Ripe* in a future article.
3 The reproduction of this painting is sourced from and with the permission of Bridgeman Images. On their webpage it can be found in color: https://www.bridgemanimages.com/en-GB/search?filter_text=cherry+ripe&filter_group=all&filter_region=DNK (Accessed August 1, 2019). Another, high quality reproduction of the painting can also be found on Sotheby's webpage: http://www.sothebys.com/en/auctions/ecatalogue/2004/important-british-pictures-l04121/lot.21.html (Accessed August 1, 2019).
4 The pedophile would, on the contrary, in fantasy construe the child as an object that fulfils desire and thus as an answer to the question/lack of desire (cf. André and Gosselin 2008).

References

André, S. and G. Gosselin (2008), *Qu'est-ce que la pédophilie?* Bruxelles: Éditions Luc Pire.

Bradley, L. (1991), "From Eden to Empire: John Everett Millais's *Cherry Ripe*," *Victorian Studies*, 34 (2): 179–203.

Campion, T. (1912 [1617]), "Cherry-Ripe," in A. Quiller-Couch (ed), *The Oxford Book of English Verse, 1250–1900*, Oxford: Clarendon Press. Available online: https://archive.org/details/cu31924011997909 (accessed September 1, 2018).

Didi-Huberman, G. (1985), *La peinture incarnée*, Paris: Minuit.

Eyers, T. (2012), *Lacan and the Concept of the "Real,"* Basingstoke and New York: Palgrave Macmillan.

Funnell, P. (1999), "Introduction: Millais's Reputation and the Practice of Portraiture," in P. Funnell and M. Warner (eds), *Millais: Portraits*, London: National Portrait Gallery Publications.

Gallati, B. D. (2004), *Great Expectations: John Singer Sargent Painting Children*, New York: Bulfinch Press.

Greenberg, M. L., "Victorian Visions of Youth: The Child in Art and Psychoanalysis," in D. Henderson (ed), *Psychoanalysis: Philosophy, Art and Clinic*, Newcastle upon Tyne: Cambridge Scholars Publishing, 2015.

Higonnet, A. (1998), *Pictures of Innocence: The History and Crisis of Ideal Childhood*, London: Thames and Hudson, 1998.

Lacan, J. (2007 [1966]), "The Subversion of the Subject and the Dialectic of Desire in the Freudian Unconscious," in *Écrits*, trans. Bruce Fink in collaboration with Héloïse Fink and Russell Grigg, London and New York: W. W. Norton.

Lacan, J. (1998 [1973]), *The Seminar of Jacques Lacan: Book XI: The Four Fundamental Concepts of Psychoanalysis*, trans. Alan Sheridan, London and New York: W. W. Norton.

Mavor, C. (1996 [1995]), *Pleasures Taken: Performances of Sexuality and Loss in Victorian Photographs*, London: I.B. Tauris.

Millais, G. (1979), *Sir John Everett Millais*, London: Academy Editions.

Pointon, M. (1997 [1993]), *Hanging the Head: Portraiture and Social Formation in Eighteenth-Century England*, New Haven and London: Yale University Press.

Polhemus, R. M. (1994), "John Millais's Children: Faith, Erotics and *The Woodman's Daughter*," Victorian Studies, 37 (3): 433–50.

Reis, P. T. (1992), "Victorian Centerfold: Another Look at Millais's *Cherry Ripe*," Victorian Studies, 35 (2): 201–5.

Warner, M. (2009), "Millais in reproduction," in M. Giebelhausen and T. Barringer (eds), *Writing the Pre-Raphaletites: Text, Context, Subtext*, Surrey: Ashgate.

4

Color between Materiality and Signification

Lilian Munk Rösing

From its beginning, psychoanalysis has had an interest in the materiality of the signifier as something that escapes its function of representation. When Freud listened to the words from his clients, he often turned his attention from the things they represented to the material (sounds and letters) from which they were made. When the Wolfman pronounced the word "Wespe," for instance, Freud heard the sounds "es" and "pe" and noticed their likeness to the sound of the Wolfman's initials "S. P." (Sergei Pankejeff). This gave Freud a clue to how to interpret the Wolfman's phobia of winged insects.

The primary pragmatic function of the signifier is to signify, to refer to, to represent something. But the signifier is also made from some material that does not in itself refer to anything, but still may produce something, whether alternative chains of signifiers, as in psychoanalysis (Wespe—SP), or some kind of aesthetic enjoyment of the material in itself, as in art (or in jokes, where Freud found sexual and aggressive fantasies at work, but also plain and simple "pleasure at words," *Wortlust*, "the thought... revisiting its erstwhile home of the ancient play with words," Freud 2002: 166–7).

Psychoanalysis and aesthetics seem to join in a common attention to that dimension of the enunciation (be it the client's talk or a work of art) that does not represent anything, the material dimension. When it comes to painting, color seems to highlight the signifier's lingering between representation and materiality. Color may represent something, either through mimesis (a tree on a painting may be green because a real tree is green) or through codified signifying systems (green for hope, red for love, black for mourning, etc.), but color also draws attention to the material presence of the artwork (away from the absent phenomenon or concept that it represents).

Georges Didi-Huberman has pinpointed this ambiguity of color by his concept of *pan*, taken from a passage in Proust's *In Search of Lost Time* when the character Bergotte is standing in front of Vermeer's painting *View from Delft*. Bergotte is completely captivated by a little patch (French: "pan") of yellow that represents a piece of wall in Delft, but just as much makes itself present as yellow paint on the cloth. To Bergotte, who is himself a writer, this experience of *pan* is a kind of aesthetic shock experience; it is literally killing him. "Why didn't I write that way?" he says to himself—and then he dies on the spot, on a settee in the museum!

There is something in color that escapes representation and signification. This something may be some kind of *real*, as Didi-Huberman suggests by his concept of *pan*, but it may also be some kind of *imaginary*, related to a phantasy of escaping the cut of the signifier. Such a phantasy seems to be at work when Merleau-Ponty regards color as a smoothing tissue nourishing the thing, a kind of visualization of what he calls "the flesh."

In this chapter I will discuss the ambiguity of color between representation, materiality, and abstraction. What dimension of the artwork do we capture when we focus on color? Is the fascination with color a fantasy to escape the cut of the signifier, that is, the symbolic order, or could it testify to a traumatic or/and revelatory encounter with the beyond of the symbolic order, the cut or opening in the symbolic order itself? In that case, could that explain why color in our culture is connected to femininity, given that Lacan defines the feminine position as the one related to the cut in the symbolic order? I shall start by reflecting on the connection between color and femininity at stake in the "chromophobia" of our culture and finish by affirming a more "chromophile" (and femininity-friendly) liaison. The argument will pass through the different conceptions of color involved in Didi-Huberman's concept of "pan" and Merleau-Ponty's concept of "flesh," and the different conceptions of "flesh" to be found in Merleau-Ponty and Eric Santner. A last important concept will be the concept of "incarnation" as used by Didi-Huberman to designate what happens when signifiers do not so much signify an abstract meaning as materialize it. Could color, like the yellow in Vermeer's painting, be an "incarnation" in that sense?

Chromophobia

In Western history you may speak of a certain contempt for or even phobia of colors, as argued by the artist and writer David Batchelor in his book *Chromophobia*. Plato called the painter "a grinder and mixer of multi-colored drugs" (Batchelor 2000: 31). Aristotle writes in his *Poetics*: "[A] random distribution of the most attractive colors would never yield as much pleasure as a definite image without color" (Batchelor 2000: 29). Seen as excessive on the one hand, and superficial on the other, color has been connected to the feminine, the oriental, the queer, the vulgar. Well known in art history is the big debate in renaissance Italy between *disegno* and *colore*, drawing and color, Florence and Venice, Michelangelo and Titian. Michelangelo pitied the colorist Titian for not knowing how to draw. The founding father of art history as a discipline, Giorgio Vasari, preferred Michelangelo's clear lines to Titian's blurred colors, clearly associating the lines with the masculine and the colors with the feminine. In Paris in 1848, the art critic Charles Blanc seemed driven by his name (Blanc/White) when comparing the union of design and color to the union of man and woman, declaring that design/man must maintain its preponderance over color/woman—otherwise color will lead art to its fall, just like Eve led man to his (Batchelor 2000: 23). Herman Melville writes that "nature paints like a harlotte" (Batchelor 2000: 16), and Shakespeare's Hamlet goes mad because women paint their faces: "God has given you one face and you make yourselves another, that hath made me mad" (*Hamlet* Act III, Scene 1).

On the other side you have the chromophiles. Roland Barthes celebrates and eroticizes color, here in his essay on Cy Twombly: "Color... is a kind of bliss ... like a closing eyelid, a tiny fainting spell" (Batchelor 2000: 32). Yves Klein (the painter of blue monochromes) sees color as "enslaved by the line" and the line as a prefiguration of writing. Klein even compares the line/writing to the mark of Cain (the cut of the signifier) separating man from the paradise of color (Batchelor 2000: 77–8). Roland Barthes' erotic is always of a gentle, caressing unaggressive kind. When explicitly searching for that "happy, gentle, jubilant sexuality" that he sees as expelled from the literature of his time, he finds it "in painting, or better still, in color," as he writes in his autobiographical essay *Roland Barthes par Roland Barthes* (Batchelor 2000: 68). Painting and color could also be connected to a more explosive kind of sexuality, though. Color can be splashed onto the cloth in a more or less ejaculatory way, as we know from action painting.

Color as abstract and concrete

In a scene from Jacques Demy's film musical *Les demoiselles de Rochefort*, color is clearly connected to some kind of phallic, violent ejaculation, as we see a gallery owner shooting at suspended plastic bags with paint, thus producing a drip painting on the paper underneath. The scene is altogether a piece of color philosophy, discussing the relation between color and representation. Delphine (Catherine Deneuve) is visiting the gallery owner who is her fiancé. The art in his gallery is abstract, except for one figurative painting that seems to be a portrait of Delphine, but which is really a phantasy of the ideal woman painted by the young soldier who has not yet met Delphine, but who will be her lover in the end.

Delphine (singing!) breaks up with the gallery owner, accusing him of only valuing her as a beautiful doll in his gallery. As she enters and as she leaves, the gallery owner shoots at the suspended paint-bags. After Delphine has left, we see two girls and two sailors stopping in front of the gallery, looking at an abstract, blue painting in the window. One of the girls compares the painting to one of the sailor's eyes: "Your eyes are the same blue as the picture." This makes the other sailor pronounce this highly philosophical statement: "They say that the painting is abstract, but that's wrong, since it resembles his eyes."

To the gallery owner, figurative painting is a bad representation. When Delphine asks him about the portrait: "Is that me?" He answers: "No, not at all, it is figurative in the simple way, and you are spiritual." Considering the other pieces in his gallery, one may guess that to him true representation, the one that captures the spirit, would be an abstract painting. So here we already have several different ideas of painting: figurative painting as either mimesis or inventing an ideal, abstract painting as capturing the spirit. The sailor's line gives us a fourth idea: abstract painting as mimesis of color. Actually the line captures color's ambiguous or mediating state between abstraction and representation. Color is always the color of something, but at the same time, it is abstractable from this thing, like some kind of visible essence. Color seems to be both concretion and abstraction, both phenomenon and idea.

Color as flesh

In *Le visible et l'invisible* (*The visible and the invisible*) Maurice Merleau-Ponty connects color to his central and a bit mysterious concept of "la chair," "the flesh." At one point he even seems to identify flesh with color, or rather what he calls "naked color," "la couleur nue." Naked color is "less a color or a thing, than a difference between things and colors" (Merleau-Ponty 1968: 132).

I think this thought is close to the philosophy of color that we find in the scene from *Les demoiselles de Rochefort*. Color is always the color of a thing, yet it also seems detachable from the thing, having an abstract, yet still visible existence of its own, like the blue of the abstract painting seemingly extracted from the sailor's eyes. In painting color is both a representation and an abstraction. What Merleau-Ponty calls "naked color" is this detachable or abstractable color. By the way, "naked color" is almost an oxymoron. We would conventionally think of color as a layer or veil, covering some naked thing; here it is naked itself.

Interestingly, Merleau-Ponty's "naked color" seems to be equivalent with his concept of "the flesh." Right after having told us that "naked color" is the difference between things and colors, he situates "the flesh" in the same place, the same interstice between colors and things. He further defines "the flesh" as the tissue, the possibility, the latency of things: "Between the alleged colors and visibles, we would find anew the tissue that lines them, sustains them, nourishes them, and which for its part is not a thing, but a possibility, a latency, a flesh of things" (Merleau-Ponty 1968: 132–3).

If color can be some kind of equivalent or visualization of Merleau-Ponty's "flesh," it is because it has this status between abstraction and concretion, idea and thing. Where Merleau-Ponty desires to dwell is in the chiastic zone where the idea is incarnated and the flesh is sublimated. He puts this in a clear chiasm when aligning the "carnal existence of the idea" with the "sublimation of the flesh" (Merleau-Ponty 1968: 155). Here the Christian inspiration for Merleau-Ponty's "flesh" becomes clear. The carnal existence of the idea and the sublimation of the flesh are exactly what are at stake in the Christian *incarnation*, the quite scandalous story of Jesus Christ, the abstract idea of God taking on flesh and blood.

Differently from Merleau-Ponty's flesh, flesh is to Eric Santner what is created through symbolic castration as a kind of excess. Flesh is "the fleshy surplus we take on when we are taken in by the cultural, historical modes by which we are 'naturalized'" (Santner 2011: 122). Flesh is the "surplus of life" that is created because we are "beings of language, as animals compelled to live [our] lives in the field of the Other." Flesh is "a spectral materiality… that forms at the impossible jointure of body and letter, soma and signifier, enjoyment and entitlement" (Santner 2011: 95). Flesh is not an uncut mass from which the symbolic castration cuts a subject; rather, flesh is produced by that very symbolic castration that Santner calls "incarnation." To become a subject is to incarnate a position in the symbolic order (a name, a title), and that incarnation produces our vulnerable "flesh." When a man is made to incarnate, say, a pope, his "flesh" is produced at the junction of "enjoyment and entitlement" as something almost unbearable, as you can see it from one of Santner's most illuminating examples: the scream of Pope Innocent painted by Francis Bacon in porous layers of color clearly conveying a sense of "spectral materiality."

What Merleau-Ponty wants to avoid by his chiasm of flesh and idea is of course the dualism of the Christian incarnation; flesh and idea are always-already one in his world of eternal chiasm and reversibility. What Merleau-Ponty smoothly avoids, though, or represses, is the *violence* of incarnation. The story of God taking on flesh and blood is a very violent story, as you know from the most bizarre image in Christian culture, still meeting us everywhere in the Western world, the dying, bleeding God on the cross.

In Western art history the theme of incarnation has produced paintings in which color is not a soothing tissue nourishing the thing, but the result of a violent cut, the cut in the body of Jesus Christ, from which the red color pours. As we saw, this side of color is also represented in the scene from *Les desmoiselles de Rochefort* when we witness the gallery owner shooting at the bags with paint, thereby producing a painting in the manner of Niki de Saint Phalle's famous shooting paintings from the 1960s (*Tirs!*). The gallerist's shooting is a repercussion of other discrete violent features in the film, which paints a colorful, idyllic picture of the town of Rochefort, but also suggests war and murder in its margins, corresponding to the description of the town given by Delphine's sister: "a town full of warriors, sadists, and disregarded painters".

The medieval painter that splashed red paint over Christ's body acted like a phallic action painter, but the bleeding Christ rather belongs to the feminine side of Lacan's sexuation formulae. The feminine position is marked by the cut in the Big Other: $\cancel{A}$, and the wound in Christ's body may be said to be a very concretizing image of this cut, the cut in God. The wounded, mortal God on the cross could be seen as the very image of the wounded, lacking Big Other: $\cancel{A}$. Produced by the painter, the blood drops are phallic; produced by Christ, they are signs of the lack of the big Other.

Color uncut

To Luce Irigaray, Merleau-Ponty's fascination with color is a fantasy of a prenatal, intra-uterine existence. As something flooding my gaze, recalling the fluidity of its very first dwelling, color takes me back before division and separation, back to a "preconceptual, preobjective, presubjective life," "preceding or following a determinate incarnation into subject-object duality" (Irigaray 1993: 156). Altogether, Irigaray reads Merleau-Ponty's phenomenology of the flesh as a fantasy of staying in the uterus, or as she puts it most bluntly: "Merleau-Ponty's seer remains in an incestuous, prenatal situation with the whole" (Irigaray 1993: 173). To Irigaray, Merleau-Ponty's "tissue" of the world, his "flesh," is the tissue of the placenta; the "intertwining" or "the chiasm" by which he describes the osmotic exchange between subject and object, seer and visible, is an eternal crossing of umbilical cords (Irigaray 1993: 183). There is no cut, no division, no other, no sexual difference in this prenatal state of eternal reversibility.

Irigaray's criticism of Merleau-Ponty is basically the same as Mladen Dolar's in his brilliant essay "Touching the Ground," in which he proposes the moebius strip to think "the flesh" in a way that includes the cut that Merleau-Ponty excludes. Dolar pinpoints his criticism in this way: "Merleau-Ponty's endeavor is a disavowal of the cut, or a circumvention of the cut. Psychoanalysis would agree with everything else except for this: there is a cut" (Dolar 2008: 89).

But is color always related to this imaginary fantasy of a state before division and differentiation? Is color always an imaginary attempt to overcome the division and differentiation of the symbolic order, to escape the cut of the signifier? Or does it also have a dimension, which exceeds or transcends the symbolic order, that is, a dimension of the real?

First of all, you may say that colors (rather than color) are part of the symbolic order, the logic of the signifier. The colors of the rainbow are a classical example to explain the coincidence claimed by structuralism between our linguistic and perceptive differentiations. What is really a gradual flow of colored light is divided by language into seven definite colors, and through this naming and division, these colors are actually what we see when looking at a rainbow. In this sense, colors are names by which we divide some undivided real into palpable categories. The contingency of this division is clear from the fact that different languages have different color distinctions; for instance, there are two distinct color names in Russian for what are in English just different shades (lighter or darker) of blue. Another, secondary way that colors are inscribed into the symbolic order is of course their culturally determined allegorical significations (green for hope, red for love, white for innocence, etc.).

So color has an imaginary dimension (the fantasy of presymbolic nondivision), and it has a symbolic dimension (as category and allegory). I shall argue that it even has a real dimension. As excess, as "pan," as something pointing to the materiality of the signifier, color touches upon the real.

Color as shock

In his book *La peinture incarnée*, Didi-Huberman states that color is both caress and shock. You can feel touched by color, and it has this haptic quality, but this touch is not always a gentle caress; it can also be "an effect of pan, of shock, of tear, of stigma, of poignant shot" ("un effet de pan, de choc, de déchirure, de stigma, de plan poignant") (Didi-Huberman 1985: 54). Even to Roland Barthes, the great eroticist of color, color can be "like a pinprick in the corner of the eye," as he writes in his essay on Cy Twombly (Batchelor 2000: 74). Color can reach out for you in a violent way—you can feel as if color were looking at you, as David Batchelor writes (Batchelor 2000: 74). Rather than a decorative surface, color can be a stain, and it can have the quality of the stain in the Lacanian theory of the gaze: something looking back at you, like the famous anamorphous skull in Holbein's *The Ambassadors*.

In the universe of Marcel Proust, you can even die from color, as we have learned from the scene of Bergotte's death in *In Search of Lost Time*. Bergotte dies from his aesthetic shock experience of the yellow patch or "pan" in Vermeer's painting. To Didi-Huberman the "pan" becomes a concept, a word for the moment when representation and materiality, sense and being, the subject and the big Other face or efface each other. The moment when the patch of yellow in Vermeer's painting is both a piece of wall and a stain of color. "Pan" is the moment when the signifier oscillates between its signification and its materiality. It is the moment of the symptom, and it is the moment of non-sense, the kind of non-sense created by the soma (the yellow patch as paint) being occupied by the sema (the yellow patch as a representation of the wall), being invaded by sense, the body animated by the signifier. It is here that Didi-Huberman, like Eric Santner, situates the "flesh." With Merleau-Ponty the flesh is some kind of undivided mass before the cut of the signifier; with Didi-Huberman and Santner, it is rather produced by the cut of the signifier, as this "spectral materiality… that forms at the impossible jointure of body and letter, soma and signifier, enjoyment and entitlement" (Santner 2011: 95).

Didi-Huberman's "pan" is also situated at the level of this "impossible" jointure of soma and signifier, materiality and representation. It would not be a "pan" if it did not linger between being a sign (representing the wall in Delft) and being pure materiality (yellow paint)—the aesthetic shock experience is produced by the switch from the signifier as signifying and the signifier as material. In *Seminar XI* Lacan draws a diagram of two circles, representing respectively "being" (or subject) and "sense" (or the big Other) in order to point out their overlapping field as the field of "non-sense." The "non-sense" that calls for Lacan's (and every psychoanalyst's attention) is not some kind of non-sense beyond sense, but the non-sense that arises exactly when pure "being" tries to make sense, when the subject (who is really not a subject until this moment) tries to make sense out of itself, responds to the interpellation from the big Other. In *La peinture incarnée* Didi-Huberman draws the same diagram, letting the first circle represent "the flesh" and the other one "the plane," whereas the field of their overlap is called "pan." This is to show that "pan" is not pure materiality (yellow paint) that does not signify anything (yellow wall), but arises exactly as some excess of or other side to representation. In modern abstract painting, it is the other way round: Representation arises as some excess of or other side to pure materiality, as we do not stop to search for recognizable forms and figures even in the most abstract painting.

Like "flesh" in general, the flesh of color is also produced by the cut of the symbolic order. It is the excess resulting from this production. The aesthetic shock experience is produced by the switch from the signifier as signifying and the signifier as material. Still, what is thus produced by the cut of the symbolic order, as excess, is also a cut *in* the symbolic order, pointing to its lack, to that which escapes its ordering of the world. This cut in the symbolic order once again takes us to Lacan's feminine position: Ⱥ, as "A" can be understood as the whole of the symbolic order, the whole system of categories and the rules of their interconnection, to which the subject is subjected. The cut or the flaw in A is a cut or flaw in the symbolic order, and the feminine position is associated with this cut.

In Balzac's story *Le chef-d'œuvre inconnu*, which is Didi-Huberman's main reference in *La peinture incarnée*, it seems that the chaos of color triumphs over representation, as the aging artist Frenhofer strives to paint his masterpiece of the ideal woman, but ends up with "a chaos of colors" from which just a part of a foot sticks out. The idea of Woman has been drowned in color. One may say that color here functions like the bar across "La" in Lacan's sexuation scheme; the bar that says "Woman does not exist." But at the same time, it functions like another bar on the feminine side of the sexuation scheme: the bar across the big Other. Woman does not exist, but the feminine position does, as exactly the position pointing to the lacks and excesses of the symbolic representation. So when we talk about color, I would like to insist on the sexual difference that Merleau-Ponty uses color as flesh to elude. I would actually like to embrace our culture's association of color with the feminine, and point to that dimension of color that is the stain, the excess, the lack of the signifying chain, bleeding from the wound in the side of Christ, that is from the lack in the big Other, that is from here: Ⱥ.

References

Batchelor, D. (2000), *Chromophobia*, London: Reaktion Books.

Demy, Jacques (1967), *Les demoiselles de Rochefort*, dir: Jacques Demy, 1967, Parc film/Madeleine films.

Didi-Huberman, G. (1985), *La peinture incarnée*, Paris: Les éditions de minuit.

Dolar, M. (2008), "Touching the Ground," *Filozofski vestnik*, XXIX (2): 79–100.

Freud, S. (2002), *The Joke and Its Relation to the Unconscious*, trans. Joyce Crick, London: Penguin.

Irigaray, L. (1993), *An Ethics of Sexual Difference*, trans. Carolyn Burke and Gillian C. Gill, Ithaca: Cornell University Press.

Merleau-Ponty, M. (1968), *The Visible and the Invisible*, trans. Alphonso Lingis, Evanston: Northwestern University Press.

Santner, E. (2011), *The Royal Remains. The People's Two Bodies and the Endgames of Sovereignty*, Chicago: University of Chicago Press.

Index

absence, presence of 149–50, 156
Alvarez, Alfred 158 n.9
The Ambassadors (Holbein) 222
The Anatomy of Violence (Raine) 55
anxiety 39
    fantasy and 7, 60
    and genes 52–3
    Hobson's 51
    over death 50–1
    people with cancer 52
applied Marxism 122
applied psychoanalysis 1, 122
archeology 187
    coda 195
    historical conditions 188–90
    subjective aporias and ignorance 190–2
    truth, love and dimension 192–3
Aristotle 49, 217
Attridge, Derek 133–5, 143
Aufbau 42 n.12

Baader, Andreas 48
Badiou, Alain 80, 139, 145
Barthes, Roland 217, 222
Batchelor, David 216–17, 222
Bayout, Abdelmalek 54–5
Beckett, Samuel 149–50, 151, 155
    absences, importances 10
    characters 153
    non-knowledge 157
    nothingness 155, 157
    positivized negativity 150
Benjamin, Walter 127–8
Bennett, Jane 187
Beyond the Pleasure Principle 79
Bjerre, Henrik Jøker 7
Bjerre, Ida Nissen 11
Blanc, Charles 217
Blanchot, Maurice 149
body, secrets of
    Christmas tree effect 49
    genetics 49

Hobson's Choice 50
hormonal castration 51
language and disciplines 49
patient's anxiety attacks 50–1
speculations 49
substantial form 49–50
Bogerts, Bernhard 48
Boltanski, Luc 187
Bonaparte, Marie 176
boredom 86–7
    according to Heidegger 88–90
born criminals 47
Botha, P. W. 141
Braidotti, Rosi 136, 144
Brown, John 33
Burke, Kenneth 39–40
Butler, Judith 146 n.1

Caillois, Roger 71
Campion, Thomas 203
capitalist discourse 109
    alternatives 113–15
    anxiety 110–11
    demands 110
    dominance 110
    foreclosing of castration 114
    imaginary ideas 111–12
    plus-à-jouir 111
    psychoanalysis 115
    racism 112
    smartness 111
Carlsen, Nikolaj 10
Cherry Ripe (Millais) 12, 197, 208, 209, 210, 212 n.2
    cultural phenomenon 201
    girl and cherries 204
    lack of realization 205–6
    recovering 201–6
    sexual symbolism 202–3
    signifier-in-isolation 204
    symptomatic reception 198–201
    telescopic push-pull effect 202

Chiapello, Eve 187
Christian spirituality 190
Christie, Agatha 47
Christmas tree effect 49
Chromophobia (Batchelor) 216–17
Civilization and Its Discontents 65–6
Coetzee, J. M. 10, 131, 136–7, 140–1, 146
Colarusso, Calvin 51
color 215–16
    as abstract and concrete 217–18
    as flesh 12, 218–20
    as shock 220–3
    uncut 220–1
computer music 169
concerts 160
    obscuring transference 167
    performance and perversion 161–3
    perverse environments 161
    realization 165
    transference 165–6
Copjec, Joan 134, 138, 184 n.4
    Antigone 144
couch to culture 8–9
courtly capitalism 103–5
courtly love code 193–4
crainology 47
criminology 48, 60
cultural institutions 72
culture
    couch to 8–9
    discontent in 8
    drives (*see* drives and culture)

Daniel, Arnauld 106
Das Unbehagen in der Kultur (1929–30) 65
de Beistegui, Miguel 152
De la Grammatologie (Derrida) 29
Demy, Jacques 217
der Trieb 65
Derrida, Jacques 30, 41 n.7, 43 n.16
    De la Grammatologie 29
    Ear of the Other 41 n.6
    graphematic universal 41 n.7
    La Carte Postale 38
    Parisian psychoanalytic work 7
Didi-Huberman, Georges 12, 205, 215–16, 222
Disgrace (Coetzee) 10, 131–2
Dolar, Mladen 8, 26 n.2, 182, 221

drives and culture 65
    auto-referential project 67
    and civilization 67, 82 n.4, 82 n.7
    clinamen 80
    conflict 77
    deviation and substitution 80–1
    Eros and Death 77–8
    Greek's theory 78
    issue 78
    and libido 79
    multiplicities 80
    nature and 81
    traits (*see* traits of culture)
Duras, Marguerite 11, 173, 178, 184 n.5, 193

Eagleton, Mary 145
Ear of the Other (Derrida) 41 n.6
Écrire (Duras) 173
Electronic Dance Music (EDM) 167–8
electronic music 162
    analyzing 11
    modern 10, 159, 167
    technê 163
Essay on the Origin of Language (Rousseau) 27, 40 n.1
ethical capitalism 106
ethics (unconscious) 131
    abandoned dogs 133
    Disgrace 132, 134
    Freud 131
    hearing committee 140, 143
    ideological ethics 145
    minimal difference 139–40, 145
    New South Africa 140
    psychoanalytic reading 135
    racial and sexual exploitation 140
    sexed acts of resistance 139–46
    and sexual difference 133
    subtraction, concept 139
    theme of disposability 144
excessive hermeneutics 125–7
Eyers, Tom 204

Febvre, Lucien 193
Ferrara, Alessandro 121
Fink, Bruce 174
Fisher, Mark 131
Flaubert, Gustave 121

Foucault, Michel 11, 184 n.5, 187–9
Fox Keller, Evelyn 54
Fragonard, Jean-Honoré 203
Franzén, Carin 11
Frege, Gottlob 24
Freud, S. 1–2, 4–8, 10, 41 n.8, 42 n.10,
    65–8, 72, 92, 96, 110, 122, 129. *see
    also* traits of culture
  deviations and perversions 79–80
  discontent in culture 8
  drives 31, 37, 42 n.10, 42 n.11, 73
  drunkard and his bottle 77
  expressions 75
  materialism 11
  materialist examples 123
  Neurosenwahl 8, 59
  olfactory sense 43 n.15
  Platonic myth 79
  psychoanalysis 2
  question to Bonaparte 176
  rivalry 5
  sexuality 77
  stumbling 123
  sublimation and desexualization 74, 77
  Three Essays on Sexuality 42 n.11, 42
    n.13
  tool 69
  unconscious 4, 6, 10
  Wisstrieb 69
Fukuyama, Francis 98

Gall, Franz Joseph 47
genes
  anxiety and 52–3
  for crime 55, 59
  epigenetics 59
  example 54
  Hobson's anxieties 51
  information 53–4
  Landrigan's story 55–8
  neurogenetic real 54
  program 53
  refashioning life 54
  for violence 55
genetic predisposition 52
The Graphic 198–201, 211

Hansen, Brian Benjamin 10
Harvey, Irene E. 125

Hegel, G. W. F. 7, 19–21, 24–5
Heidegger, Martin 150, 157 n.3, 158 n.6
  boredom 86, 88–9
  Es ruft 154
  language 152
  openness, modes 152
heliocentrism 194
History of Astronomy (Smith) 19, 22
Hobson, Allan 50–1
Human Genome project 54
humanity, lack of 159
Hyldgaard, Kirsten 8

Imagination Dead Imagine 151
Imagine There's No Woman (Copjec) 134
Interpretation of Dreams (Freud) 4, 122
invisible forces
  agent's intentions 21
  cunning of reason 20
  freedom 21
  God 17–18
  human passions 20
  Providence 19
  reductionism 19
  self-realization 20
  The Theory of Moral Sentiments 18–19
  Wealth of Nations 18

Jegerstedt, Kari 10
J.M. Coetzee and the Ethics of Reading
    (Attridge) 133
Jones, Ernest 158 n.7
jouissance 11, 31, 33–4, 37, 54, 105, 109,
    111–12, 158 n.5, 179–80, 184 n.4

Kael, Pauline 85, 87
Kant, Immanuel 26 n.1, 125
Kay, Sarah 189
Kierkegaard, Søren 127–8, 158 n.6
Kivland, Sharon 42 n.15
Klein, Yves 217
Klotz, Jean-Pierre 192
knowledge 9, 87–8
  acephalic 70
  capitalist market 117
  Cartesian approach 191
  genes 53
  hysterics and obsessionals 91–2
  of language 23

literary reading 138
psychoanalysis 131
sexual symbolism 202
totalizing 32
Wisstrieb 69

La Carte Postale (Derrida) 38
La peinture incarnée (Didi-Huberman) 222–3
La Rochefoucauld, F. de 191
Lacan, Jacques 1, 4, 36, 40, 41 n.3, 41 n.7, 49, 68–9, 73, 107 n.2, 124, 150, 164, 173, 187
  Achilles 183
  analyst 174
  anxiety 90
  capitalist discourse 9, 112–14
  communication system 25
  courtly love code 193
  dehumanization 48
  discourse of university 87
  drives 31–2, 76
  fake satisfactions 34
  Freudian materialism 11
  historical references 190
  Hommelette 5
  image of woman 180–1
  jouissance as *jouis-sens* 158 n.5
  language 10, 29–30, 41 n.10
  masculine and feminine positions 10
  masculine universal, sexuation 43 n.18
  mathemes 184 n.1
  morra 178
  poetry and psychoanalysis 115–17
  psychoanalysis 7, 11–12
  Rome Discourse 41 n.6
  Seminar V 23
  Seminar VII 104
  Seminar VIII 190
  Seminar XI 188, 191–2
  Seminar XVII 41 n.9, 43 n.16
  sexuation 6
  signifier 30
  skepticism 191
  social tie, discourse 37
  symbolic and proper acts 142, 144
  unconscious 2–3, 7
Lacanian theory 1, 8
Laclau, Ernesto 146 n.1

Landrigan, Jeffrey 55–8
language 152–3
  Allure 35–6
  capitalism 33, 37
  of devotees 41 n.3
  drives 37–8
  existence 28
  fake satisfactions 34
  fragrance, description 35
  functioning of drive 33
  gnawing 156
  human 33
  imperatives 34
  impulse 28
  jouissance 33–4
  La Carte Postale 38
  literature 40, 43 n.20
  metaphoric distinctions 43 n.19
  metonymy 40 n.2
  new signifier 32
  olfactory 34–5
  symbolic law 36–7
  techno-capitalism 38
  telecommunications, new regime 38
  theories of 27
  tonality 39
Latour, Bruno 187
Lawton, J. F. 107 n.1
Le ravissement de Lol V. Stein (Lacan) 11, 173
  archeological metaphor 176
  game of love 177–9
  jouissance 179–80
  knowledge 177
  Lacanian terminology 182
  non-gaze 182
  primal scene 174–5
  recurring scene 175
Lectures on the History of Philosophy (Hegel) 7
Lehman, Andree 52
Leibniz, G.W. 17–18, 20–1, 24
Les demoiselles de Rochefort (Demy) 217
Less Than Nothing (Žižek) 155, 157 n.1
Lévi-Strauss, Claude 2, 4, 188
Levinas, Emmanuel 158 n.8
Lombroso, Cesare 47
Lurie, David 132–3, 136, 140
  disciplinary committee, withdrawal 142

MacCannell, Juliet Flower 7
machine music 167
  lack of lacks 164–5
  transference 159, 163
Manet, Edouard 203
Marshall, Gary 95
Marx, Karl 20, 42 n.15, 100
  capitalism 112
materialism
  Freudian 11, 194
  Žižek 122
  naturalistic and post-human 11, 187
  origins 80
  psychoanalysis 6
materialist use, examples 122
  breakdown of concepts 128
  excessive hermeneutics 125–6
  Freud's work 123
  Irma's injection 123–4, 126
  ontology 129
  reconceptualization 125, 128–9
  relocation 125
  universal Singular 122
  user 127
materiality 2, 173, 187, 189, 215
  and ethics 194
  signifier 4–5, 11–13
  spectral 220, 222
  technique and 167
McGowan, Todd 43 n.18, 122
Medusa (Caravaggio) 182
Meinhof, Ulrike 47–8
Melville, Herman 217
Mencius on the Mind (Richards) 41 n.3
Merleau-Ponty, Maurice 216, 218–21
Millais, John Everett 12, 197
Miller, J. Hillis 38–40
misery 67
Munch, Edward 182
The Mysterious Affair at Styles (Christie) 47

Neiman, Susan 26 n.1
neoliberal subjectivation 187
neoliberalist discourse 109
neuroscience and genetics 48–9. *see also* genes
Neurosenwahl, concept 8, 59
New Introductory Lectures on Psychoanalysis (Freud) 79

The New Spirit of Capitalism (Boltanski & Chiapello) 187
Nietzsche, F. 98
nothingness 152–5
Noys, Benjamin 157 n.2
Nymphomaniac (von Trier) 8–9, 85–6
  boredom 86–7
  Heidegger, boredom 88–90
  hysterics and obsessionals, knowledge 91–2
  identification, question 92–4
  knowledge 87–8

Olympia (Manet) 203
ordinary language 149
Orpheus 156

pan, concept 215–16, 222–3
Peele, L. T. 204, 211
Penelope Boothby (Reynolds) 197, 200
performer and audience 160
Pfaller, Robert 122
Pfeiffer, Jürgen 47–8
Phenomenology of Spirit (Hegel) 26 n.2
philanthrocapitalism 106
Philosophy of History (Hegel) 19–20
phrenology 47
played music 159
poetry and psychoanalysis 115–17
Poirot, Hector 47
political beliefs
  biological cause 47
  in body 47
  person's embracement 48
popular music, drop 167–8
Pretty Woman (Marshall) 95, 107 n.1
  courtly capitalism 103–5
  depersonalization 105
  money shot 98–103
  myth 96–8
Project for a Scientific Psychology (Freud) 41 n.8, 42 n.12
psychoanalysis 2, 82 n.1
  and aesthetics 215
  application 9–11
  applied 1, 122
  capitalist discourse 115
  challenges 59
  crime 60

knowledge 131
materialism 6
   and natural science 2
   poetry and 115–17
   strategies 22
   subjectivization 60
psychoanalytic theory 60
The Psychopathology of Everyday Life 123

Raine, Adrian 55
Rasmussen, René 9
reality principle 67
Reynolds, Joshua 197, 200, 207
Richards, I. A. 41 n.3
Richardson, Michael 178
Rosendal, Jakob 12
Rösing, Lilian Munk 12, 131
Rothenberg, Molly Anne 141
Rousseau, Jean-Jacques 27–8, 40 n.1, 40 n.2
Ruby, Anders 11

Salecl, Renata 7–8
Samuelson, Meg 141
Santner, Eric 12, 66, 216, 219, 222
Saramago, José 126
Saussure, Ferdinand de 2–3, 7, 27–9
schizophrenia 48
The Scream (Munch) 182
secondary revision 96
Seeing (Saramago) 126
self-evidence 66–7
self-othering 21, 26 n.2
sexual difference 10, 35–6, 133–4, 138, 140–1, 145, 181, 223
sexuality 12, 34, 58, 66, 70, 74, 76, 77, 79–80, 121, 134, 136, 138, 140–1, 199–200, 202–3, 217
signifier 1, 152
   articulation 28
   by-product of 30–2
   Cherry Ripe (*see Cherry Ripe* (Millais))
   lack of 156
   language (*see* language)
   materiality (see materiality)
   metaphor 28
   play of 188
   radiant energy 30
   Saussure's discovery 27

science 3, 7–8, 22–4
semiodicé 24–5
semiology 28
sex and race function 143–4
   and signified 3, 29–30
   stringent theory 29
   succession 28
   work of 5–7
Siméon, Jean-Pierre 117
Smith, Adam 18–22, 24
Söze, Keyser 126
sphere theory 96
Spivak, Gayatri 132, 137–8, 143
"star" 160
Strachey, James 65
subjectivity 154
   contemporary 187
   manifestations 190
   materiality and ethics 194
   modern electronic music 159
   Western 189
The Swing (Fragonard) 203

Tesla Model S 33
Thanatos 77
theory of money 102
The Theory of Moral Sentiments (Smith) 18–19
Three Essays on the Theory of Sexuality (Freud) 66, 74, 79
Todorov, Tzvetan 43 n.20
training analysis 161
traits of culture
   cleanliness, endeavor 72–3, 76
   futility 70–1
   indications 70
   mastering of nature 68–70, 76
   order 73, 76
   otium 71
   parergon 71, 76, 82 n.3
   social nature 75–6
   spiritual elevation 73–4, 76
   utility 70

unconscious 123–4, 128
   by-product of signifier 30–2
   connections and structures 5
   de-constructible differences 136
   discourse and 43 n.16

Disgrace 135
drive 7, 42 n.12
feminist critiques 138
Freud 4, 6, 10
institutionalized critique 136
instrumentality 136
intersectionality 136
Lacan 2–3, 7
Lucy syndrome 137–8
mechanisms 60
The Unnameable (Alvarez) 150
   murmurs 150–2
   nothingness 152–3
The Usual Suspects (Söze) 126

van der Vlies, Andrew 132, 134
Verfremdung, technique 92–3
Vibrant Matter (Bennett) 187
Vico, Giambattista 27

View from Delft (Vermeer) 216
von Trier, Lars 8, 85. *see also*
   Nymphomaniac (von Trier)

We Have Never Been Modern (Latour) 187
Wealth of Nations (Smith) 18
The Woodsman's Daughter (Millais) 199
Worstward Ho 151, 155

Zeitgeist 81
Žižek, Slavoj 36–7, 70, 122, 126, 142, 146 n.1
   idealist and materialist approach 124
   Less Than Nothing 155
   person and subject 150
   subtraction 139
   true act, examples 127
Zupančič, Alenka 3, 82 n.9, 96
Zwitterwesen (Heidegger) 90